THE CREATIVE PROCESS:
A FUNCTIONAL MODEL BASED ON
EMPIRICAL STUDIES FROM EARLY
CHILDHOOD TO MIDDLE AGE

PSYCHOLOGICAL ISSUES

HERBERT J. SCHLESINGER, *Editor*

Editorial Board

THE CREATIVE PROCESS: A FUNCTIONAL MODEL BASED ON EMPIRICAL STUDIES FROM EARLY CHILDHOOD TO MIDDLE AGE

GUDMUND J. W. SMITH
and
INGEGERD M. CARLSSON
In Collaboration with Anna Danielsson, Sven Sandström
and Bert Westerlundh

Psychological Issues
Monograph 57

INTERNATIONAL UNIVERSITIES PRESS, INC.
Madison, Connecticut

Copyright © 1990, International Universities Press, Inc.

Library of Congress Cataloging-in-Publication Data

Smith, Gudmund J. W.
  The creative process.

  (Psychological issues ; monograph 57)
  Bibliography: p.
  Includes index.
  1. Creative ability. 2. Creative ability
  in children. I. Carlsson, Ingegerd M. II. Title.
III. Series. [DNLM: 1. Creativeness.
W1 PS572 monograph 57 / BF 408 S648c]
BF408.S525 1990   153.3′5   88-25555
ISBN 0-8236-1086-1

Manufactured in the United States of America

CONTENTS

ACKNOWLEDGMENTS

This monograph is based on the results of a project supported by the Swedish Humanistic and Social Science Research Council.

Anna Danielsson coauthored Chapters 3, 4, and 5; Sven Sandström, Chapter 14; and Bert Westerlundh, Chapter 2. Ingegerd M. Carlsson coauthored Chapters 6 through 15 and was senior author of Chapters 11 and 13. She coedited the entire book.

Most experiments have been carried out at the psychological laboratory of the Department of Psychiatry I, Lund University; present head, Professor Rolf Öhman.

We thank all collaborators, including those not mentioned in the text.

Permission to use reconstructed parts of previously published material has been granted by Sage Publications (Chapter 2), *Scandinavian Journal of Psychology* (Chapters 6 and 11), *Archives of Psychology* (Chapter 7), *International Journal of Behavioral Development* (Chapters 8 and 9), *Psychoanalytic Psychology* (Chapter 10), and *Psychoanalysis and Contemporary Thought* (Chapter 15). Other chapters (3, 4, 5, 13, and 14) have appeared as reports in the *Psychological Research Bulletin,* Lund University.

1

CREATIVE FUNCTIONING: A PRELIMINARY MODEL

The concept of creativity has become highly fashionable. Many fashionable terms live a short and hectic life and end up on the intellectual garbage heap like rumpled plastic bags. The term "creativity" may also go out of fashion one day soon. But behind this term one encounters a complex of questions that has always closely concerned us, questions that have tempted us to indulge in endless speculations and have both attracted and frightened us. The creative person is commonly regarded as being filled with new ideas and projects: he[1] views life from surprising perspectives, formulates problems contrary to what he has been told by parents and teachers, turns traditional and seemingly self-evident conceptions topsy-turvy, and wants to retest the validity of accepted "truths." He may seem stimulating, but also trying and awkward. We usually accept a creative attitude as a constituent part of artistic work, research, and technical construction. But creativity permeates all aspects of human activity, including our everyday business and communication.

In evaluations of the reasons for accomplishment and failure, creativity appears to have replaced intelligence as the focus of

[1]In most of this monograph we have adopted the generic use of the pronouns "he," "his," and "himself" to describe both male and female subjects. This choice has been made primarily to avoid the cumbersomeness of the "he/she" construction. The missing female pronoun should be kept in mind by the reader.

interest. High intelligence was long believed to guarantee success within a number of areas, even practical ones. Occupational psychologists did rather well in their attempts to predict how young people would perform when studying various trades and professions, particularly if the description of their intelligence was profiled with regard to more specific components. To be sure, many intelligent people have had remarkable careers. At the same time, however, high intelligence does not necessarily mean that an individual will leave permanent traces in his field of work in the form of inventions or organizational change. His contributions could simply be the result of a first-class administrative job in a complicated area, but wholly along traditional lines. Intelligence alone consolidates but does not fertilize.

Binet seemed already to have realized the limited value of intelligence test scores when he coined the term "divergent thinking" as opposed to thinking that conforms to established rules. The conventional test psychologist measures level of achievement. Usually, however, he has no interest in how the individual attained this level and the strategies used to solve the problems presented to him. Among two test persons, one might have immediately grasped the essence of the problem, spotting the correct answer almost at once, while the other toiled along tortuous paths of reasoning to reach the same solution. These two very different minds would have been placed in the same category by the traditional psychologist because they reached the same final result. Furthermore, neither of them was ever asked to formulate problems of their own; their role in the test was rather to find a suitable key fitting an old lock. People trained in how to handle keys were favored and received high scores. It was advantageous for the final result for the person not to think too much about the deeper meaning of the problems presented.

Gradually, new viewpoints began to penetrate intelligence research. One of the psychometric pioneers, Guilford (Guilford, Wilson, and Christensen, 1952; Guilford, 1967), obviously inspired by Binet, invented new test methods to map the individual's ability to use well-known objects, like a brick or a newspaper, in unusual ways. The term "creativity" was quickly popularized and was often conceived as the antithesis of traditional intelligence. The creative person was wrapped in romantic garments and many a good person began to regard himself as the member of a creative elite. The number of articles and books devoted to the subject of creativity has since increased exponentially. In spite of all this, relatively few inventions were introduced in creativity research. It is still not uncommon to administer blunt methods with low criterion correlations in ambitious projects on creativity.

Besides the psychometric line of creativity research, there was also a psychodynamic one. In the spirit of Hartmann (1939), many students of creativity considered adaptive regression as an important prerequisite for the generation of new ideas. Thus Kris (1952) coined the well-known concept of "regression in the service of the ego." According to Nilsson (1982) adaptive regression "to a lower mode of functioning is characterized . . . by a continued relationship between the different instrumental systems" (p. 11), the lower ones in certain respects operating on the conditions of the higher ones. Despite the reactualization of more primitive modes of thinking (e.g., in daydreaming), the individual retains or has easy access to his habitual, more logical functional level. This is not true of defensive or pathological regression when primitive systems gain the upper hand and rule unrestricted (e.g., in paranoid delusions). We prefer to use the term "reconstruction" instead of "adaptive regression" with its all-too-close clinical associations (Kragh and Smith, 1974). The meaning of reconstruction will be explained in more detail in Chapter 2. The term as used by us is associated with our assumption that percepts are preceded by brief, preconscious processes (*percept-geneses*), easily automatized when repeated. Reconstruction refers to the individual's ability to recapture nonadapted, early parts of such a process and make them conscious. The more the objective endstage of a perceptual process is isolated from the preparatory (subjective, imaginary) stages, the more difficult the reconstructive operations will become (see also Kragh and Smith, 1970).

Such a dynamic model seems well suited for treating many empirical observations in creativity research, particularly if the personalities of the creators are involved. The core assumption—that primary processes play a crucial role in creative endeavors—dates back to Freud's book on jokes and their relation to the unconscious (1905). Arieti (1976) has gone one step further by assuming that in the creative person, primary and secondary processes interact to form a tertiary process where a creative synthesis takes place. Székély's (1976) descriptions of how past events can be functionally active in the generation of new scientific ideas are particularly enlightening; past events not only refer to the contents of, for instance, childhood experiences, but to the childish means used by the individual to master these events. A plasma physicist in Székély's material, for instance, actualizes motor patterns from his own early years when struggling to solve his present cognitive problems. This falling back on primitive processes does not imply broken contact with the present habitual levels of adaptation. The plasma physicist, in fact, bears his complicated theoretical problems in mind all the time and eventually succeeds in solving them. Similarly, Erikson (1977) describes the relation between Einstein as an adult theory builder and as an avid blockbuilder and fitter of jigsaw-puzzle pieces as a child. In psychometrically oriented research, lists of traits have often been employed to characterize creative persons and their activities. As we see it, such lists will never be able to capture the kind of functioning specific to the creative act in the same way as a dynamic model might.

However, by using the term "reconstruction" we emphasize a certain distance between ourselves and Kris. Among other critical authors we particularly wish to mention Rothenberg (1979). One reason why Rothenberg does not accept the concept of "regression in the service of the ego" is his view of the creative process as adaptive and initially conscious. Thus creative work does not imply that the individual sinks into what psychoanalysts call "primary-process functioning," where the unadapted side of personality is steered by unconscious needs. As a matter of fact, there seems to be a fundamental difference between creative activity and dreaming, the latter activity being closely tied to the primary process. The function of dream imagery is to protect the dreamer and, in an indirect and evasive manner, to express personal wishes and needs. The creative process, Rothenberg claims, is rather the mirror image of dreaming: it starts as a conscious intention that may, thereafter, open the doors to unconscious, foreign, and perhaps frightening contents and tendencies. Creative activity not only leads to new artistic and scientific products but also to increased control over relevant aspects of the individual's unconscious life. This last consequence of creative work probably acts as an important motive for the creative person to embark upon such a cumbersome enterprise. Our own criticism of Kris and his followers may be summarized in two points: (1) He did not focus on intentionality in creative work because the creative "process" in the real sense was not his primary concern; and (2) in spite of his fascination with artistic work in general, his dominant interests were clinical. Typically, in his model, regression to primary process thinking preceded secondary process revision.

At this point we would like to define creativity. The definition will be made in connection with a new test instrument developed to describe creative functioning and within the framework of the percept-genetic model to which the instrument refers. Thereby we depart from the cognitive test tradition within which creativity usually has been defined, and place the term, at least partly, in the context of a psychology of perception. We thus speak of creativity as a generative or productive way of experiencing reality, including the perceiver's own self. In accordance with other researchers in the field with an orientation toward personality or psychodynamics, we assume that the generative quality of the reality contact is favored by open communication between different levels of experience. Primitive or "unadapted" types of experience and mental functioning should be accessible to reconstruction and "re-use." In this lies our chance to start anew and break away from ingrained patterns of experience.

The percept-genetic (PG) methodology is based on gradually prolonged presentations of a stimulus in a tachistoscope. This technique allows us systematically to observe processes "behind" everyday perception, optimally the entire process from its roots in the individual's early, primitive experience to its culmination in an objective reflection of reality. A long series of investigations have shown that reconstruction of these processes is often blocked by defensive structures. We therefore presume that the PG technique will be able to disclose whether early experiences and forms of functioning are still within reach of the individual or whether they are more or less completely withdrawn from his reconstructive attempts. Since the microprocesses reflect the individual's subjective history and individual style of adaptation, the PG techniques do not only take perception—in the traditional sense of the term—into account but also the broader aspects of the individual's personality. Thus the information revealed about the perceptual process by a PG experiment—i.e., its richness or relative poverty, its freedom from restrictions or distortion through defensive activities—is therefore very probably a characteristic of the whole person.

The usual PG technique, with its successive prolongation of stimulation time, reflects the person's ability to reconstruct early experiences or forms of functioning or, in other words, his acceptance of the existence of an inner dimension and his openness to the world of emotions. But this "straight" technique does not suffice to map the creative function; it must be supplemented by an "inverted" technique. Consequently, in the latter half of the experiment, when the stimulus picture has been correctly recognized, each subsequent exposure is successively shorter in duration. By using this technique we hope to learn something about the perceiver's *inclination* to abandon his correct stimulus interpretation and to accept, instead, more unfinished and subjective ones, perhaps those used in the introductory straight PG. It is important to emphasize that the correct interpretation necessarily acquires a strongly authoritative stamp. Once the perceiver has learned the correct meaning, he is greatly tempted to retain it, not indulging in subjective, perhaps markedly deviant imaginations.

The model for a creative attitude associated with this technique could be formulated as follows: Perceptual processes operating within the framework of a traditional view of reality do not allow subjective contents to break the frame. As already mentioned, it is typical of everyday perception that the processes "behind" it easily become automatized when repeated, even when personal feelings and experiences have been involved at the beginning. But passive "retainment" of subjective contents from the early parts of the process to its final stages is not enough to guarantee a creative set. In creative work the subjective material is utilized for constructing alternative views of reality. To create is to be active, not passive; it is to restore contact with the early stages of constructive processes. The straight PG illuminates the communication between surface and depth in the individual's experience, his readiness for emotional engagement in creative work. The inverted PG more directly mirrors the intentional side of creative functioning—the courage to break conventions and challenge one's own anxiety.

In our presentation of the field of creativity work we have omitted many important names, partly because they will appear later in this monograph, partly because we never intended to write the history of studies in creativity. But we have touched upon the psychometric and psychodynamic traditions. An advantage of the former is its emphasis on exactitude, and a disadvantage is its limited scope. An advantage of the latter is that it endeavors to make penetrating analyses, and a disadvantage is its dependence on anecdotal material. As must be obvious by now, the present project has adopted more of a psychodynamic approach than a psychometric one, even if it has been partly experimental and our theoretical background has been the percept-genetic process perspective. Perkins (1981) has made a commendable attempt to demystify the romantic, speculative side of creativity research and to puncture the anecdotal balloons used to support the speculations. But Perkins's allegation—i.e., that creative people differ from uncreative ones mainly in terms of their greater energy expenditure and stubbornness—does not seem to hold.

Even if Perkins's warnings are useful for a personality psychologist entering the mined area of creativity research, he does not convince us that our preliminary creativity model is basically wrong. We assume that there are clear functional differences between creative and uncreative individuals and summarize our model thus, using Nadine Gordimer's paraphrase of Lucàcs: Creative work implies turning inwards toward our own self and outwards toward reality, at one and the same time. By planting external concepts in the personal soil, the creative person can give them new powers of growth. The series of empirical studies presented here should facilitate the development of a model more detailed and clearly delineated than our preliminary one.

2

THEORETICAL BACKGROUND:
THE PROCESS PERSPECTIVE

More than three decades ago a group of psychologists in Lund (Smith, 1952b; Kragh, 1955) advocated a developmental frame of reference for psychology or, to be more precise, a *process* perspective (Smith, 1963). The common outlook at that time was felt to be more of a concern with the end products of processes than with the processes themselves, thus dealing more with traits or other reified "factors" than with adaptation and growth. There was reason to be optimistic at that time. It was still highly opportune to study cognitive style (Gardner et al., 1959), and the study of subliminal perception had not yet been forced underground (see Dixon, 1971, 1981). Even if investigating cognitive style did not necessarily imply a concern with processes per se, processes could very well be handled in terms of style or form: slow–fast, continuous–discontinuous, etc. Moreover, research in this area was often associated with an adaptive perspective, with an interest in coping strategies, and with a biological approach in the widest sense. Subliminal perception is not necessarily associated with a process perspective but becomes indispensable in a theory about microprocesses.

Today, to be sure, the word "process" is exploited more often than before, even in such traditional research as that on intelligence. Sometimes, however, it seems to be handled merely as an ornament. Not uncommonly, the term refers to a physiological level rather than to a psychological one, or to a long ontogenetic perspective rather than to processes unfolding within the span of the present moment. Moreover, all too often, processes are represented by hypothetical flow charts—e.g., in theories about information processing—which describe, as it were, the voyage of stimulus messages from one reified structure to another. These could at best be called pseudoprocesses. The development of more genuine process models seems, however, to be on the way, notably in the field of vision (Marr, 1982).

What, then, designates a process—as opposed to a pseudoprocess? To most of us the concept of a process would seem rather self-evident: an event over time, time being seen not only in a macro- but also a microperspective, as a qualitative change which, at least as a first approximation, can be conceptualized as a series of stages. It is tempting to understand process in terms of adaptation—that is, as a means for the organism to accommodate itself to a variable outer situation. Such a definition would easily become too narrow, however, at once too "positive" and too passive. Processes can be pathogenic and self-destructive, or they can be creative and constructive. Whatever the outcome of a process, its most important characteristic, besides being an event over time, would be the *successive determination* from one stage to the following. This does not necessarily exclude apparent discontinuities (Hinde and Bateson, 1984). Successive determination implies that one section of a process cannot be comprehended without reference to the foregoing sections, even if the change from one section to the next one might seem like a complete metamorphosis. The last example particularly actualizes the need to supplement a merely descriptive approach to processes with an understanding of the laws governing them.

When studying processes, before-and-after measurements are not enough. In psychotherapy research, for instance, studies designed in that manner are correctly called *outcome*, as distinct from *process* studies. Processes can be grasped only by means of responses to systematic series of stimulation over time. There are many ways of accomplishing this. Here we will consider the percept-genetic methodology and just mention in passing another approach taken at our laboratory in Lund, namely, the serial one. Serial methods are usually adapted to the study of behavioral change over macrotime. A simple prototype would be the analysis of how an individual endeavors to master, step by step, a situation turned topsy-turvy by forcing him to observe his field of work (his hands) in a mirror instead of directly (cf. Smith, 1952a). Another objective of serial research is visual afterimages. Here the subject is stimulated to produce one afterimage after another until he has adapted this new, subjective phenomenon to the world of real objects (projection screen, etc.), reporting size, color, brightness, etc., after each stimulation (Andersson, Nilsson, Ruuth, and Smith, 1972; Hentschel and Smith, 1980; Smith and Kragh, 1967).

How to Study Perceptual Processes

The historical roots of percept-genesis cannot be covered in detail here. Instead, we refer to a review by Flavell and Draguns (1957), to a later article by Draguns (1961), and to the first international symposium on microgenesis and related issues (Fröhlich et al., 1984). The idea of a genesis "secretly" preceding everyday perception seems to have occurred to Sander (1927) in Germany and Gemelli (1928) in Italy at about the same time and independently. Schilder's (1928) and Werner's (1927) early formulations are also worth considering in the historical context. The genetic approach to perception became widely known through the German term *Aktualgenese* and inspired a number of research endeavors, even after World War II (Linschoten, 1959; Graumann, 1959; Drösler and Kuhn, 1960; Draguns, 1961, 1963; Fröhlich, 1964). The original framework of this research was a general psychology concerned with the structural properties of percepts, and the methodological approach was mainly descriptive-phenomenological, at least in Sander's laboratory.

The Anglo-Saxon public became acquainted with this "genetic" perspective through Werner's (1956) *microgenesis*. Werner's term was meant to be an approximation of Aktualgenese, but his approach came to differ from the German one in many ways. There was more emphasis on the similarity between the principles governing the microprocesses behind perception, on the one hand, and on those intrinsic to the macrodevelopment from infancy to adulthood, on the other. Early stages in a microprocess as well as in ontogeny were thus supposed to be characterized by a high degree of fusion between feeling and perception (physiognomic perception) and at the same time by lacking integration of different functions. Later stages would be distinguished by increasing differentiation, articulation, and integration.

The central assumption in Sander's Aktualgenese as well as in Werner's microgenesis was thus that percepts do not come about instantaneously but are the end products of processes extending over time. Because these processes are generally very brief—they may be completed in fractions of a second—percepts appear to come about as soon as the perceiver confronts the external stimulation. This quasi-instantaneity may be regarded as a functional illusion because the individual's attention is directed toward the Concluding *C-phase,* not the Preparatory *P-phases.* When, through repetition, the microprocess becomes more and more abbreviated and automatized, the instantaneity naturally becomes less illusory (cf. also below).

This process model would seem rather trivial if it did not include the additional assumption that percepts do not come about as the result of a series of quantitative increments of process intensity, resulting from repeated fixations of one and the same stimulus, but via a succession of qualitative changes. As formulated by Kragh and Smith (1970, p. 25): the microprocess cannot be conceived as "a cumulative reinforcement of an initially weak but correctly transcribed pattern of excitation." The end stage of perceptual development

> appears to be related to the prestages, not as a sum to its parts but as a differentiated and specific part-component to the complex component pattern from which it has gradually evolved. With reference to the stimulus motif, the perceptual process would be subtractive (eliminative) rather than additive as it proceeds from composite to more unambiguous meanings, from global formations to less "syncretic" and more isolated ones.

Special techniques were invented to reveal these processes which only rarely, or only indirectly, came to the perceiver's own attention. These techniques should prevent the final C-phase from appearing quasi-momentarily and thus prolong the preparatory sections of the genesis and make them accessible to inspection. Among commonly exploited early techniques were tachistoscopic fragmentation and systematic reduction of brightness and clarity. The first presentation of a stimulus was thus so brief or faint or blurred that the perceiver could just barely sense its existence. Only after a series of prolonged (or more intense or less blurred) exposures was he supposed to give a correct report (reach the C-phase). The succession of reports from the first presentation to the final correct one was treated as a reflection of the perceptual process. The credibility of such an assumption will be dealt with later in the text.

PERCEPT-GENESIS: INTRODUCTORY DEFINITION

The term "microgenesis" is very general and therefore easily becomes misleading. The Lund University group adopted the more concrete term "percept-genesis" (PG) instead. PG particularly refers to the analysis of percepts and perceptual processes. The PG model is defined by the methodology employed in this analysis. The operational or, rather, operativistic mode of theorizing (cf. below) implied by the explicit reference to methodology is not, however, the only difference between the PG perspective and the Akualgenese tradition, and is not even the major difference. The hallmark of the PG model is its association with problems of personality.

The early study of Aktualgenese, with its ultimate roots in Wundtian psychology, had no interest in personality, not even in differential psychology. Heinz Werner, to be sure, made room for individual differences within his developmental psychology and sensory-tonic field theory, but he showed no intention of letting such concepts as personality or "self" become points of crystallization in this theorizing. His observations of similarities between micro- and macroperspectives of development concerned general, not individual characteristics. Studies in the Werner (1956) tradition by Stein (1949), Phillips and Framo (1954), and others made use of group data, for example, the similarities between the microgenesis of Rorschach responses in a group of adults, on the one hand, and the typical change from early to adult age in Rorschach response preferences, on the other.

In Lund, students of PG tried particularly to exploit the process perspective to describe personality organization and functioning. Perceptual processes as revealed by means of various PG methods were thus supposed to represent personality in its historical-hierarchical dimensions. Early sections of a "full-fledged" PG were, in this view, more closely related to deep-seated, archaic levels of functioning than middle or late sections which, in their turn, reflected more advanced levels. At the threshold of the C-phase, finally, the individual again attained his present or manifest level of adaptation. Simultaneously, the personal life history of the individual was unfolded in his PG, early experiences in early P-phases and later experiences in subsequent ones. This direct before-after parallelism between various aspects of the PG (the aspect to be emphasized partly depending on the choice of stimulus motif), on the one hand, and life history, on the other, has been most explicitly advocated by Kragh (1955, 1960, 1962, 1980, 1986; Kragh and Smith, 1970). C-phase contents usually dominate the focus of attention, but P-phase contents may nonetheless remain as an aura around the focus giving the perceptual world a personal touch of emotion and early reminiscences.

Since a PG is supposed to proceed from preparatory to fully adapted stages, the issue of subliminal perception must be central. The well-established fact that it is possible to correctly interpret messages sent via subliminal channels could mean either of two things, most probably both: (1) Awareness is not necessary for a stimulus to be correctly apprehended. Much evidence from research in subliminal perception supports this conclusion (Dixon, 1981). (2) A correct interpretation has somehow already been embedded in early P-phases. As a matter of fact, subliminal stimulation can be effective far below the recognition threshold. However, this "directional force" of the stimulus probably could not make itself felt in competition with other, more subjective themes until the PG had gotten well under way.

THE PERCEPT-GENETIC MODEL

As stated, the PG treats the perceptual act as a process moving from subjective prestages to the final correct meaning of the stimulus. In optimal cases, the series of reports to iterated tachistoscopic presentations will reflect the "historical personality," i.e., the psychic structure formation during the individual's ontogenesis. The degree of condensation of personal meaning is bound to be high in the beginning of a PG, and the influence of intersubjective meaning tends to dominate at the end. This means that the clearest relationship between a PG and life history will be found in the middle part of the series of reports. As the PG proceeds toward the C-phase, the principles of visual organization become less archaic, less dreamlike and condensed, and more adapted to ordinary space-time categories.

LEVELS OF MEANING

A number of levels of meaning are involved in PG analysis. As explained by Kragh and Smith (1970, p. 27):

> The concept of *organization* will denote the visual form reported by the subject verbally and/or in the form of a drawing. The *meanings* are also given by the subject in the report ("primary meanings"), in terms of associations to the organization ("secondary meanings"), and as recollections ("tertiary meanings"). The tertiary meanings may be amplified from sources other than the subject himself—e.g., from parents' reports. *Structure*, finally, is a construct; its contents are derived from information provided by organization and meanings. It refers to the concept of personality and its definition will agree closely with the one used in psychoanalysis.

RELATIONSHIP BETWEEN THE PG MODEL AND THEORETICAL CONSTRUCTS

Up to the level of structure, PG analysis is descriptive, representing continuity and change in perception as related to personality. The explanatory constructs are found at the structural level. PG has not developed unique constructs of this type. Instead, PG results have been interpreted in terms of general personality and cognitive theory. However, the basic PG assumptions about the microprocesses of perception and their relation to personality and life history clearly articulate the nature of those theories which can be used to explain PG results. Roughly, we can differentiate between mechanistic and dynamic theories. Mechanistic theories regard development as a quantitative increase or decrease, such as change in performance with age, an addition or subtraction of qualitatively uniform parts (e.g., habits). Dynamic theories claim that the development of structure over time is characterized by qualitative changes, according to principles that change and complicate during development. PG is compatible with dynamic theories, such as psychoanalysis and the cognitive genetic structuralism of Piaget. It is incompatible with mechanistic theories, such as various behavioristic or cognitive ones.

The explanatory background of the PG system can be offered only by the individual's developmental history. This is one reason why it seems tempting to use psychoanalysis in combination with the PG approach. But psychodynamic theory seems natural not only because of its developmental perspective but also for many other reasons. The hierarchical point of view of psychoanalysis, one aspect of which is that mental processes exist on different levels of a primary-secondary process continuum, is paralleled in the PG by development from subjective to intersubjective contents in the series of reports. Further, PG theory has developed working operationalizations of concepts derived from the psychoanalytic theory of defense. However, the relation to psychoanalysis, or any other theoretical system used in combination with the PG approach, must necessarily be dialectical in a give-and-take manner.

CONSTRUCTION AND RECONSTRUCTION

The direction from the subjective prestages to a stimulus-proximal perception is called *construction in the direction of the objects* in PG. What happens here has a double aspect psychologically: the stimulus is interpreted in terms of meaning, and this meaning is related to successive layers of the life-historical meaning system. Early prestages carry a great amount of diffuse and condensed subjective meaning. Later stages are primarily characterized by an elimination of subjective contents and a preponderance of the consensus C-phase meaning.

However, for a conscious percept or interpretation to come into being, a further psychological activity is necessary. The individual must grasp the significance of the constructed contents outgoing from his present cognitive and motivational level of functioning. This is called *reconstruction*. From a formal point of view, the direction of reconstruction is opposite to that of construction. Especially in the early phases of a PG, the individual must make contact with his own subjective levels of functioning. For certain minds, this is threatening. Many compulsives will exclude all subjective material from consciousness and only report in a PG when they have grasped the correct meaning of the stimulus.

The concept of reconstruction thus comprises a number of determinants of perception of a primarily cognitive order. Two such important groups are *set* and *defense mechanisms*. Sets will influence reconstruction in certain directions. An "objectivistic" setting will easily induce a set only to report veridical information, with exclusion of prephases as a consequence. Defense mechanisms are activated by anxiety signals and lead to specific transformations of the reconstructive activity.

The relationship of construction to reconstruction is as follows: during our lives, we are constantly adding to our conscious experience (reconstruction). This successive experiencing is incorporated in the life-historical meaning system and is thus activated in later acts of construction. In terms of the historical personality, the act of construction implies an activation of the individual's earlier reconstructions.

The PG conceptualization of the processes just discussed can very briefly be described as follows: reconstruction refers to what we consciously perceive on the screen (and verbalize) at each exposure of the stimulus. These interpretations are, in their turn, dependent on the (mainly preconscious) constructive processes (see Figure 2.1). In the diagram, the technique of

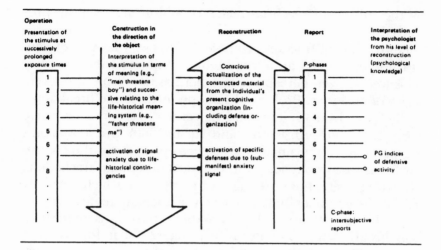

FIGURE 2.1

SCHEMATIC REPRESENTATION OF THE PG MODEL OF PERCEPTION-
PERSONALITY.

fractioning is represented vertically as the successive presentations of the stimulus. The directions of construction and reconstruction are shown as arrows. The activation of a defensive operation is illustrated.

METHODS AND DATA

Iterated tachistoscopic presentations of a stimulus provide data as a series of perceptual reports. Are the contents studied here comparable to those in everyday perception? There are two issues involved: protraction of the perceptual act and fractioning of the stimulus presentation.

Ordinarily, perceiving serves immediate adaptive ends. Perceptual acts in an average expectable environment are abbreviated in the service of adaptation (cf. below). However, given comparable conditions, the time intervals involved in uninterrupted and tachistoscopic vision are not incommensurate. If a subject is presented with an object that is not too familiar and not too simple and of rather weak intensity, the time needed

by the subject to reach correct recognition may well be pro-
tracted.

Equivalents of fractioning are found in everyday perception.
Fractioning implies an intermittent repetition of the stimulus.
As is well known, percepts come about as the result of discrete
series of fixations. Prolonged fixation leads to the breakdown
of the perceived stimulus and its return in a more primitive
form (e.g., Pritchard, Heron, and Hebb, 1960). Eye movements
are necessary for maintaining the percept and can thus be regarded as a neurophysiological equivalent of stimulus fractioning.

In the PG situation, prestages of perception, which normally
do not reach phenomenological representation, are apprehended and verbalized. Further, this reporting is reiterated.
Will this affect the contents of the process? Will it, for instance,
lead to a tendency to consolidate material once reported? Possibly some such factors operate in the PG situation. "Since any
scientific measurement is likely to interfere with its object, a
fact accepted long ago in physics, we have to be content with
giving as faithful a reflection of perception as possible within
the framework of a well-defined analysis" (Kragh and Smith,
1970, p. 22).

However, there are a number of facts indicating that such
error factors are not too important. The end stages of fractioned perception do not differ in a phenomenological sense
from ordinary perception. Moreover, error factors of the type
discussed should have similar effects on different subjects,
whereas PGs show great individual personality-related variation. Finally, as stated above, the organization and character of
the prephases of perception have been shown to be the same
for a number of dissimilar information-reduction techniques
showing the stability and generality of these prephases. In all,
PG seems to open a channel where normally covert signals, and
not noise, predominate. (These issues are also discussed in two
recent texts: Fröhlich et al., 1984; Hentschel et al., 1986).

OPERATIONALISM AND PERCEPTUALISM

PG researchers have tried to anchor their concepts firmly to
empirical operations. The model has been called "operation-

intrinsic" in a laudatory sense by its proponents and in a derogatory one by critical workers in the same tradition (e.g., Neuman, 1978). However, the "operationalism" of PG researchers has limited itself to careful description of empirical parameters and their relations to constructs, for example, from psychoanalysis. Further, these constructs are not thought of as specified in meaning by the empirical operations in the sense of operational definitions. It is not claimed that "defenses are what a PG test measures," which would thereby specify their meaning. Instead, it is stated that responses to the PG pictures contain signs of defense, a term which has much the same meaning here as in psychoanalytic theory. The interest of PG workers in linking operations to central constructs of personality theory could perhaps better be denoted by the term "operativism" than by the old term "operationism."

STABILIZATION AND AUTOMATIZATION

The developmental principles described by the Lund group can very well be subsumed under the general heading of "stabilization." The event over time called percept-genesis obviously leads to increasingly stable perceptions or conceptions of reality; and this stabilization occurs not only according to the microgenetic perspective but according to the macroperspective of ontogenesis. Concomitant with stabilization according to the latter perspective is a growing automatization in the microperspective resulting from repetition of identical or similar microprocesses. Automatization implies that a process is abbreviated and that originally separate preparatory stages are merged with each other and eventually disappear. With the double time perspective in mind, it is natural for percept-geneticists to speculate about the reflection of ontogenesis in the PG. As a result of automatization, however, such a reflection would become increasingly more fragmentary. In other words, the PG gradually loses its personal flavor. At this stage the classical stimulus-response paradigm may reign undisputed.

Stabilization as well as automatization may be viewed as biological necessities. Through stabilization one creates not only a world recognizable to oneself but a world where one can communicate with others of one's kind with a reasonable amount of mutual understanding. The successive automatization of adaptive microprocesses is the key to an effective energy economy. Energy invested in present enterprises has to be released as soon as possible to meet future demands. Automatization makes this release of energy possible, or—to use more concrete wording and eliminate the dubious energy concept—automatization facilitates the redistribution of attention and intentional effort.

One conclusion would be that percept-genesis cannot lead to a fully stabilized end stage until ontogenesis has allowed the person to reach a definite (internalized) conception of reality. Because the PG of a child does not end in a percept as stable and unanimous as that of an adult, it has room for more possibilities. As we have seen in our work with children 4 years of age and older (Smith and Danielsson, 1982), many normal children typically tend to retain several alternative meanings close to the end stage of their perceptual processes. In adults there is a clearer line of demarcation between the prestages and the concluding end stage. Creative renewal and reconstruction in an adult thus involves much more complicated retrogressive operations than those in the child. Because readaptive efforts are thus likely to meet greater resistance in the adult, they are more likely to resort to ingrained, automatized alternatives.

Stabilization and automatization do not necessarily imply that reactions to stimulation from the outside have been permanently settled in a fixed pattern. Various kinds of changes may even occur in normal adults; they may be gradual or sometimes more abrupt and disruptive and may imply retreat from external reality or serve the continued adaptation to it.

APPLICATIONS OF PERCEPT-GENETIC METHODS

In applications of the PG methodology, threatening stimuli were used to provoke anxiety signals and defensive reactions—i.e., reports of distortions of the perception of the threat. The prototype was the Defense Mechanism Test or DMT (Kragh, 1969).

A variant, the Meta-Contrast Technique or MCT (Smith, Johnson, and Almgren, 1982), was based on early experiments with subliminal stimulation (Smith and Henriksson, 1955, 1956). Other thematic pictures have been used to activate conflicting experiences—i.e., the Mother-Child Picture Test or MCPT (Smith, Almgren, et al. 1980). We are not going to dwell on these techniques here. A special Identification Test, or IT, particularly utilizes subliminal stimulation (Smith, Carlsson, and Danielsson, 1985). The MCT, the IT, and a creative functioning test, the CFT, are going to be presented in detail in Chapters 3, 6, and 11. Otherwise, we refer to recent review articles (Hentschel and Smith, 1980; Smith and Westerlundh, 1980; Westerlundh and Smith, 1983).

3

THE CREATIVE FUNCTIONING TEST:
AN INTRODUCTORY EXPERIMENT

Before exploiting the methodological innovation mentioned in Chapter 1 for its ultimate purpose as a diagnostic tool, we wanted to test how sensitive it is to changes in the kind of "attitude to reality" that we presume are associated with creativity. To this limited end we chose to design an experiment where subjects were induced either to focus on outside reality or on their own inner experiences. The more the individual's attention is diverted from outside reality and directed toward his own inner mental processes, the less an irrevocable C-phase motif should dominate his inverted PG.

If, as before, we use the term C-phase to designate the final, correct percept, and P-phase to designate the preliminary stages, we can formulate the following hypotheses: Attention directed inward should result in (a) more sensitive changes in the description of the C-phase motif, i.e., changes in size, perspective, etc., indicating flexibility in the reality contact; (b) more alternative interpretations (associations) even if the C-phase motif is maintained; and (c) more regenerated P-phase interpretations replacing the correct one. These characteristics will be defined in more detail later. It suffices to say here that in (a) the subject retains his basic impression of the stimulus, whereas in (c) he completely loses the C-motif. Obviously, the latter kind of effect should be considered more pronounced than the former.

As a means for bringing about the inward-outward polar-

22

ization between two groups of subjects, we used placebo pills together with instructions about their effects: relaxing, on the one hand, and concentrating, on the other. Previous experiments (Smith and Sjöholm, 1974) have demonstrated that instructions with an apparent realistic-scientific association are likely to have a good suggestive effect.

The stimulus motif selected for the experiment had been tried on a considerable number of individuals and proved to be capable of producing many and varied P-phase reports. The general three-step design of the experiment is more or less self-evident: to begin with, a complete, straight PG in order to capture the essential characteristics of each subject; thereafter, the placebo pill with instructions; and finally, the inverted PG.

The problem of matching the two groups receiving different instructions will be dealt with later. In line with what has just been said, it follows that the richer and more varied the "straight" PG is—i.e., the inner life of the perceiver—the more effective the relaxing placebo should be and vice versa. The thematic diversity of the straight PG should, therefore, be the main matching dimension.

METHOD

The stimulus motif presented in the tachistoscope was a black-and-white still life by the Finnish artist I. Aalto depicting a rounded glass bottle and a wide bowl beside it. This still life has rather obvious physiognomic qualities. The stimulus was projected (from behind) on a half-transparent screen, 35×35 cm, placed about 1.6 m in front of the subject. The illumination of the room, as measured at the screen surface with a Lunasix light meter, was 1.2 lux. When the stimulus was exposed the value was increased to 1.5.

Starting with 0.01 sec., exposure times were arranged in a geometric series with a quotient of $\sqrt{2}$. At the longest or eighteenth exposure level the exposure time was 3.62 sec. There were two presentations at each level. The straight PG culminated when the subject had given three consecutive correct

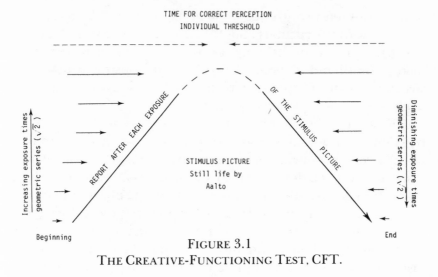

FIGURE 3.1
THE CREATIVE-FUNCTIONING TEST, CFT.

descriptions of the stimulus picture. Thereafter, the subject was given a placebo pill and one of the sets of instructions. The inverse PG started one level below that where the straight PG had ended. There were still two presentations at each level and the series ended with the 0.01 sec. exposure time (see Figure 3.1) or when the subject could no longer see anything on the screen. Before the experiment started the subject was given the following instructions: "We are going to show pictures on the screen. They will come in brief flashes. I will therefore say 'now' before each presentation. Look at the screen when I say 'now' and tell me afterwards what you saw. You need not be certain; just say what you believe."

INSTRUCTIONS: RELAXATION (RELAX)

"This pill is usually taken in much larger doses and is known to be harmless. It has a mildly relaxing and tranquilizing effect. The relaxation is accompanied by an increased sensitivity to one's own mental life. In other words, the medicine makes you more 'inner-directed.' Basically, it is a question of stimulating certain structures in the central nervous system."

"It may seem odd to you that we tell you about the medicine's effect in advance. We do it for ethical reasons. Controls against conceivable suggestion effects are built into the experimental design."

"We are going to wait another minute for the effect of the pill to begin."

Instructions: Concentration (CONC)

"This pill. . . . leads to increased attention and concentration. The increased attention is accompanied by an increased alertness to outside stimulation. In other words, the medicine makes you more 'outer-directed.' Basically, it is a question of stimulating certain receptors in the eye."

"It may seem odd. . . ."

The subject reported what he had seen after each exposure. He was also encouraged to make simple drawings of his impressions. For this purpose, he was given sheets of paper with six empty squares, 7 × 7 cm, on each sheet.

A few subjects were not able to give a correct description of the stimulus even at the longest exposure. They were asked whether the correct interpretation seemed a plausible alternative to their own and were then presented with the picture yet another time (see also below).

Subjects

Twenty-nine subjects took part in the experiment. They were all university students or trained hospital employees and were paid a nominal fee for their participation. Allotment to either of the two experimental conditions was random to begin with. Later we had to make some slight adjustments in order to equalize the groups in certain basic respects (see below).

Four subjects were excluded. One did not report anything at all before his correct recognition of the stimulus in the straight PG; three subjects did not perceive the motif correctly even after being told what it could possibly be.

This left twelve subjects (seven men and five women) in the RELAX condition and thirteen (seven men and six women) in the CONC condition, all of them in their early or middle twenties. The crucial matching variables will be presented later in the text.

Scoring

The Straight PG

The first P-phase (P_1) was scored when the subject reported his first meaningful visual structure. A report of something like a diffuse light or flash was not accepted as a meaningful structure, but a report of "a cone of light from a car," etc., was accepted.

The first partial C-phase (C_0) was scored when either the bottle or the bowl was correctly identified and *the final C-phase* when the entire picture was recognized. The number of phases (exposures) was counted between P_1 and C_0 and between P_1 and C.

The number of themes was accounted for in the following way: Generally, the P_1 theme was given 1.0 point. When this theme changed into an entirely new theme (e.g., from a landscape to a person) another 1.0 point was given. A partial change of theme (e.g., from a human being to a human being holding a newspaper) was not alloted more than 0.5 point. The scoring was similarly continued until the C-phase—the correct report not being considered—and the number of points was added up.

The Inverted PG

The following symbols will be used to characterize the inverted PG: *XX, X, (X), O, S, –*. It can be used as a quasi-scale, *XX* representing the highest creativity score and –, the lowest or no creativity.

XX: The C-phase theme eventually disappears and makes room for a meaningful but "incorrect" interpretation, often directly matching a P-phase reported in the straight PG. One example: "I had expected to see the bowl again but I saw somebody waiting at a pedestrians' crossing or perhaps somebody looking out of a window." Similar themes were actualized at the beginning of this subject's straight PG.

X: The C-phase is temporarily replaced by another meaning, or it never really disappears, the subject entertaining both meanings. One example: "I see the same old bottle but I also understand why I saw a statue earlier in the session." *X* is also scored when the change is not reported until one or two exposures before the end of the inverted series.

(*X*): The C-phase is retained but details in the picture are given deviant interpretations. One example: "I saw a parrot's beak on the front of the bottle."

O: Fleeting feelings reported by the subject that some of the old impressions are coming back but with no explicit verbal reference to a definite structure. However, drawings can be quite revealing here.

S: The C-phase is retained as far as its contents are concerned, but the form of the picture changes with respect to size, distance, depth, and perspective. Naturally, since exposure times are actually decreasing, we paid no attention to reports of increasing darkness, more blurred contours, and the like.

−: The C-phase motif is retained unchanged until it eventually fades away.

The scoring was performed by two persons, first each one by himself and thereafter both together. There were few differences between them. In cases of doubt we always preferred to work against our own assumptions.

A typical creative protocol may be exemplified by excerpts from a 50-year-old male artist:

The straight PG   4 . . .

P_1 5 A figure, crooked, and some other small figure or a shadow. It could be the body of a human being.

6 The same.

7–11 . . .

12 More complex. Something is happening there. The picture has got more volume. We are on the way to some other contents.

13–15 . . .

C 16 A bottle, and a bowl behind it.

The inverted PG 15 About the same, but the motif is tighter, more tangible, less diffuse.

14 . . .

13 Nothing really new. Perhaps darker.

12 . . .

11 Like before. A form in the middle with a diagonal light behind. A bottlelike form.

X 10 Now only a shadow. Like a body, a human being.

XX 9 Back to previous impressions. A tree and a body. A silhouette against a sky that is illuminated. A configuration.

8 Still a shadow in the foreground. . . .

7 Very diffuse impression.

RESULTS

The two groups differed slightly with respect to the P_1-C_0 distance in the straight PG (9.6 phases in the RELAX group, 11.0 in the CONC group), the P_1-C distance (13.3 and 16.2, respectively), and the exposure level where the inverted PG was started (9.9 and 11.2). Using individual group medians, we compared the subjects above the median with those below with respect to the scoring categories for the inverted PG. There were no correlations at all, not even slight tendencies.

Repeating a similar comparison for the number of themes in the straight PG (where a common median can be used), we found a noticeable but statistically nonsignificant correlation. Subjects with themes above the median number were more often scored in the XX and X classes (7 to 3) than subjects below the median (5 to 10), the fourfold table yielding a G-index of agreement (Holley and Guilford, 1964) of 0.36. However, the two instruction groups were almost identical with respect to the number of themes and the standard error of the mean: 3.1 ± 0.41 for the RELAX group, 3.2 ± 0.41 for the CONC group.

Incidentally, there was hardly any correlation between the number of phases P_1-C_0 or P_1-C, on the one hand, and the number of themes, on the other, the G-indices being -0.04 and -0.20, respectively.

It could possibly be argued that because RELAX subjects had slightly more themes per number of P-phases in the straight PG, they were also relatively more "creative" than the CONC subjects. As can easily be determined from Table 3.1, however, a great number of themes over a small number of P-phases does not in itself guarantee an XX or X scoring in the inverted PG.

TABLE 3.1
GENERAL SURVEY OF RESULTS

Condition	Subject	Sex	The straight PG		No. of themes	The inverted PG					
			No. of phases			Start at exp. levels	XX	X	(X)	O	S
R	1	m	7	20	3.0	14					4
E	3	m	10	10	3.5	7	+	+			1
L	5	m	1	4	1.0	4	+		+		4
A	8	m	4	8	2.0	9		+			2
X	10	m	3	5	1.5	8				+	5
A	20	f	8	8	3.5	7	+	+	+		4
T	24	f	6	10	3.0	8	+	+			0
I	26	f	8	12	3.5	7	+	+			5
O	30	f	9	11	3.0	8	+				3
N	31	m	17	27	6.5	16		+	+	+	5
	35	f	11	13	2.5	11					1
	37	m	31	31	4.0	17		+			7
C	2	m	25	31	4.5	18			+		2
O	4	m	13	28	6.5	18		+			0
N	6	m	9	9	2.0	10		+		+	0
C	9	m	5	11	2.5	7					1
E	11	m	6	6	4.0	7					5
N	12	f	8	13	4.0	10					3
T	14	m	12	14	2.0	9					2
R	21	f	13	24	5.0	13	+				10
A	23	f	6	7	2.5	7				+	2
T	27	f	7	10	3.0	7					4
I	29	f	14	27	3.0	16					3
O	32	f	12	13	1.5	11			+	+	1
N	34	m	13	17	1.5	12					1

An overview of the basic results is presented in Table 3.1 and Figure 3.2, and the groups are compared in Table 3.2. There were significantly more subjects in the RELAX group who were able to reconstruct P-phase themes in the inverted PG. In most cases the C-phase theme finally disappeared, in other cases it was somehow retained in the background or reappeared after a brief interval. Even if most CONC subjects clung to their correct impression of the stimulus, they sometimes reported fleeting associations pertaining to the beginning of the first PG or, more often, to changes in size, perspective, etc., of the C-phase structure. Still, this kind of sensitive change tends to be more common in the RELAX group.

By combining instructions and number of themes, we obtained two extreme groups: one group consisting of RELAX subjects with themes above the median number and the other of CONC subjects with themes below the median number.

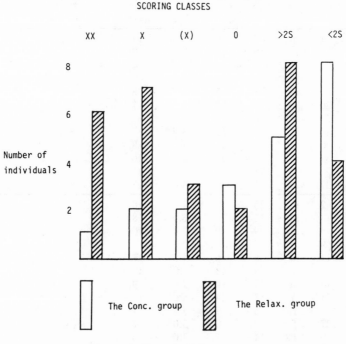

FIGURE 3.2
RESULTS OF THE PLACEBO EXPERIMENT.

TABLE 3.2

COMPARISON BETWEEN THE INSTRUCTION GROUPS
WITH RESPECT TO THE INVERTED PG

Dimension in Inverted PG	Relaxation group		Concentration group	
P-theme instead of C-theme	6	9	1	3
P-theme and C-theme together	3		2	
Only details in C-theme change	0		2	
Fleeting associations	1	3	1	10
Sensitive changes more than 3 times	1		2	
The rest	1		5	

Comparison (italicized figures): P = 0.013 (Fisher's exact test, one-sided)

Among the former five subjects all belonged to the *XX* or *X* classes; among the latter eight subjects only one was assigned to one of these classes (P = 0.005, Fisher's exact test, one-sided). The relaxing instructions were obviously most effective for the recovery of P-phase contents when the PG had been rich and varied.

DISCUSSION

We would first like to consider the probable influence of experimenter bias on the reporting of our subjects. It goes without saying that, to our knowledge, there was no manipulation of the subjects besides the instructions. Moreover, the critical part of the experiment was the inverted PG, where the subjects were well adapted to the experimental routines and the experimenter's questioning was reduced to the bare minimum.

It is even more important to realize that the experimenters had no interest whatsoever in manipulating the results in one direction or the other (even if they manipulated the subjects). The study concerns the usefulness of an instrument for future research. If the instrument does not prove to be genuine, our future research efforts will very likely be of no avail.

For this reason we were particularly careful when scoring the protocols. In our attempts to avoid a biased scoring we may have biased the scoring against our original hypotheses, not in favor of them.

We can thus claim that the inverted PG is sensitive to the difference between relaxed attention that is directed inward and more focused attention directed outward. The former attitude clearly facilities open communication between the C-phase and the P-phases behind it, to the advantage, we presume, of the generation of divergent imaginative ways of perceiving and thinking. However, another interesting factor to consider is the richness of a person's ordinary PG processes. We have here registered the significance of the *number* of P-phase themes. Other characteristics worth paying attention to in future studies would be reports of live creatures or of inanimate objects, movement, color perceptions, number of details registered, inclination to use alternative interpretations, and stability of impressions.

In an earlier paper on creativity, Smith and Kragh (1975) actualized Greenacre's (1971) assumption that sensitivity is an important prerequisite for creativity. The crucial characteristic of the sensitive person in PG experiments seems to be flexibility of the C-phase. It was evident to these authors that a flexible C-phase, allowing the use of more varied reconstruction strategies than an inflexible one, would be a fruitful starting point for the revival of hidden P-phase contents. The sensitive change scored in the present experiment, and most often in the RELAX condition, is related to the kind of change previously proved to be typical of sensitive individuals (Smith, Sjöholm, & Nielzén, 1974).

When scoring the inverted PGs, we noted a difference between protocols where the C-motif finally disappeared to make room for a more subjective impression and protocols where it somehow remained close at hand in spite of the subject's "P-level" associations. We did not feel that the latter way of reconstructing P-phase material was necessarily less "creative" than the former, a close contact with the C-phase (i.e., with reality) often being a prerequisite for the generation of truly useful new ideas. Neither did we distinguish between protocols where the P-phase material very obviously referred to the contents of the straight PG and protocols (a minority) where this was less clearly the case. We must presume that not all phases in an ordinary PG need be recognized, either by the perceiver himself or by the experimenter scoring his protocol.

To conclude the discussion, we believe that our new instrument (including both the straight PG and the inverted one but without placebo manipulations) can be useful in future explorations in the field of creativity. However, the relation between the ease of an individual's reconstruction of P-phase material, particularly in his inverted PG, on the one hand, and his inclination to approach real life challenges in a generative way, on the other, is probably not a very simple one. Anxiety, for instance, may be actualized and disturb the accessibility of early experiences. Nor do we claim that our instrument will cover more than a limited segment of this vast problem area, but we feel, nevertheless, that studies such as those suggested above may be worthwhile.

4

RICHNESS IN IDEAS, EGO INVOLVEMENT, AND EFFICIENCY IN A GROUP OF SCIENTISTS AND HUMANISTS

Before introducing the first applied study using the Creative Functioning Test (CFT), we would like to summarize and broaden our premises. The PG model rests on the assumption that external reality, i.e., the "objective" world of things and living creatures which we presume to exist irrespective of our own perception of it, is the terminal point of constructive processes. Such perceptual processes would usually be ultrashort and their end products well integrated with the individual's present level of functioning. Their ultimate origins, however, should be sought in his more primitive functional systems. Historically, these systems are interwoven with early, even very early, childhood experiences.

Experiences and representations actualized at different levels of the process of construction can become more or less accessible to the individual himself, often appearing as sudden associations or vague feelings. If we distinguish between focal and marginal structures in the perceptual field, the latter are more likely to reflect reminiscences of early process stages which give the individual's view of reality its background of personal coloring, not its nucleus of bare facts (cf. Westerlundh, 1984). The reconstruction of early process stages can be facilitated in many ways by the individual, but is particularly systematized by means of PG techniques which, when correctly applied, are likely to "unroll" the process in temporal order. With the CFT technique as a background, we can specify our assumption with respect to the subjects of the present study—researchers. If a rich and varied normal or straight PG reflects the degree to which an individual is ready to reconstruct an inner, personal dimension, it should also reflect his inclination for emotional involvement in his choice occupation, i.e., his research work. The measure of the individual's readiness to test possibilities other than the one finally offered by the C-phase would rather be the inverted PG. However, scientists and humanists rich in new ideas were not expected to relinquish the C-phase entirely, as did the relaxation group in Chapter 3, but rather to entertain subjective and objective meanings at the same time. To paraphrase what has been said earlier with regard to so-called adaptive regression: despite their inclination to reactualize more primitive modes of functioning (perhaps implying unconventional ways of combining ideas), these researchers should retain easy access to their habitual functional level, e.g., their critical distance and skepticism.

Even though a rich straight PG is expected to correlate to some degree with a rich inverted one, we also considered possible cases with a negative correlation. Individuals combining a meager inverted PG with a rich straight one were supposed, above all, to be hampered by their conventionality or reluctance to trust any new idea not yet approved by authoritative colleagues. The reverse constellation is more difficult to conceptualize but could perhaps be typical of intrinsically creative scientists unwilling to perform any act of introspection or to admit the relation between an inner personal dimension and their scientific work. Learning at the end of a straight PG that the stimulus has a meaning after all, they would perhaps be more willing to risk communication of alternative meanings in the inverted PG.

SUBJECTS

Two senior research counselors, one a humanist and the other a biologist, both working in very active and internationally well-known departments at a large university, were asked to write down a dozen names of possible subjects. We wanted the subjects to be students or former students of the counselor, to be actively engaged in research of their own, and, in case they had not yet taken the Swedish doctoral degree, to be close to doing so.

We received twelve names from each counselor. Three humanists and one biologist did not wish to participate, a second biologist was on the verge of going abroad, and a third biologist, who was older than the other subjects and who had a deviant foreign background, was not included. This left us nine biologists (seven men, two women) and nine humanists (seven men, two women). The median age of the biologists was 39 (30–47) and of the humanists, 34 (31–41). Five biologists (four men, one woman) held a doctoral degree as did five of the humanists (three men, two women).

The two departments were quite similar with respect to research quality and the general openmindedness of their senior members, and the subjects selected from them were as representative as possible of their "nonestablished" researchers. It was not our intention, however, to make a comparison between these two groups of subjects but first to inquire into some more general characteristics of research work. As we will see later, the groups did not differ with respect to these characteristics.

METHOD

The Creative Functioning Test (CFT) was used as described in Chapter 3. The test protocols were first of all scored according to the rules laid down in the first validation study and not changed thereafter.

In addition to these "hard" scoring dimensions, a number of more general dimensions were utilized. They included such items as anxiety (scored by analogy with other PG tests, i.e., with an eye to reports of black structures or other threatening occurrences); restrictions used by the subject to avoid anxiety; obvious joy expressed over the complications and ambiguities encountered in the test; attempts by the subject to extract as much *new* information as possible from each presentation of the stimulus; aggressive breakthroughs in the test situation; the subject becoming more and more dependent on the experimenter, appealing to him for information, etc.

The two experimenters tried to keep this general scoring independent of other impressions of the subject and also tried to control each other almost compulsively in this respect. It may still be possible, however, that in some subtle way they adjusted their dimensions to fit (or not to fit) the present sample. Therefore, we plan to use these variables only insofar as they substantiate the independent variables—in particular, the "hard" test scores and the criterion variables about to be described.

There are altogether thirty scoring dimensions emanating from the test. In many cases two dimensions referred to the same subject matter but one of them referred to a more liberal scoring principle than the other more conservative one.

RATINGS BY INDEPENDENT JUDGES

The judges, one humanist and one biologist, who were or had been counselors were asked to rate their respective students or former students in nine dimensions. They received the following letter from the experimenters:

> Please indicate the person or persons who clearly differ from the other ones with respect to the qualities listed below. The deviation should be in the positive direction. (1) Richness in ideas (without regard to originality or practicality); (2) originality (with respect to the best ideas, not considering quantity); (3) productivity (concerns quantity of finished research per time unit without regard to richness in ideas or originality); (4) ability to effectively organize research work; (5) ability to communicate results in a clear and well-structured fashion; (6) verbal ability referring to linguistic flexibility and variability (without regard to pedagogical clarity); (7) critical keenness; (8) emotional commitment to research (seeing research as a calling rather than any kind of job); (9) independence.

The final scores were not received until the test protocols had been scored and the interviews organized and utilized as a basis for the specific ratings.

In addition to these nine variables there were three variables pertaining to sex, doctoral degree, and field of work.

THE INTERVIEW

The experimenter who had not supervised the testing interviewed the subject afterwards without knowing anything about the test results. The interview was half-structured and pertained to such themes as scientific production and education, time alloted to research, working habits, basic motivation for research, other emotional aspects, research and private life, other interests, early childhood memories, social relations, etc. When choosing the interview items, we often relied on the work of Nordbeck and Maini (see Nordbeck, 1976). The interview usually took one hour, and the material was organized for scoring immediately afterwards.

The scoring dimensions included the following: does he consider research to be his "true" life; does he feel that his ideas come from within; has he clear memories from the age of 3-4; does he depend on inspiration or casual moods in his work; does he depend on other people or external circumstances; are agony and anxiety well-known ingredients in his research work; can he distinguish between research and private life; does he consider himself rather more "re-creative" than "creative"; is he afraid that the flow of ideas might dry up eventually, etc. A number of more general scoring dimensions based on the general impression of the subject were added—e.g., a tendency to be carried away emotionally, ability to control emotions, etc.

Most dimensions were scored conservatively as well as more liberally. There were altogether thirty-two dimensions. Several months after the experimentation, the researcher who had not conducted the interviews read them and checked the scoring. A few corrections were made. Disagreements most often depended on oversights.

THE INVERTED FACTOR ANALYSIS

The inverted factor analysis was based on the G-index of agreement as developed by, among others, Holley and Guilford (1964). This technique is particularly suited for the organization of dichotomous data provided that the number of persons does not considerably exceed one-third of the number of scoring dimensions. There were eighteen persons and seventy-four dimensions, all of the latter with ≥2 markings for presence (1) and absence (0). Varimax rotation was used.

In the accepted factor solution, the lowest factor loading was 0.58 and the smallest difference between the largest and the next largest (positive) loading was 0.10. Ten loadings were ≥0.70. Fifteen subjects were placed in six factors, two of them single-person factors. On the basis of the accepted solution, a D-index of discrimination was calculated (Holley and Risberg, 1972). The D-index is used to estimate the degree to which an item discriminates between the representatives of one factor and the rest of the subjects. It varies from −1 to +1.

Items with D-values <0.50 will not be considered here. Since D has a tendency to increase with a decrease in the number of representatives in a factor, an even more severe criterion should be applied with respect to the small factors; in the case of the two single-person factors, only top values of D were accepted. D-values will be presented with decimal points omitted.

RESULTS

Before inspecting the results of the inverted factor analysis, we would like to test the difference between the present group of scientists and humanists and the two instruction groups from Chapter 3 with respect to the test dimensions in which all of them were scored. Most students in the instruction groups were university students in their middle twenties.

As pointed out previously, Smith and Kragh (1975) have examined Greenacre's (1971) assumption that sensitivity is an important prerequisite for creativity. The crucial characteristic of a sensitive person seems to be flexibility of the C-phases (the

S-score in the inverted PG; cf. Smith, Sjöholm, and Nielzén, 1974). In the foregoing experiment the relaxation instruction group had somewhat more sensitive signs than the concentration group. The present sample places itself in the middle (Table 4.1).

Table 4.2 is more interesting. We note again the difference between the two instruction groups. Returning to our prediction for the present group—that they would not entirely relinquish the C-phase in favor of the P-phase meanings in the inverted PG—we now find that it differs from both the fore-

TABLE 4.1

SENSITIVITY IN THE INVERTED PG — COMPARISON WITH
PREVIOUS INSTRUCTION GROUPS

| Subjects | Number of phases with sensitive changes | | | | | Distri- |
	6	5-6	3-4	2-1	0	bution
Conc. group	1	1	3	6	2	5-8
Relax. group	1	3	4	3	1	8-4
Biologists	1	1	3	2	2	5-4
Humanists	2	1	1	2	3	4-5
Researchers	3	2	4	4	5	9-9

TABLE 4.2

RETRIEVAL OF P-PHASE MATERIAL IN THE INVERTED PG —
COMPARISON WITH PREVIOUS INSTRUCTION GROUPS

| Subjects | Classification of inverted PG | | |
	XX	X (X) O	The rest
Con. group	1	5	7
Relax. group	6	4	2
Biologists	0	9	0
Humanists	0	6	3
Researchers	0	15	3

Comparison: The middle column contra the extreme ones
Researchers/Conc. group, Fisher's exact test P = 0.014 (one-sided)
Researchers/Relax. group, Fisher's exact test P = 0.002 (one-sided)

going groups. While the instruction groups tend to represent the extremes of either abandoning the C-phase entirely or being completely dominated by it, the present scientists and humanists generally place themselves in dimensions X, (X), O, where P-phase contents are readmitted but the C-phase is never completely abandoned.

Before testing the predicted relationships between test results and various criteria, we would like to inspect the degree of association between counselor criteria, estimated by means of the G-index of agreement. Productivity and ability to organize are highly associated ($G = 0.89$) and tend to form a cluster of their own. In a more loosely structured complex of associations, we find originality-independence (0.78) and verbal ability-critical keenness (0.78). Within the same complex there are also slightly lower associations (0.67) between verbal ability, on one hand, and richness in ideas, originality, and ability to communicate results, on the other. One of the crucial variables, richness in ideas, is associated to some extent with originality (0.55) and independence (0.55) but hardly at all with emotional involvement (0.22). Among thirty-six G-indices in the matrix, $8 \geqslant 0.67$ and $11 \leqslant 0.22$.

First of all, richness in ideas as judged by the counselors should correlate with a rich inverted PG. We find a significant correlation in Table 4.3. This correlation would probably have been higher if the counselors had not been slightly reluctant to consider other than useful ideas (cf. the correlations just presented). From the interview we tried to extract two variables that also should correlate with the inverted PG: a tendency to regard new ideas as emanating from within, and a (highly) correlated readiness to reconstruct early childhood memories. The contrast is not significant if tried on the basis of a 2×2 contingency table with median cutting, but a cutting just above (indicated by a broken line in Table 4.3) yields a P of 0.009.

Personal involvement in research work, according to our predictions, should correlate above all with a rich and varied straight genesis, i.e., with a readiness to let early PG stages be reconstructed, even more so, it would seem, in cases where the

TABLE 4.3
THE INVERTED PG AND PREDICTED CRITERIA

Inverted PG		Richness in ideas		Ideas emanating from within and early childhood memories	
P-phase material	Sensitivity +/(+)/−	+	−	Both dimensions +	At least one −
X		4	1	5	0
(X)	+ or (+)	2	0	1	1
(X)	−	1	1	0	2
0	+	1	0	0	2
−	+	0	3	1	1
The rest		0	5	1	4
		Fisher's exact $P = 0.008$ (one-sided, median cut)		Fisher's exact $P = 0.077$ (one-sided, median cut)	

TABLE 4.4
THE STRAIGHT PG AND PREDICTED CRITERIA

Straight PG	Emotional involvement according to supervisors		Research their life according to interview	
	+	−	+	−
With articulated P-phase themes, incl. persons	5	1	4	2
The rest	2	10	1	11
	Fisher's exact $P = 0.013$ (one-sided)		Fisher's exact $P = 0.022$ (one-sided)	

prestages depict live persons. Accordingly, Table 4.4 reveals a correlation between the straight PG and emotional involvement in research, as judged in the interview. The reader may remember that, according to the counselors, emotional involvement correlated only slightly with richness in ideas.

Finally, we would like to consider cases where the degree of richness of the straight and inverted PGs correlates negatively.

Let us first contrast a long, straight PG with a meager, inverted one. As just mentioned, people with a rich and varied straight genesis should be well motivated researchers, but, lacking an inverse genesis, inclined to bind their ideas close to existing paradigms or to the surface patterns of their empirical material. Such people might be characterized as lacking both originality and independence even though they have taken their doctoral degree (and in the cases concerned, even proceeded beyond it). There were six such people in the group, four of them with 1.0 or 0.5 markings for themes in their straight PGs but not more than *0* markings (combined with no markings for sensitivity) for their inverted PGs. No other people showed this scoring combination. A 2 × 2 contingency table with these figures yields a Fisher's exact P, one-tailed, of 0.005.

There was only one subject showing a very brief, straight PG combined with a rich, inverted one. This person should be able to generate new ideas but is reluctant to identify himself with them. Among five subjects with very rich, inverted PGs in the material, he is the only one who does not really consider research to be of central personal concern to him even though he is judged by his counselor to be both rich in ideas and original.

The latter hypothesis, but also the former one, will be tested again in studies to follow upon the present one.

THE COUNSELORS' RATINGS IN THE FACTOR SOLUTION (see Figure 4.1)

Factor I (four subjects representing both humanistic and biological fields). Three variables received high D-values: productivity (79), ability to organize (71), and critical keenness (64). If we calculate D based on all three variables, we obtain a value of 86. This factor appears to encompass effective and intelligent scientists—in brief, competent people.

Factor II (three subjects from both fields). Six variables obtained high D-values: richness in ideas (67), originality (67), verbal ability (67), independence (67), critical keenness (60), ability to communicate results (53). The D-value considering these variables together is 93. This factor includes the really

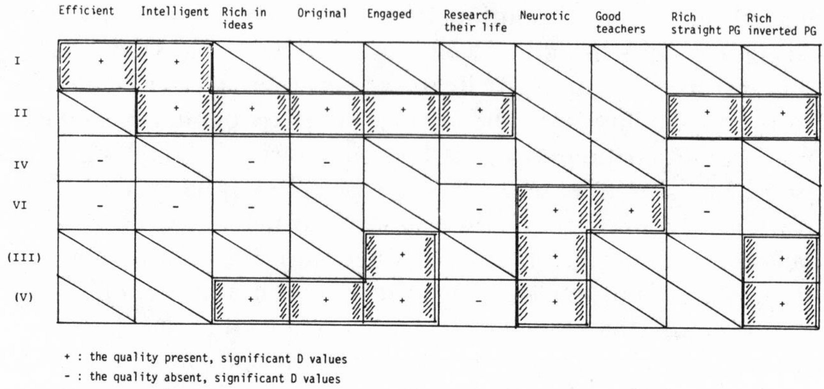

	Efficient	Intelligent	Rich in ideas	Original	Engaged	Research their life	Neurotic	Good teachers	Rich straight PG	Rich inverted PG
I	+	+								
II		+	+	+	+	+			+	+
IV	-		-	-		-			-	
VI	-	-	-			-	+	+	-	
(III)					+			+		+
(V)			+	+	+	-		+		+

+ : the quality present, significant D values
- : the quality absent, significant D values

FIGURE 4.1
SCHEMATIC SUMMARY OF THE FACTOR ANALYSIS.

creative subjects, those who do not respect current paradigms (Kuhn, 1962), but who are not necessarily the most efficient ones.

Factor IV (four subjects from both fields). Five variables obtained high negative D-values: richness in ideas (-57), originality (-57), ability to organize (-57), independence (-57), productivity (-50). The D-value for absence of all these variables is 79. In this factor we find persons not characterized by the traits descriptive of factors I and II. They appear to represent the academic mediocrity, producers of acceptable papers but not more.

Factor VI (two subjects). The following D-values were noted: absence of critical keenness (56), no richness in ideas (50), no ability to organize (50), but having the ability to communicate scientific results (50). The values are admittedly quite low for such a small factor, but the summarizing D rises to 93. This factor is difficult to define solely on the basis of the counselors' ratings. Let us note, however, a pedagogical ability not correlated with appreciable critical keenness, effectiveness, or richness in ideas.

Factors III and V are single-person factors which we will mention briefly when all results have been compiled.

The Interview Variables in the Factor Solution

Factor I. The three best variables received D-values >60: re-creativity (71), ideas not emanating from within, liberal scoring (64), or this variable combined with absence of early childhood memories, liberal scoring (61). These competent research workers apparently consider themselves as mainly re-creative, dependent on other people's ideas and not particularly inclined to reconstruct their own private experiences.

Factor II. Somewhat higher D-values should be demanded from this factor. There are five values >70 and two additional ones at 67: concern about the flow of ideas eventually drying up (93), extremely dedicated to their research work (87), ideas emanating from within together with early childhood memories, liberal scoring (80), problem orientation (80), ideas emanating from within, conservative scoring (73), relief and joy frequent experiences in research work (67), deep rather than shallow social contacts (67). These creative researchers are keenly aware of the subjective roots of scientific ideas and consequently also of the risk of the flow of ideas drying up, a risk which seems to be all the more deeply felt since they are strongly identified with their work. Associated with this generally inner-directed orientation is an ability to reconstruct quite early childhood memories.

Factor IV. There are no D-values >60 but three just below: no inner compulsion to do research work (57), no frequent experiences of relief and joy (57), no deep social contacts (57). This is wholly in line with our previous picture of the normal, little ego-involved research worker. It is particularly instructive to note that these people, lacking true identification with their research, are not inclined to have deep social contacts, unlike the representatives of factor II. Many seem to do research work because they cannot do anything better, some of them perhaps because they cannot manage human relations very well.

Factor VI. In this small group we prefer to mention D-values >70: research not being their true life (82), tendencies toward neurotic compensation (82), problems with the scientific material (77), tendencies toward narcissistic compensation (77), no frequent experiences of relief and joy (71). The compensatory variables suggest that for them research is an instrument for self-assertion. They generally encounter serious problems in their research work and have yet to complete their dissertations (56).

THE GENERAL RATINGS IN THE FACTOR SOLUTION

Factor I. These people were characterized, according to us, by an ability to rid themselves of emotions when necessary because of their work (79), a trait in line with their efficiency.

Factor II. Here we found a tendency to be carried away by emotions (60).

Factor IV. The opposite tendency, liberally scored (64), was noted.

Factor VI. The positive emotional tendency reappears in this factor, particularly if scored conservatively (81), but also an inability of the subjects to rid themselves of emotions, liberal scoring (81).

These additional ratings may help us better describe factor VI. The individuals representing this factor let themselves be absorbed by their research work, but for reasons other than the research proper. This neurotic tendency of theirs is likely to make their emotionality difficult to control. Even if factor II persons may also let themselves be carried away, they are still capable of ridding themselves of emotional influences.

THE PRE-DETERMINED TEST VARIABLES IN THE FACTOR SOLUTION

Factor I. Only sensitivity in the inverted PG, liberal scoring, is vaguely differentiating (50).

Factor II. The strongest sign is an inverted PG with clear P-phase themes (87). One may also note at least two 1.0 themes in the straight PG (67), the D-value rising to (73) if person motifs, liberal scoring, are considered at the same time. These results imply a validation of the basic assumptions of the present paper. Incidentally, the association of this factor with a well-structured straight PG is rather self-evident, but the combination with person motifs is particularly interesting in view of the early childhood memories and deep social contacts typical of these subjects.

Factor IV. These subjects—and it is no surprise—show no sensitive signs, liberal scoring, in their inverted PGs (79) and no clear P-phase themes (64).

Factor VI. The straight PG does not include person motifs (75), a result in line with these subjects' narcissistic-compensatory tendencies.

THE ADDITIONAL TEST VARIABLES IN THE FACTOR SOLUTION

Factor I. No anxiety was scored in the protocols of these efficient workers (71).

Factor II. Two things are particularly characteristic: joy expressed over the complications and ambiguities in the test (93) and attempts to extract new information, liberal scoring (80). These results nicely round off the creative profile of this factor.

Factor IV. Anxiety is vaguely characteristic (57).

Factor VI. Most typical are clear aggressive breakthroughs (1.00). The subjects became frustrated when they could not grasp the meaning of the tachistoscopic glimpses, obviously in the same way as when they meet with obstacles in their research work.

DISCUSSION

In view of the rather complicated results of the factor analysis, in particular, we shall begin the discussion with thumbnail sketches of the factors. Thereafter, we will consider the single correlations between test results and criteria and, after a brief evaluation of the various groups of variables, compare the present findings with a selection of findings from other studies. Finally, we shall take up a few questions relating to anxiety and psychopathology and to outline in a very preliminary way a model of how neurotic persons may be able, in spite of everything, to function creatively.

According to criteria supplied by the counselors, *factor I* includes efficient and intelligent scientists (biologists as well as humanists) who are not particularly rich in new ideas or original. They consider themselves to be re-creative rather than creative, depending on impulses from outside to facilitate their scientific activity. Accordingly, they see no reason for applying an introversive perspective on their scientific work, which they prefer to consider as akin to any other kind of qualified occupation. They can easily rise above emotions, are free from signs of anxiety in the PG test, and show little evidence of subjective involvement.

Factor II individuals, coming from both fields, were rated as rich in ideas, original, independent, and intelligent but not necessarily very efficient or productive. They are strongly identified with their scientific endeavors and are aware of an inner, subjective dimension as the ultimate source of their innovations. Knowing that scientific ideas are not somehow buried in the empirical material but grow out of the scientist himself, they are prone to worry about the future supply of fruitful ideas. They are typically problem oriented. In their straight PGs they describe many different motifs, often with human beings involved, and they return to P-phase motifs in their inverted PGs—but without entirely relinquishing the C-phase. They obviously enjoy being confronted with new aspects of reality and tend to seek out rather than avoid complications. These subjects are genuine discoverers and inventors and represent what we perceive to be creative scientists.

Counselors' ratings describe the *factor IV* individuals as an intermediate group with no outstanding characteristic, craftsmen who have learned to handle the tools of science in an acceptable manner. They are not identified with their research and are not particularly efficient. The inverted PG has no or very vague P-phase themes. Even the sensitive C-phase changes suggesting openness to new impressions are conspicuously absent from their protocols.

The two *factor VI* persons were rated as good teachers. Apart from that they are characterized by few triumphs in the scientific arena but all the more by a strong, narcissistically colored search for compensating rewards. It is difficult for them to cope with frustrating experiences, and they are prone to react with aggressive outbursts.

Factor III includes one person who, according to his counselor, has a strong emotional commitment to research (65). The picture of him is supplemented by a rich inverted PG (77) and an ability to reconstruct early childhood memories (88). At the same time, the test protocol is marked by restrictions employed to avert anxiety (1.00) and by dependence on the experimenter (94). The interview reveals tendencies toward neurotic compensation (82). This person is potentially creative but handicapped by two things: low tolerance for anxiety and lack of critical keenness.

The *factor V* individual is characterized by the following counselor ratings: richness in ideas (59), originality (59), and emotional commitment (77). His inverted PG is similar to those found in factors II and III, liberal scoring (53). But he more closely resembles factor III persons in his strivings for neurotic compensaton (82) and is unique in his inability to control his emotions (88). This potentially creative person does not consider research to be his true life (82) because it implies a painful burden to him; he dwells very much on problems in handling the empirical material (77). Even if he is creative and somehow emotionally tied to his work, he cannot enjoy it and thus differs from the factor II individuals.

The two basic assumptions of the present study were (1) that a rich and varied straight PG should reflect a subject's ability to commit himself to his research work, and (2) that the degree to which he actualized P-phase themes in the inverted PG should correlate with the fertility of his scientific imagination. Both these assumptions were substantiated. We were also able to show that scientists, even if rich in new ideas, did not entirely relinquish their contact with reality but rather played with P-phase material besides remaining aware of the correct C-phase theme. Attention was also given to those cases where a rich straight PG was combined with a meager, inverted one and vice versa. The hypotheses advanced to explain these combinations were tentatively supported by the present material but obviously need to be tested in a new sample. As far as the main results are concerned, however, we feel entitled to consider them as cross-validations because they are in line both with previous findings based on the straight PG technique and with the results of our introductory study using the inverted PG version.

We have exploited our variables differentially, emphasizing the predetermined test variables and the counselors' independent ratings more than, for instance, our own general ratings. Because of the high correlation between the former two groups of variables, they have dominated the factor solution. Our supply of relatively soft data has mostly served to expand on relationships suggested by the hard data. Thus the factor solution, however illustrative in its various details, does little more than reflect the basic correlations just mentioned, correlations we considered to be cross-validations of previous findings. The details of the solution might change, however, if a new sample of researchers were to be tested. Still we cannot resist pointing out the beauty of the factor pattern where creativity and efficiency in research work are not confounded with each other and where various neurotic variants, even including potentially creative individuals, emerge as small factors, around the periphery of the core pattern formed by the three factors. By most accounts, factor II corresponds to our preconceived notion of the creative researcher, exploring the depths of his imagination with awe but still never losing contact with the harsh light of reality around him.

Individuals combining a generative approach to research with personal dedication and high intelligence were comparatively rare in our study, even though it encompasses quite competent, sometimes very successful research workers. People not judged as intellectually outstanding were not included in factor II even if they generated many ideas. Some potentially creative neurotics, who tended to bind their emotions and energies in irrelevant contexts, form factors of their own. In the remaining group we find persons reminiscent of those described by Eiduson (1962) in her broad investigation of scientists, i.e., persons eager to find new combinations, challenged by complications and ready to accept the anxiety accompanying their demands for relentless cognitive reorganization. According to Eiduson, however, their anxieties were limited mostly to the scientific task at hand. Regarding the primary process material actualized by deep-reaching reorganizations, sometimes material of a problematic kind, we may also refer to Barron's (1963a, 1963b) findings that creative individuals are more tolerant of ambiguity than noncreative ones (cf. Maini, 1973). We agree with all this but would like to place more emphasis on the anxiety dimension: the primitive material reconstructed during an innovative process may be explosive and even dangerous to the integrity of the scientist's self.

Factor II was codetermined by two items, both with relatively high positive D-values, which have not yet been scrutinized. One of them pertains to the interview where these subjects described their social contacts as deep rather than shallow, the other to the test where they scored for person motifs in their straight PGs. Roe's (1951, 1953) scientists, particularly her biologists and physicists, did not exhibit any noticeable interest in social contacts. Her definition of social contacts seems to agree most closely with the shallow end of our variable. The preference of our subjects for a limited number of more intimate contacts and their inclination to reconstruct persons in their PG processes fit together with their personal involvement in and persistent dedication to research work. After the conclusion of the present investigation, we have also come to realize, partly due to observations made by one of the counselors, that the factor II people are characterized by feeling deep responsibility for other people, among them the younger doctoral students to whom they offer advice and counsel. They even experience a conflict between their "egoistic" wish for being alone in pursuing their own research, on the one hand, and this or similar social responsibilities, on the other.

Apropos the one person mentioned above whose inverted PG is rich but whose straight PG is meager, but also regarding tendencies to deny the personal side of scientific work observed in other, professionally successful subjects in our sample, we would finally like to venture the term "projective functioning." Because these subjects are anxious not to reveal their private experiences, they look for roundabout ways to generate new ideas. One subject told us that ideas dismissed by other scientists often supplied the best tinder for igniting his own fantasy processes. He advanced the hypothesis that all scientific work was purely cognitive. For him copious reading was a necessity, while others can be obsessed with advanced technical manipulations of empirical data. By thus placing the center of creativity outside themselves, these people may diminish the risk of directly involving their own problematic selves. Basically, it seems to be a strategy to avoid anxiety and such defensive deadlocks as might endanger the whole creative process. Projective functioning would sometimes allow even severely neurotic scientists to generate new ideas.

5

THE INFLUENCE OF ANXIETY ON THE URGE FOR ESTHETIC CREATION

According to Arieti (1976), both the esthetic field and the field of science are expanded by the formation of new classes and categories. This information, we assume, is facilitated by contact with nonadapted ways of functioning. If creative activity in the field of science were not basically different from creative activity in other fields, it would be possible to cross-validate our findings by applying the PG technique to the field of artistic-literary creation. Creative people in such a field would be similar to our creative researchers with respect to their ability to reconstruct subjective material in the inverted PG. However, we do not believe that this ability is restricted to individuals with a certain degree of literary-artistic talent but that it is more or less typical of individuals with a serious *urge to create*, even if the products of creation may seem clumsy and provincial to the seasoned critic.

At this point we shall highlight our thinking about creativity by discussing symbolic functioning. We have chosen this theme because a symbol represents something above and beyond itself. A symbol has more than just annotative character. People who do not comprehend symbols are not very likely to comprehend dreams or care very much about them. When dream images no longer represent something more than their sensory surface they become meaningless, provided that they do not express very open wish fulfillments. Lack of understanding of symbols will also adversely affect art and poetry appreciation. In the esthetic area, says Arieti (1976), the concrete representation, i.e., the symbol or the metaphor, "not only is not incongruous with the original abstract concept, it actually reinforces it" (p. 146). Greenacre (1957), among others, underscores the ease and wealth of symbolization in people with artistic talent.

The understanding of symbols need not, however, refer to a cultural highbrow level. Even everyday things can acquire symbolic meaning for people who are capable of adding a depth dimension to the tangible surface of reality. For example, to a child a pencil may not merely be a pencil, it can also be a sword, a fish, a submarine, a man, etc. In PG experiments, at stages where presentation times are still too short for the subject to perceive the stimulus correctly, children gladly entertain several interpretations of one and the same structure simultaneously. At one stage in the presentation series, the child may see a blackbird which at the next step changes into a hat—but the blackbird is still there, sitting on the hat. Adults are more likely to let one interpretation exclude all alternatives. Creative individuals, like children, would be more inclined, we believe, to perceive several meanings behind a correctly perceived object or, in the words of Niederland (1976, p. 192), to show an "attenuation of the demarcation between self and nonself." In other words, they would treat the object as a symbol or a representative of their own personal universe.

The oceanic feeling as described in 1927 by Romain Rolland in a letter to Freud, i.e., the feeling of harmony between oneself and some larger context, the forerunner of which may be the experience of awe in childhood (Greenacre, 1957), can be seen as the positive pole of symbolic functioning. In *Pilgrim at Tinker Creek*, Annie Dillard describes how she one day sees the back yard cedar "charged and transfigured, each cell buzzing with flame. I stood on the grass with the lights in it, grass that was wholly fire, utterly focused and utterly dreamed. It was less like seeing than being for the first time seen, knocked breathless by a powerful glance." The opposite pole would be not a feeling of dark apprehension or universal threat, but of flatness and boredom, the feeling that everything is merely surface and nothing else. In this view, periods of boredom are periods lacking creativity.

Because sensitivity is a scoring dimension in the test, a few words ought to be said about the relation between sensitivity and symbolic functioning (see also Greenacre, 1957). Sensitivity refers to a plastic perception of reality, a susceptibility to what is marginal, just liminal, or even subliminal. In previous studies (Smith, Sjöholm, and Nielzén 1974) this characteristic has been shown to correlate with susceptibility to nuances in subject-subject relations and even tendencies to projective perceiving. Symbol understanding as just described refers to the density of perceived meaning. An inclination to perceive objects as symbols rather than signs, however, presupposes sensitivity to marginal cues. The sensitive person registers not only a word or a gesture but the whole spectrum of nuances that can give the word or gesture surplus meaning. Basically, we are talking about sensitivity to one's own as well as other people's primary processes or, to phrase it more in terms of the PG model, to the marginal, personal zone of human experience as it is revealed not in the last correct phase (the C-phase) of a PG, but in previous phases (P-phases) far removed from the last phase. In the creative person, we presume, the P-phases are never wholly disqualified for the benefit of the consensus of the C-phase; they remain as a corona in the background, accessible to an adaptive regression when needed (cf. Hartmann, 1939; Kris, 1952).

It is well known that sensitivity has a pathological, paranoid side, where the condensed meaning of reality reaches ominous proportions. The symbolic functioning of paranoid people is intense but has gone astray and is wholly focused on an aggrandized self. In these cases one might be tempted to talk about pathological creativity. As Arieti (1976) points out, however, the unquestionably new experience in such cases is actually a reduction from a metaphoric to a concrete level and implies a restriction, not an enlargement, and restriction is incompatible with creative activity.

Before introducing another aspect of the present study, we would like to summarize our *hypotheses* as they have been presented so far. A rich inverted PG is above all assumed to correlate with an urge to create. Among associated dimensions we particularly want to mention oceanic experiences and appreciation of dreams. Domino (1976), in his creativity research, has used an intricate classification of dreams as more or less stamped by primary-process thinking. We have tried a simpler approach by asking subjects about color in their dreams. An affirmative answer would, we presumed, reveal closeness to dreaming and primary process functioning, a hesitant or negative answer, remoteness. In the study of researchers there was a tendency for the more creative ones to be close to their childhood memories. We expect the same tendency in people with an urge for esthetic creation.

Since anxiety seemed to be a companion of creative research work (see also Eiduson, 1962) and since, according to many students of creativity (e.g., Hammer, 1975), a certain level of tension and anxiety is necessary for personal growth and creativity in artists, we planned to introduce a threatening picture as an independent variable in this study by presenting it subliminally just before the inverted PG in part of the sample. Silverman used subliminal stimulation as a means of activation of primary process derivates of affective ego functioning, particularly in pathological cases (Silverman, 1976; Silverman and Geisler, 1986). Aggressive stimuli were especially effective when thus used. Antell and Goldberger (1986), on the other hand, observed more positive effects on literary creativity when using subliminal sexual stimuli. Aggressive stimulation could even have a disruptive effect if subjects were noncreative and the task demanded secondary process activity.

The PG task does not require much secondary process activity. We might, therefore, predict a positive effect of threatening stimulation, above all in creative subjects or, since we would get a ceiling effect in the most highly creative ones, in subjects with a less articulate creative urge. This prediction could be questioned because an increase in defensive activity might be a possible result of subliminal threat stimulation. Since our creative researchers seemed reasonably tolerant of anxiety—perhaps because creativity itself can be used as an instrument to handle dangerous emotions—and since the sample is supposed to be normal, we vouch for the prediction of a facilitating effect of the threat. We shall elaborate on it later.

METHOD AND DESIGN

SUBJECTS

We wanted subjects with an urge to create but we also wanted a mixture of creative and uncreative subjects. All subjects were full- or part-time students at the university; some of them were studying drama or culture communication, others were majoring in history, social science, medicine, etc. Altogether, forty-three subjects participated in the experiment. All subjects received a nominal fee for their participation. There were eight men and thirteen women in the threat group, aged 20 to 41 years with a median age of 25 years; there were six men and sixteen women in the control group, aged 19 to 49 years with a median age of 22 years.

The subjects took the CFT first and were then interviewed. The experimenter and the interviewer were different persons. There were two experimental (subliminal) conditions to which the subjects were assigned according to a list of random numbers. The design was strictly double-blind, i.e., the experimenter did not know which subliminal stimulus was being presented.

THE CFT

The stimulus motif was again the bottle and the bowl. In previous studies, the straight PG culminated when the subject had given three consecutive correct descriptions of the stimulus picture. Here the first correct reporting was followed by five additional presentations where the CFT picture was paired with either a threatening or a control stimulus (see further below). Thereafter the inverted PG started one level below that at which the straight PG had ended. The scoring was the same as before.

Among other things, we distinguished subjects with at least two 1.0 point themes from the remainder. Otherwise, subjects were assigned to the following classes representing the sum of points for all themes: (a) $\geq$ 4.0 themes (N = 12); (b) 2.5–3.5 (N = 13); (c) 1.5–2.0 (N = 10); (d) 0–1.0 themes (N = 8).

There were eleven subjects (including some slightly marginal cases) in the *XX* category, eight in the *X* category and seven in the (*X*) and *O* categories combined, six in the *S* category, and eleven in the rest (–) group.

In addition to the usual scoring dimensions, a number of anxiety signs were utilized in the straight and inverted sections of the test. These signs were defined by analogy with anxiety signs in the MCT (a test of anxiety and defense mechanisms *ad modum* percept-genesis; see Chapter 6) where they have been validated. We thus scored (a) reports of stimulus-incongruent blackness-darkness with ominous overtones—for example, a black hole, a dark cave, or an alley; (b) reports that someone in the picture is frightened or anxious; (c) the picture seems frightening or disagreeable to the subject; (d) reports of dissolving or broken structures; (e) deprecatory remarks about the picture—i.e., attempts to make it harmless (denial in the MCT); (f) reports of stiffened persons, etc. (signs of repression in the MCT). Most signs were noted in the straight PG; the inverted PG did not add any new information. The test was not specifically designed to reveal anxiety, and the anxiety signs played a rather subordinate role in the factor analysis. It might even be asked if it was correct to generalize from the MCT to the present test. On the other hand, we only use signs appearing to be related to anxiety and defense in a very obvious way.

Test Reliability

Since we have already been able to demonstrate high correlations between test results and criteria, we are entitled to conclude that our data are reliable. The only kind of reliability that we can calculate here is the inter-rater correspondence. A high agreement between two independent raters primarily implies that the scoring dimensions have been defined in such a way as to render the choice of scoring classes easy for the judges. We chose the most difficult part of the test, the inverted PG, to examine the inter-rater correspondence. It was 88%. When scoring the protocols, both judges were unaware of the contents of the subjects' interview protocols.

The Subliminal Presentation

When the subject had reported the CFT picture correctly, it was presented another five times at the same exposure level with a new stimulus preceding it. This stimulus was either a drawing of a horribly grimacing face covering most of the screen or a neutral drawing with the same outer contour as the face but striped, with similar proportions of black and white stripes. The subject did not know that an extra stimulus had been presented and the experimenter did not know which stimulus had been shown. A total of twenty-one subjects were assigned the threat stimulus and twenty-two the control stimulus.

The exposure time for the subliminal stimulus was 0.014 sec. Since the CFT picture was always presented using the exposure level at which the subject gave a correct report, the exposure time for that stimulus varied among subjects (not among conditions). The shortest time used in this group of subjects was 0.06 sec., which was reached after not less than ten presentations. The median time was 0.23, reached after not less than eighteen presentations. Seven subjects needed more than thirty presentations to give a correct report.

No subject gave the slighest hint of having discerned any trace of the subliminal stimulus, in spite of the instruction to report even the vaguest impressions. Even though subliminality is not the issue here, we wanted to keep the stimulus subliminal to maximize the effect of the threat. Also in our favor was the fact that the same stimulus had been used before with good results (Andersson, Fries, and Smith, 1970).

Comparing their own technique of influencing subjects subliminally with previous techniques, Silverman, Ross, et al. (1978) found the latter rather tentative and inefficient. We did not knowingly try to model our method after that of Silverman. The design, nonetheless, includes some elements of the priming procedure recommended by Silverman: the subjects were in the middle of a reconstructive activity when the subliminal stimulation was presented. Moreover, there was no risk here of the kind of bleaching that Silverman, in accordance with Cornsweet (1970), felt would hamper any effects of subliminal manipulation (cf. the illumination values presented above).

The Interview

The interview—led by the investigator who had no knowledge about the experimental results—was semistructured and encompassed the following main fields: (1) studies and/or work; (2) main interest, above all in "creative" fields, and spare-time activities; (3) ways of thinking and remembering; (4) dreaming; (5) day dreaming; (6) going to sleep; (7) childhood memories; (8) emotional life, including oceanic experiences and anxiety; (9) play; (10) the subject's view of himself in terms of creativity, independence, etc.

The interview formed the basis for a number of scoring dimensions pertaining to factual information, statements by the subject, and evaluations made by us. Some of these evaluations are particularly important for the main theme of the study and will therefore be described in detail below. When scoring the protocols, the judges did not have access to the names of the interviewees. This meant that none of the judges could connect interview protocol and test performance.

Artistic-Literary Creative Activities

Subjects were placed in one of the following three categories representing different degrees of artistic talent or creative urge.

a. Genuinely artistic-creative activities with emotional involvement and a need to express something personal; activities to which the person is presently committed or would like to commit himself given the opportunity (N = 12).

b. Such activities belonging to the person's past: he does not get inspired by them any longer; his creativity is at best latent (N = 11).

c. Creative activities, if any, are not genuine: too rational, more like a superficial hobby, dry exercises by people with some talent and dexterity (N = 20; 6 of these reporting no activity at all).

The independent judges agreed in 78% of the cases. The dimension was considered quite difficult. Nevertheless, disagreements did not concern more than one step on the scale.

OCEANIC FEELINGS

Subjects were placed in one of the following categories representing different stages of true oceanic experiences.

a. True "oceanic experiences" that might still be actualized: reports of overflowing happiness, of total absorption in something far beyond the confines of one's own self, often combined with feelings of a religious-mystical nature (N = 8).

b. More doubtful experiences in which the oceanic component represents manic feelings, good humor, hysteroid exaggerations, etc., and lacks the "mystical" absorption in some greater context (N = 26).

c. Total incomprehension of the subject matter or just reports of successful problem-solving occasions (N = 9).

The independent judges agreed in 81% of the cases. Disagreements did not concern more than one step on the scale.

CHILDHOOD MEMORIES

Subjects were placed in one of the following three categories representing different degrees of closeness to early childhood memories.

a. Early, vivid and sensual memories located at or, most often, before the age of 3 years. Solitary islands of traumatic scars do not belong here (N = 18).

b. Early, empty, or frightening memories, often solitary, or memories from the age of about 4 years (N = 14).

c. No such early memories (N = 11).

The independent judges agreed in 88% of the cases. Disagreements were mostly due to carelessness and never concerned more than one step on the scale.

COLOR DREAMS

Subjects were placed in one of the following three categories on a color scale.

a. Current dreams definitely in color (N = 16).

b. Uncertainty about color dreams or such dreams occurring in the past (N = 13).

c. Subjects who never thought about whether their dreams were in color or deny dreaming in color (N = 14).

The independent judges agreed in 88% of the cases, disagreements never concerning more than one step on the scale.

ATTITUDE TOWARD DREAMING

Subjects were placed in one of the following four categories representing different degrees of understanding and familiarity with their own dream life.

a. Genuine understanding of the nature and function of dreams, i.e., appreciation of dreams as an expression of the dreamer's private self. Considers dreaming an important part of his own life (N = 7).

b. Interested in his own dreams but misunderstands their function and advances home-made dream theories such as "dreams open up your future" or theories of a very ungenuine, artificial nature (N = 9).

c. Dreams, wants to dream, thinks dreaming is pleasant, remembers occasional dreams, but shows little interest in the nature and function of dreaming (N = 20).

Totally devoid of interest in dreams and dreaming (N = 7).

One of the judges, considering himself inferior to his partner in evaluating this category, abstained.

ANXIETY

Subjects were placed in one of the following four categories representing different degrees of anxiety manifestation plus one category (*e*) representing denial.

a. Very obvious experiences of anxiety: moments close to panic, hunger for air, globus, cramps, sweating, tendencies to faint, attacks of palpitation of the heart, etc. The symptom reliability increased by demanding present nightmare dreams as an additional sign for all subjects (N = 9).

b. Less obvious manifest anxiety: no moments close to panic, but more diffuse symptoms, passing phobic fears, etc. Subjects with more severe signs either in waking life or when dreaming, but not both, are also placed here (N = 13).

c. The so-called anxiety is more reminiscent of normal apprehension or fear or belongs to a previous period of the subject's life. Occasional nightmares with no counterpart symptoms in waking life are accepted in this category (N = 11).

d. Subjects do not comprehend the meaning of anxiety (N = 5).

e. Subjects deny anxiety. This denial does not necessarily imply total isolation of anxiety; subjects who very pointedly refer their symptoms to an earlier "distant" period of life are included here (N = 5).

The evaluation was left to one of the judges who had more practical-clinical experience than the other.

THE INVERTED FACTOR ANALYSIS

The inverted factor analysis was based on the technique described in Chapter 4. With twenty-one persons in the threat group and twenty-two in the control group, there were sixty-nine scoring dimensions in the first factor solution and sixty-four in the second. In all dimensions there were ≥ 3 markings for presence or absence. Varimax rotation was used, down to Eigenvalues ≥ 1.

The factor solutions were guided by the rule that no factor loading $< +0.45$ should be accepted. If a subject was to be assigned to a factor, the difference between his two largest (positive) loadings should be ≥ 0.10. In the accepted factor solution the lowest factor loading was $+0.47$. There were seven loadings > 0.70 in the control group and eight in the threat group. A D-index (see Chapter 4) was calculated for each item.

First, discarded factor solution. This solution gave seven factors in the threat group, one of them being a one-person factor. Fifteen subjects were placed. There were eight factors in the control group, two of them including only one person. Seventeen subjects were placed.

Second, accepted factor solution. To eliminate the one-person factors we searched for their key items. Five items had D-values >0.50 in a one-person factor and D-values <0.50 (with a difference of at least 0.20) in all other factors of ≥2 persons. These were eliminated—i.e., oceanic feelings (category *a* + *b* vs. *c*), visual set (no visual set at all vs. the rest), perseverating memories (pleasant memories vs. unpleasant or none), scientific interests, color reports on the PG test. The following items were allowed double weight, instead: *XX* scores vs. the rest, *XX* + *X* scores vs. the rest, creative activities (category *a* vs. the rest, and category *b* vs. the rest), early childhood memories (category *a* vs. the rest), color dreams (category *a* vs. the rest), attitude toward dreaming (category *a* vs. the rest), oceanic feelings (category *a* vs. the rest).

A limit of five factors was set for each group. In the threat group, seventeen persons were placed in two two-person factors, two three-person factors and one seven-person factor. In the control group sixteen persons were placed in four three-person factors and one four-person factor.

RESULTS

Following the hypotheses formulated in the introduction, we have constructed a criterion scale including literary-artistic activity (summarized as esthetic activity in the tables) plus early childhood memories (category *a*), color dreams (category *a*), understanding of dreams (category *a*), and oceanic feelings (category *a*). Subjects given scores on at least one of the last four dimensions have "other signs" in the tables. Considering present esthetic activity as the crucial criterion, we constructed the following scale: aesthetic activity *a* (i.e., still active); esthetic activity *b* (i.e., once active) plus "other signs" (as reinforcement); esthetic activity *b* only (i.e., without reinforcement); "other signs" only; the rest of the subjects.

When correlating the distribution over this scale with the distribution over categories in the inverted PG, we combined classes (*X*) and *O* because of their small size. Cross-validation of previous results should be most reliable when using a sample

TABLE 5.1
THE INVERTED PG AND CREATIVITY CRITERIA

Control group (threat group)	Inverted PG				
	XX	X	(X) 0	›2S	The rest
Esthetic activity a	3 (3)	4 (0)	0 (0)	1 (0)	0 (1)
Esthetic activity b plus "other signs"	2 (2)	1 (0)	1 (0)	0 (0)	1 (0)
Esthetic activity b only	0 (0)	1 (1)	1 (0)	0 (0)	0 (1)
"Other signs," only	0 (1)	0 (1)	0 (3)	1 (3)	3 (1)
The rest	0 (0)	0 (0)	1 (1)	1 (0)	1 (3)

Control group (median cutting): $P = 0.004$ (Fisher's exact text, one-sided)
                                    $G = 0.64$
Threat group (same cutting): $P = 0.014$ (Fisher's exact text, one-sided)
                                    $G = 0.62$
Groups combined (same cutting): $G = 0.63$

with an experimental setup differing as little as possible from that in the sample of researchers. We therefore used the control group when drawing medians for the 2 × 2 comparisons in Table 5.1. The P-values in the table refer to Fisher's exact test for such tables while the G refers to the G-index of agreement, which approximates a correlation coefficient.

It is evident that the inverted PG correlates very well with the criterion scale in both subgroups. We also expect a correlation between the straight and inverted PGs and, therefore, at least some correlation between the straight PG and the criterion scale. The former G-value is 0.43 in the combined groups (0.64 in the control group, 0.33 in the threat group). The latter G-value is 0.35 in the combined groups (0.55 in the control group, 0.14 in the threat group) (see Table 5.2). We shall return to the correlational discrepancy between the two subgroups.

It may also be instructive to compare the present groups with previous groups as regards their results on the inverted PG. Table 5.3 clearly reveals that the present group of humanistically oriented students is more similar to one of the placebo instruction groups, the group with the inward-directed instruction, than to the group of researchers.

TABLE 5.2
THE STRAIGHT PG AND CREATIVITY CRITERIA

Control group plus	Number of themes in straight PG			
Threat group	≥4.0	2.5-3.5	1.5-2.0	≥1.0
Esthetic activity a	7	3	2	0
Esthetic activity b				
plus "other signs"	2	3	1	1
Esthetic activity b only	0	1	1	2
"Other signs," only	3	4	5	1
The rest	0	2	1	4

G = 0.35

TABLE 5.3
DISTRIBUTION OF SCORING CATEGORIES ON THE INVERTED
PG IN THE PRESENT GROUPS AND IN PREVIOUS GROUPS

Group	Inverted PG				
	XX	X	(X)	0	The rest
Instruction: inward-directed.	1	2	2	1	7
Instruction: outward-directed.	6	3	0	1	2
Researchers	0	5	4	6	3
Present control	5	6	1	2	8
Present threat	6	2	2	2	9

The correlational differences, as shown above, between the control and threat subgroups seem to indicate a disruptive influence of the subliminal threat. It is also obvious, however (see Table 5.1), that the two subgroups are dissimilar with respect to the distribution over the criterion scale, in spite of the random assignment of subjects to the two experimental conditions—i.e., there are more control subjects in the upper reaches of the scale. Consequently, to estimate the effect of the threat an attempt was made to neutralize the influence of group differences, but there are other things to consider before testing the subliminal threat.

First, we wanted to inquire into the association between anxiety, on the one hand, and a creative urge or an understanding of one's own inner mental life, on the other. The relationship

TABLE 5.4
ANXIETY AND THE CREATIVITY CRITERIA

Criteria (groups combined)	Anxiety in interview	
	$a + b$	The rest
Esthetic activity a	8	4
Esthetic activity b plus "other signs"	5	2
Esthetic activity b, only	0	4
"Other signs," only	8	5
The rest	1	6

is presented in Table 5.4, where anxiety refers to levels a and b on the interview scale, level a representing too few subjects to be used alone. Anxiety was characteristic of a majority of subjects on all steps in the criterion scale except two: subjects who have left their creative activity behind them and have no additional signs of interest in their own mental functions plus the group lacking all creativity signs.

The association between anxiety and a present urge to create, or, at least, an understanding of one's own inner life, supports our tentative assumption of a beneficial effect of the subliminal threat, above all in subjects who are susceptible to that kind of stimulation. We would therefore consider d and e subjects on the anxiety scale as at least doubtful. To equalize the two subgroups with respect to the criterion scale, we divided the entire sample into three levels. Level A includes the two upper steps in the scale: esthetic activity a and esthetic activity b plus "other signs"; level B includes the next two steps: esthetic activity b only, and "other signs" only. A and B were relatively homogeneous in themselves and clearly different. Below A and B we found subjects lacking all signs of creativity.

The following prediction can now be made. Level A subjects are expected, optimally, to score XX as a result of the subliminal threat. It is more difficult to be precise about the B subjects, but they should at least score $>2S$ or better. The low-level subjects cannot be expected to move upwards on the creativity scale and are excluded in Table 5.5. The prediction is substan-

TABLE 5.5
EFFECTS OF THE SUBLIMINAL THREAT

Group	Optimal result	Non-optimal result
Control	8 (6)	11 (11)
Threat	14 (13)	3 (2)

The parentheses: when subjects in anxiety categories *d* and *e* are excluded.
Comparisons (Fisher's exact test, one-sided): P = 0.015 (0.004).

tiated even better when subjects lacking anxiety () or denying it (*e*) are excluded (see also Figure 5.1).

By quantifying, in five equidistant steps, the esthetic scale as written in Table 5.4 and the inverted PG scale as represented in Table 5.1, we were also able to compare the two groups with respect to their inverted PGs by performing an analysis of co-variance (where an adjustment is made for group differences with respect to the independent variable, the aesthetic scale). Even if the F-value for the dependent variable, the PG scale, was adjusted upwards, however, it failed to reach a significant value. This failure could be due to the erroneous equalization of the steps on both scales. When cautiously reconstructing the scales according to the reasoning underlying the arrangement in Table 5.5, we obtained an F of 4.69 (P<0.05). On the new esthetic scale, with the remainder group excluded, the scale values were 5, 4, 2, 1, while on the new inverted PG scale they were 7, 5, 4, 3, 1. We must add, however, that the distribution of values on the esthetic scale is bimodal rather than normal and that the first, nonparametric test for Table 5.5 may be the more correct procedure.

FACTOR SOLUTION, THE CONTROL GROUP

Factor I (three subjects). The highest D-index referring to the inverted PG (84) describes the subjects as scoring from (X) to >2S. In the straight PG they are scored for 1.5–3.5 themes (68). They report no or infrequent sleeping difficulties (74) and show

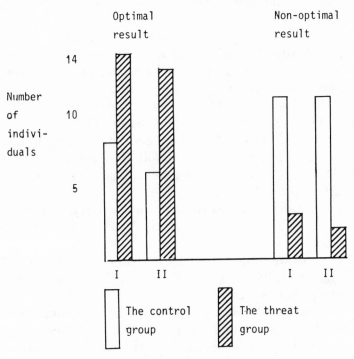

The inverted percept-genesis
(in individuals at creativity
levels A and B)

FIGURE 5.1
THE THREAT EFFECT.

little genuine understanding of dreams (53). Their memory is mainly visual (63).

We see this as a factor including, by and large, uncreative subjects, probably well guarded or, at least, with little interest in their own inner functions.

Factor II (three subjects). These subjects score *XX* in the inverted PG (94) and have ≥4 themes in the straight PG (74). In addition, there are relatively clear signs of anxiety in the test protocols (68). They are actively engaged in creative work at the present time (74), have a genuine or near genuine understanding of dreams (68), report color dreams (58), but do not consider themselves as particularly creative (63). Tendencies to participate in compulsive rituals, now or previously, are also reported (63).

Whatever they say about themselves, these subjects seem to be our creative subjects. As expected, their reconstructive efforts are often accompanied by anxiety and reports of sporadic compulsive rituals do not seem surprising.

Factor III (3 subjects). These subjects receive no scores in the inverted PG (90). They report color dreams (58) but also nightmares (63) and have a less than genuine understanding of dreams (84). They memorize visually (63) and are free from compulsive signs (53). There are clear symptoms of depression in the interview with this group (51).

Here neuroticism in one form or another seems to block the subject's access to his primary-process derivatives and ways of functioning.

Factor IV (four subjects). There are no convincing D-indices in this factor. Subjects score XX or X in the inverted PG (61) and were previously engaged in creative activities (53). Their understanding of dreams, however, is much less than genuine (56). They have a strong need for physical movement (56).

As the reader may have noted, a relatively rich inverted PG here is not necessarily combined with a relatively rich straight PG. The previous finding that a low straight PG score (where many themes without live persons were also considered a low score) is often associated with low emotional involvement in research work suggests that subjects in the present factor have left their creative activity behind them. But they would probably still be able to resume this activity.

Factor V (three subjects). The straight PG includes >4 themes (74). The inverted PG scores were XX and X (58) or XX, X, and (X) (53). Signs of anxiety occur in the test protocol (68). The subjects are not one-sidedly visual (63), have no strong need for physical movement (63), report no compulsive rituals (53), no color dreams (58) but occasional sleeping difficulties (58). Some of them consider themselves creative (53).

In spite of their relatively rich protocols and claims to creativity, these people are not actively engaged in creative work. The factor is difficult to really grasp but seems reminiscent of factor V in the threat group.

FACTOR SOLUTION, THE THREAT GROUP

Factor I (two subjects). This small factor is mainly characterized by anxiety signs on the test (90) and medium scores on the inverted PG (79).

Factor II (seven subjects). The inverted PG score is *XX* or *X* (93) and the straight PG includes ≥4 themes (57). Nightmares (50) and at least occasional sleeping difficulties (50) are reported by many subjects. Although these subjects, perhaps understandably, show little appreciation of dreams (50), they are presently or have previously been engaged in creative activities (50).

This factor obviously encompasses the bulk of creative and formerly creative subjects in the threat group. It is reminiscent of factor II in the control group, but differs from it in that rich inverted PGs are here, as a result of the subliminal activation, combined with more marginal signs of creativity and symbolic functioning. Signs of anxiety are also scored but not, as we know already, in those subjects who have left their a esthetic activities behind them and show no interest in their own inner life.

Factor III (two subjects). This small factor is determined mainly by a genuine understanding of dreams (90), color dreams (84), and esthetic activities (90). The subjects are exceptions to the general correlation found in this material because they do not score highly on their inverted PGs.

Factor IV (three subjects). These subjects report <1.5 themes in their straight PGs (100) and represent the low pole of the inverted scoring (83). They know nothing of color dreams (78) and do not show the slightest understanding of dreaming (50). They cannot retrieve early childhood memories (56) and do not like to play with children (50). Socially, they are relatively isolated (61). This is a factor of manifestly uncreative subjects, totally devoid of any interest in their own inner life. They strike us as very dull persons.

Factor V (three subjects). These subjects either show clear anxiety or defensively deny such symptoms (89). They describe themselves as creative (67) and independent (67) and obviously enjoy social contacts (56) and playing with other adults (61). Occasional sleeping difficulties are reported (56) and some test signs of medium anxiety are noted (56). In the straight PG they report 1.5–2.0 themes (56), and on the inverted PG they get (*X*) or *O* marks (94).

What is most obvious in these people is the discrepancy between a rather meager inverted PG (meager in spite of the subliminal threat), together with lack of other signs of creative functioning, on the one hand, and open claims of creativity, on the other. They also differ from most truly creative people with respect to their social contacts, which tend to be wide but shallow. We feel tempted to call these people *pseudocreative*, and shall return to them in a later context.

Among the variables given double weight in the second factor analysis were the four variables called "other signs" in the tables. It is difficult to ascertain their correlation with the inverted PG in the control group because among fourteen subjects with *a*-scores in one or more of these variables, ten were also scored for esthetic activities *a* or *b*. However, three of them appeared in 2–4 factors each, with D-values >50. The fourth variable, oceanic feelings, got relatively low Ds in both groups.

DISCUSSION

The present investigation implies a cross-validation of the previous one. What was called richness in ideas in the group of researchers and an urge to artistic-literary creation in the present group, both correlate with retrieval of subjective themes on the inverted PG. To be creative in any field, the individual must apparently escape the dominance over his experience of conventional conceptions of reality and play with unconventional alternatives. The breeding ground for these alternatives is to be found mainly within the individual himself. In scientific and humanistic work, as in esthetic creation, the individual must let his childish self question his rational, adult self in order to transgress the surface meaning of reality, i.e., to function symbolically. As we know, this has been called adaptive regression (Hartmann, 1939; Kris, 1952); we prefer to call it reconstruction (Kragh and Smith, 1974). The functional shift implied by the reconstruction of P-phase material, when the C-phase meaning is already known, has not only cognitive implications, however. Besides making new combinations and ways of thinking possible (cf. Arieti, 1976), this reconstruction is also bound to imply more closeness to motivational sources, i.e., increased emotional involvement and a rising urge to create (see also, below).

The similarities between various creative groups tested in the present program should not lead us to efface the characteristic differences between them. Given the scoring categories used for our subjects, there are four different ways of functioning on the inverted PG: (1) complete dependence on the C-phase meaning; (2) retention of the C-phase meaning together with a simultaneous reconstruction of P-phases; (3) construction of a C-phase but, thereafter, a wholehearted return to stimulus-distant motifs; (4) inability to construct the C-phase meaning. The first alternative was typical of people with little interest in or aptitude for creative work; the second typified researchers who were original and rich in ideas, while the third alternative was characteristic of people with an urge for esthetic creation as well as those in the placebo group (Chapter 3), instructed that their medicine would make them relaxed and inward-directed. The fourth alternative was not typical of our subjects. It is a pathological variant that we have encountered in cases of serious alcoholism (refusal to recognize the bottle) and which also might be associated with certain psychotic patients.

We have already attended to the difference between the researchers and the aesthetic group. In their exploitation of unconventional ways of cognitive functioning, our creative researchers apparently did not venture as far from an ordered and rational reality context as many of our esthetically creative subjects were inclined to do. The constant checking of new conceptions against established ones is part and parcel even of pioneering research endeavors. However, the difference between creative researchers and esthetically creative subjects may be overstated in the present study because the latter subjects were selected on the basis of their urge to create, not their ability to deliver consummate esthetic products. The close similarity between these subjects and the "passive" placebo group may be instructive. Professional artists and writers who pay particular attention to the problem of esthetic integration and communication would be more likely to retain some C-phase contact in their inverted PGs (see Chapter 14).

Another difference between the researchers and the present sample is indicated by the relatively high correlation between the straight and inverted PGs in the control group (G = 0.64). The same correlation was lower in the research group (G = 0.44). As already mentioned, there was a *special* correlation in the latter group between the straight PG and emotional involvement in research work: the subjects involved had at least two 1.0 point themes and reported live people. The correlational difference just mentioned perhaps reflects a difference between creative research work and esthetic creation, implying that creativity and emotional involvement would be more closely associated in the esthetic group. The figures do not, however, support such an assumption. Among six emotionally involved researchers, as defined by the test, four received an X score in the inverted PG; only one researcher outside this group received the same score. XX scores were not given. Among eight subjects with similar straight PGs in the present control group (the group most analogous to the research group), four received XX scores and three X scores; one additional member of the control group received XX and three received X. There were eighteen subjects altogether in the group of researchers and twenty-two in the present control group. In both groups there was clearly a close association between high creativity in the test situation and signs on the straight PG that indicate emotional involvement. This accords with our original assumptions.

It was assumed that the interview variables listed as "other signs" in the tables would have something in common with creativity. In fact, in the group of research workers, the more innovative ones often reported early, sensual childhood recollections and also maintained that their scientific ideas were generated from within. Since "other signs" are closely tied to what has been called esthetic activity *a* and *b*, they are difficult to evaluate independently. However, their presence seems to lend new meaning to esthetic activity *b* and transform this latent possibility into a revived urge for reconstruction (see Table 5.1). Like esthetic activity *a*, "other signs" are often combined with symptoms of anxiety (Table 5.4). At the same time, it is precisely in the threat group that many subjects characterized by one or more of the "other signs" (even without an activity *a* score) respond positively to the subliminal threat. As a matter of fact, these very subjects lie behind the main effect in Table 5.5. The D-values show that the "other signs," except for oceanic feelings, decisively codetermine the factor solution. Chosen to reflect the subject's degree of insight into his own mental life, they thus seem to represent some sort of sensitivity to subliminal cues, the kind of sensitivity we have presumed to be a prerequisite for, but not analogous with, symbolic functioning. Or to express it in PG terms: in these people the P-phases are not permanently disqualified but remain accessible.

But let us not leave the problem of anxiety. Table 5.5 was assumed to reflect an effect of subliminally induced anxiety. The same would be true of the correlational differences between the threat and control groups presented previously. The correlation just mentioned between the straight and inverted PGs in the control group, however, reappears in the threat group. Among six subjects in the latter group with at least two 1.0 point themes and reports of live persons, four receive *XX* scores and one an *X* score; among the remaining fifteen subjects, only three received such scores. And why should the two groups differ in this respect? The factor analysis is, again, most revealing. In the threat group, creative and formerly creative people blend within one common factor. The creative factor (II) is purer in the control group. Even though the positive effect of the subliminal threat—increasing the inclination to reconstruct P-phases—was also registered in subjects not distinguished for their creativity, this effect was not found in all subjects. If we lump the remainder group together with other subjects lacking clear signs of anxiety (categories *a* and *b*), a rather insensitive group is obtained. There are seven such subjects in the threat group, five of whom received the lowest possible score on the inverted PG; but the numbers are small and should invoke caution.

It is possible that other kinds of subliminal stimuli, e.g., sexual motifs, could have had a more pronounced effect. They might even have influenced the low group on the creativity scale. The results presented by Antell and Goldberger (1986) indicate such a difference between threatening and sexual stimuli. The present study, however, concerns anxiety in its relation to creativity. The kind of anxiety we have tried to inject into the experimental situation naturally bears a special relation to the oral-sadistic stimulus theme. We can only guess about similar effects of other threatening motifs. Nor can we know for sure how less anxiety-tolerant, e.g., severely neurotic, subjects would have reacted; but we have learned from previous experiments (Kragh and Smith, 1970) that subliminal threat is likely to increase the defensive activity in such people. Nevertheless, we may conclude with some certainty that anxiety—but probably not far above some optimal level (Hammer, 1975)—is a natural companion of the urge to use one's inner resources creatively, and that the slight sharpening of this anxiety, effected by the subliminal threat, sensitizes rather than dulls many a subject to his early P-phase material. Endowed with instruments, even if sometimes rusty and imperfect, to master the potentially dangerous, stirred-up unconscious forces by integrating them into a creative product, these subjects are thus inclined to receive the extra subliminal influx of anxiety as a positive challenge (cf. the statement by an introspective artist in Rosén, 1975, pp. 142–143). Moreover, the inverted PG supplies information not found in the straight protocol—e.g., the difference between XX and X. As shown in the group of researchers, the discrepancies between the two PGs may be particularly illuminating. Factor IV in the control group, for that matter, partly rests on such discrepancies. Here we find subjects who, in spite of their ability to reconstruct P-phases in the inverted PG, often receive medium or low scores in the straight PG. These are the potentially creative people that just do not care to work creatively any longer; and according to their thin, straight PGs they are no longer emotionally involved.

6

CREATIVITY AND ANXIETY: A CLINICAL STUDY

An impressive body of studies, ably summarized by Suler (1980), supports the assumption that in acts of creation we utilize primary-process functioning. In our own studies, the transcendence of boundaries between rationality and irrationality and between conscious experiences and preconscious ones is considered a *conditio sine qua non* for creative activity.

But creative activity also presupposes willingness and opportunity to take risks. A strong need for personal safety and convenience is often assumed to be detrimental to creative work. This seems to be a reasonable assumption, already partly supported by our work (Chapter 5). Lack of safety could also, however, prevent the person from taking risks, as Kubie (1958) among others has pointed out. An excess of anxiety or a rigid system of defenses (cf. Fitzgerald, 1966; Suler, 1980) would very likely prevent the engagement of new and unusual thoughts and ideas if these in any way involve tabooed sections of the unconscious. According to our *first hypothesis*, anxiety-ridden or rigidly defensive subjects are thus likely to score comparatively low on our creativity test, even if when interviewed their expressed urge for creative activity was similar to that of normal subjects.

As shown in Chapter 5, a subliminal threat (a horrifying face) administered together with the still life, just before the inverted PG, significantly enhanced the revival of P-phase themes. Subjects were normal people who, according to the same kind of interview as used in the present study, reported a wish to engage in creative activities. The subliminal threat evidently caused an increment of discomfort which raised the "creative temperature." At the same time, our *second hypothesis* is that in cases of excessive anxiety or low tolerance of it, and in cases with a concomitant inclination to use rigid defense strategies, this increment would have no positive effect.

To test these hypotheses, we applied the subliminal design just mentioned to a group of psychiatric patients with anxiety as one of their main symptoms. We encountered a mixed group of depressive, phobic, hysteric, compulsive, etc., reactions but no psychotic or organic symptoms. The subjects included in the previous chapter were used in the present study as normal controls.

We would also like to repeat here that creativity is not necessarily associated with great talent but with a basic attitude toward living—an urge to change and enrich one's everyday existence from within. This attitude presumes that the person keeps an open line of communication between surface and depth in his world of experience.

METHODS

SUBJECTS

There were thirty-one subjects in the clinical group, thirty of whom were inpatients at a psychiatric clinic. The remaining subject was an outpatient in psychotherapy. There were seventeen men and fourteen women. They ranged in age from 29 to 60 years, although most (27) were between 29 and 49. As we selected patients with anxiety as one of their main symptoms, we also tried to reach as many patients as possible with creative interests. We were careful to avoid psychotic and organic cases. Most patients had resided for some time in the hospital and, if not actually cured, were well enough to consent to take part in the investigation. Reactive depression and anxiety neurosis were among the most common diagnostic labels.

There were forty-three subjects in the normal group, fourteen men and twenty-nine women, with an age range of 19 to 49 years. Since neither age nor sex, have been found to correlate with performance in the CFT or with placement on the interview scales among adults, the slight age or sex differences between normal and clinical subjects were not a matter of concern. For instance, in a group of nineteen professional artists with an age range of 32–57 years, eight subjects received high scores in the PG test, five of them being above median age. When administering subliminal stimulation in the backward masking design we could also observe that older subjects did not seem more insensitive to the subliminal stimulation than younger ones. The normal group was also selected to get a sizable proportion of subjects with creative interests.

DESIGN

All subjects in both the clinical and the normal group took the Creative Functioning Test (CFT) and participated in a half-structured *interview*. The clinical subjects also took an additional test, the *Meta-Contrast Technique (MCT)*. The testing always preceded the interview, and the experimenter and interviewer were different persons.

On the basis of the interview, a *Creative Activity Scale* was formed. While the CFT aimed at disclosing the ability to function creatively, the scale was used primarily to establish the subject's urge to be creative. This distinction is particularly important with regard to the first hypothesis. Associated scales on dreaming, childhood memories and "oceanic experiences" were also used. Furthermore, a scale was constructed to measure degree of anxiety.

Our main differentiating tool in the present study was the *Subliminal PG Design*. All subjects in both groups were randomly exposed to one of two stimuli in the CFT: a subliminal threat stimulus, or a subliminal neutral counterpart. Only the very last subjects in both groups were an exception to the randomization, because the threat and nonthreat subgroups had to be better balanced with respect to age and sex. Fifteen subjects in the

clinical group and twenty-one in the control group were assigned to the threat condition.

The MCT was given to the clinical subjects to help us find
out some of the obstacles preventing a patient with an obvious
urge to create (as measured by the interview) from actually
abandoning the safety of an objective (conventional) conception
of reality (as measured by the inverted PG). The MCT is particularly designed to show the subject's level of anxiety and the
kind and intensity of his defensive functioning (see section on
MCT, below). In spite of the fact that both the MCT and the
CFT use fractioned stimulus presentation, they cannot replace
each other because they reveal very different functions in the
individual.

THE CFT

The CFT was administered as described in Chapter 5, but
a new contrivance allowed the use of two additional exposure
steps (up to 7.24 sec.). No subject gave the slightest hint of
having discerned any trace of the subliminal stimulus, in spite
of the instruction to report even the vaguest impressions. Although subliminality is not the issue here, we wanted to keep
the stimulus subliminal in order to maximize the effect of the
threat. During the paired presentations the reports did not
change appreciably, i.e., the final impression remained stable.

As reported in Chapter 5, inter-rater correspondence in the
normal group was 88%. Only two one-step discrepancies were
noted in the clinical group.

THE MCT

The MCT has been described in detail elsewhere (Kragh and
Smith, 1970; Smith and Danielsson, 1982; Hentschel and Smith,
1980; Smith, Johnson, and Almgren, 1982). Although both the
MCT and CFT utilize the same tachistoscope, presentation of
the former involves *pairs* of stimuli (A and B). Stimulus A, in
the version used here, depicts a forbidding face. Stimulus B
depicts a young person sitting at a table with a small window

in the background. B was first presented with gradually prolonged exposure times (0.01, 0.02, 0.04 sec. etc.). Once the
subject had reported B correctly, the exposure time was reduced to a standard value (0.06 sec.), which, unnoticed by the
subject, continued into the main series where A was exposed
immediately before B. While the exposure time of B was kept
constant, that of A was gradually prolonged (0.01, etc., as in
the CFT) until A + B had been correctly reported in three
consecutive trials (if possible). A + B was exposed twice at each
exposure step. Subjects were told to report everything they
caught a glimpse of on the projection screen at each trial.

The scoring dimensions pertinent to the present study concern the subject's defensive strategies, i.e., the strategies used
to ward off or distort the threat (stimulus A) directed at the
young person in stimulus B, and also the anxiety evoked by it.
A is projected on the same area of the screen as the window in
B. Here we need to describe only a few dominating defensive
categories.

Stereotypy. A stereotyped repetition including at least five—and
often many more—consecutive phases, of the same interpretation of A or of a noninterpreted A ("something in the window"). This is a sign of depression.

Empty protocols. Except for a few details, the picture appears
similar to the subject and there is no mention of the A stimulus
until the correct A is recognized. Common in subjects described
as compulsive characters, sometimes also found in depressed
individuals.

More open or vague defenses. Here we refer to protocols in
which defense signs appear only in single phases or are very
vague or tentative or do not appear at all.

The above dimensions were easy to score.

Four subjects in the clinical group had no MCT protocols.
The test was not used in the normal group.

THE INTERVIEW AND CREATIVE ACTIVITY SCALE

The interview was structured as described in Chapter 5. Subjects in the clinical group were placed in one of six categories
representing different degrees of their artistic/creative talent,

as well as their urge to create. Only the four top categories will be presented here.

A +. Genuine artistic/creative activities with emotional involvement and a need to express something personal; activities to which the person is presently committed or would like to commit himself given the opportunity.

A −. At least partially handicapped in this respect by their present psychic condition; hampered, locked, or screened off; resisting a too deep personal engagement, etc. The creativity problems, involving an urgent need to express something personal, are still very much in the foreground, however.

B +. Such activities belong to the person's past; he does not get inspired by them any longer or believe in them; his creativity is at best latent or "undelivered."

B −. The person's creativity belongs to the past. But he also seems handicapped as described in A −.

The independent investigators in the clinical group disagreed in ten cases, nine of them involving one step on the scale and eight referring to the A − level. The judges agreed on all changes except for one, which was left to a third judge to decide.

The only categories used for the normal group were A, B, C, and D, since they had no hampering psychic conditions.

The reliabilities of the associated interview scales were as follows:

Oceanic feelings. The independent judges in the clinical group disagreed in two cases. Disagreements did not concern more than one step on the scale.

Childhood memories. The independent judges in the clinical group disagreed in four cases. Disagreements never concerned more than one step on the scale and only one involved the *a* class (see Chapter 5).

Color dreams. The independent judges in the clinical group disagreed in two cases, disagreements not concerning more than one step on the scale but both involving the *a* class.

Attitude toward dreaming. The independent judges in the clinical group disagreed in seven cases, none of them involving the *a* class.

Anxiety. There were no disagreements.

A five-step anxiety scale used in the control group differed from the clinical scale above all by not including the paroxysmal anxiety typical of stage *a* in the clincial group (see Chapter 5).

RESULTS

In both the normal and clinical groups the threat and non-threat subgroups were practically identical with respect to placement on the interview scales, attainment of a C-phase, subjective human motifs in the straight PG, age, and sex. There were four patients with grave anxiety (stage *a*) in the clinical threat subgroups and five in the nonthreat subgroup.

Among the thirty-one clinical subjects, sixteen placed in the A level of the creative activity scale; compared with twelve of the forty-three normal subjects. Two clinical and eleven normal subjects placed in the B level. However, fourteen of sixteen clinical A subjects were at least partially handicapped by their present condition, even if "to create" was still their focal concern. We placed them in a special subcategory (A−), not applicable to the normal group. The clinical subjects were, on the whole, more seriously involved in their creative activities than the normal subjects, a difference tending to work against our hypothesis. The creative activities in both groups were generally of an artistic or literary nature; a few of the individuals composed popular music.

In Table 6.1 letters A and B refer to the creative activity scale, and the letter *a* refers to top placements in the associated four scales. A subject placed in the creativity category B + ≤ 1*a* scored B on the creative activity scale and *a* on at least one of the associated scales.

If A and B + ≤ 1*a* are separated from the lower steps on the creativity axis, we obtain two contrasts, one in the normal group and one in the clinical. The G-index of agreement (Holley and Guilford, 1964; Starvig, 1981) is 0.63 for the first contrast and 0.23 for the second. Comparing the contrasts (15–4) and 6–12) by means of Fisher's exact test we get a P = 0.006 (one-tailed). Clinical subjects on the highest level of the creative activity scale

TABLE 6.1
COMPARISON BETWEEN THE NORMAL AND CLINICAL GROUPS

Group	Inverted PG	
	XX/X	The rest
Normal		
Subjects with A or B + $\geq$1a on		
the Creative activity scale	15	4
The rest	4	20
Clinical Subjects with A or B + $\geq$1a on		
the Creative activity scale	6	12
The rest	0	13

recover fewer themes in their inverted PGs than their normal counterparts. The inverted PG is obviously sensitive to the difference between subjects who want to resume their habitual creative work but cannot, and subjects who are not prevented by their present condition to do so.

The subliminal effect was estimated in the first study of the normal group (Chapter 5). To replicate this estimation, we referred our subjects to three levels. Level 1 included subjects with an A score on the creative activity scale or a B score if the subject received at least one a on any of the other scales (level 1 = A or B+ $\geq$ 1a); level 2 included subjects with B scores and no a score on the other scales, or C scores on the creative activity scale but at least one more a score (level 2 = B + 0a or 0+ $\geq$ 1a). The rest of the subjects were placed in level 3. Level 1 subjects were expected to receive top scores (XX) on the inverted PG test as a result of the subliminal threat while level 2 subjects were expected to have at least some sign of creativity (the lowest step on the scoring ladder being more than two sensitivity signs [S]). Level 3 subjects were not expected to move upwards on the scoring ladder of the inverted PG and were not further considered.

The results are presented in Table 6.2. No effects of the subliminal threat emerged in the clinical group. The difference between the normal threat group (14–3) and the clinical one (2–8) is highly significant (P = 0.005, Fisher's exact test, one-

TABLE 6.2
EFFECTS OF THE SUBLIMINAL THREAT

Group	Score in the inverted PG	
	Optimal	Not optimal
Normal subjects receiving threat stimulation	14	3
Subjects receiving nonthreat stimulation	8	11
Clinical subjects receiving threat stimulation	2	8
Subjects receiving nonthreat stimulation	2	12

For further explanation of the table, see text.

tailed). Since there are eleven level 2 subjects in the normal group and only two in the clinical group, the difference might be attributable to that disproportion. However, even when we randomly diminished the number of level 2 subjects in the normal group from eleven to two, the 14–3 distribution in Table 6.2 became a 7–1 distribution, and the difference between the two threat groups remained highly significant (P = 0.008).

In Table 6.3 we have attempted to illustrate the two factors which, according to our first hypothesis, should be most detrimental to creative activity: grave anxiety and rigid defense strategies. In the first column we have included subjects where depressive or compulsive reactions block practically all reconstructive activity in the MCT, the protocols being empty or characterized by long sections of stereotyped repetitions; the second column included subjects with tentative, vague or isolated signs of defense, i.e., protocols of a more near-normal variety. Subjects who reported symptoms of grave anxiety in the interview (also scored for anxiety in the MCT) were added to the first column. The results, summarized in Table 6.3, confirmed our assumptions.

The interview scales were also analyzed. The clinical creative activity scale was quantified by assigning the scale steps the following values: A+ = 4; A− = 3; B = 2; and C = D = 1.

TABLE 6.3
THE INVERTED PG IN THE PSYCHIATRIC GROUP ESTIMATED
AS A OR B CREATIVE IN THE INTERVIEW

Scores in inverted PG	MCT and/or interview	
	Stereotypy, empty protocols, and/or grave anxiety	More open or vague defenses, no grave anxiety
Subjects scoring		
XX/X/(X)/0	1	6
The rest	7	1

P = 0.009 (Fisher's exact test, one-tailed).

The remaining four dimensions were quantified with *a* receiving a value of 2; *b* a value of 1, and lower scale steps a value of 0. The product-moment correlation in the clinical group between the creative activity scale and the sum of other scales is 0.43 (P = close to 0.01). The analogous correlation in the normal group is 0.18. This value might be somewhat misleading, however, because the creative activity scale covers a more limited range in that group. The best cut in a four-field table yields a G-index of agreement of 0.40. The regression areas look very similar in both groups. Thus, the present clinical group appears not to differ from the normal group with respect to the association between the creative activity scale and the sum of other scales.

The scores in associated dimensions are generally lower in the clinical group (md = 2.5 when the dimensions were quantified as above) than in the normal group (md = 3.5).

It might also be enlightening to compare correlations between the creativity dimension and certain other dimensions. When computing G-indices of agreement, we distinguished between A scores and other scores on the creativity axis and chose the cut yielding the strongest contrast on the other axis. One interesting difference emerged. The correlation between the creative activity scale and the color dream and dream appreciation scales were 0.44 (P = 0.015, Fisher's exact test, one-sided) and 0.26 in the normal group, but only 0.10 and 0.03 in the clinical group. Many clinical subjects with a strong urge to create apparently blocked access to their dream life. Judging by the severe nightmares reported by these people, dreaming can be a frightening activity indeed.

DISCUSSION

The present study rests on three cornerstones: the CFT, the MCT, and the interview. The two tests were scored according to principles laid down in previous investigations, principles that have proved to possess a high degree of inter-rater reliability and did not present any difficulties for previous and present raters when comparing their independent scoring sheets. One of the raters did not have access to interview data when scoring the tests, the other rater had not seen most of these data for many months and could not match names and protocols. In the few instances of disagreement the former rater's opinion carried more weight. Even if we succeeded in obliterating halo effects between interview and test, it is still possible that the interview scales were not used independently of one another. However, the interview protocols were first rated by each of the authors; they rested more on factual information supplied by the interviewee than on the interviewer's impressions. As shown by an inverted factor analysis in the first study of the normal group, the intercorrelations between the interview scales varied considerably; at least two correlations in the clinical group, as demonstrated here, were negligible. Correlations between the creative activity scale and the sum of the other scales were moderate in both groups. Because correlations were expected, halo effects would have increased these latter correlations and made the correlational landscape more even.

The main theme of the study, the relationship between creativity and mental health, may seem worn out. The two are often associated because the devouring intensity of creative genius must, to the uncreative mind, appear to be born out of madness. Thomas Mann's Doktor Faustus is a well-known case in point. This view of creativity, as we have pointed out, is not shared by Kubie (1958) and many others of the psychoanalytic ego-and-defense generation. As a matter of fact, the theorizing around "regression in the service of the ego" or adaptive regression (Kris, 1952; Hartmann, 1939; cf. Suler, 1980) partly implies that creative processing takes place outside the realm of intrapsychic conflict.

The reconstruction, in acts of creation, of very private or primitive material may involve dangers for the individual and trigger defensive reactions via anxiety signals. These dangers could be of two kinds: (1) the illogical and "irresponsible" ways of thinking associated with primary-process functioning, and (2) the nonauthorized and unconventional thought content, above all if it reactivates unacceptable infantile memories. But it would be too rash to assume that these obstacles cannot be circumvented, especially in cases where the danger areas do not cover more than part of the individual's experience. If the self-proximal content associated with primary-process functioning is not reactualized, but only the more self-distant formal qualities, this could be helpful in many instances, more often perhaps for scientists than for artists and writers. Rothenberg (1979) mentions negation as one way around direct confrontation; projective functioning is another possibility proposed in Chapter 4. It has also been suggested that in some cases only those primary-process aspects already well integrated with secondary-process functioning become involved in creative work (see Noy, 1969, 1972; Bush, 1969; Suler, 1980); therefore they do not appear foreign and dangerous.

The creative persons discussed in previous chapters were not devoid of personal problems, however. The most creative of them had to bear anxiety and disquietude as regular companions. In the present control group, for example, the subjects' placements on a five-graded anxiety scale (covering more moderate symptoms than the scale used in the clinical group) diminished with their placement on the creativity scale. Among nineteen level 1 (see above) subjects, thirteen belonged to the two upper steps of the anxiety scale, while among seven level 3 (see above) subjects, only one did. This observation has led us to assume that a certain amount of anxiety or discomfort is a necessary condition for creative functioning. The presentation of a threatening subliminal stimulus in the PG test of the control group even seemed to facilitate the resumption of subjective interpretations in the inverted PG, particularly in subjects where the urge to create had become dormant over the years, and where, typically, there were few reports of anxiety.

The results of the present study indicate that anxiety can also exert an inhibitory influence. If their tolerance for anxiety had not been relatively low, our present subjects would hardly have looked for shelter in a psychiatric clinic. In many of them, as predicted by the first hypothesis, there was a clear discrepancy between their urge to do creative work and their actual results in the inverted PG. Since the extra supply of anxiety given via subliminal channels did not help much, the second hypothesis also received support. The most obvious obstacles to creative functioning in this group were not indifference but an excess of anxiety or rigid defenses (cf. Fitzgerald, 1966), the latter most often associated with depression or compulsive isolation. It is also interesting to note that the urge to create in the clinical group did not correlate, as it did in the normal group, with closeness to one's own inner life as it expresses itself in dreams; and that low tolerance of anxiety can block performance in the inverted PG test in 10–11-year-olds (Chapter 8).

If a moderately heightened level of anxiety seems to be optimal for creative work, at least in its initial stages, total lack of apprehension or excessive amounts are likely to spoil everything. When anxiety reveals the presence of inner danger and sets defensive forces in action, or when the level of anxiety becomes unbearable in itself, the playful crossing of borders between rational and irrational functioning, between conventional order and apparent anarchy, is checked and perhaps altogether halted. But without anxiety the individual obviously lacks creative incentive—he is satisfied with himself and the world and does not want any change; he is too coy to embark on any cumbersome activity and is not made aware of his own inner territories or latent conflicts—the raw material of constructive work in creative people.

Important problems remain to be explored. It is a fact, for instance, that many neurotic or otherwise deviant persons are highly creative at the same time. If their neurosis threatens to obstruct their activities, they may try to circumvent dangerous conflict areas via some of the routes already suggested. A great

tolerance for anxiety and discomfort may help to check imped-
ing defensive reactions. Disadvantaged children who have
learned to persevere despite frustrations are thus more likely
to develop as creative problem solvers than advantaged children
who often are afraid of failure (Yando, Seitz, and Zigler, 1979).
But it is also possible that "abnormality" can have positive effects
(see Székély, 1976). Perhaps it serves to open totally deviant
perspectives which the person, if otherwise functioning reasonably well, could exploit creatively.

7

CAN PRESCHOOL CHILDREN BE CREATIVE?
(Age 4–6 Years)

In the discussion at the end of Chapter 4 we assumed that children and adults differ with respect to how new mental structure comes about. A child forms these structures at the very spearhead of their percept-genesis where they are mingled with the C-phase. When this spontaneous formation of new structure is thwarted with increasing age, new structure has to be created via reconstructive operations. This does not necessarily mean, however, that children are creative in our meaning of the term. Previous studies (Smith and Danielsson, 1982), using percept-genetic techniques, of anxiety and defense in children clearly demonstrated how incapable preschool children are of internalizing their defensive operations. At the same time, they were unable to stabilize a C-phase at the end of their percept-genesis—i.e., they could not clearly differentiate subjective and objective qualities in their experience or distinguish between their own self and that part of reality which is independent of the self. Not until children are able to stabilize a C-phase do they begin to construct an internal, representational world of their own, thereby making themselves less dependent on stimulation from the outside. If our preschool children add new structure to their percept-genesis it is, therefore, highly plausible that these structures reflect what is close at hand in the form of outside stimulation at that moment.

91

Thus, in our first study of 4- to 6-year-old children we expected only a relatively few of them, the oldest and cognitively most mature, to show real percept-geneses in the CFT—i.e., a series of P-phases gradually approaching stimulus, and no inverted geneses among the majority of children were anticipated.

In previous studies with children, it was deemed important to combine age and cognitive maturity when constructing a hierarchy of groups reflecting the gradual change of defensive strategies, starting with primitive, external ones. Therefore, a Piaget test (the Landscape or Three-Mountain Test) was included in the present study. After constructing the hierarchy of age-maturity groups we described them using the MCT. In addition to the Landscape Test, the MCT, and the CFT, an "interview" was conducted with the child to gain information about play activities and fantasy life. On the basis of these soft data we planned to construct a number of criteria to test some basic aspects of the CFT results. In addition, artistic products were utilized.

METHODS AND SUBJECTS

There was only one experimenter (I.C.). Before bringing a child to the laboratory, she spent some time getting acquainted at the nursery school. At the laboratory the child always took the Landscape Test first, followed by the CFT and then the MCT. The testing was liberally interspersed with pauses. In some cases the child was also interviewed on the same occasion and made clay figures and drawings. When time was limited or the child was impatient, the experimenter met the child on another day at the nursery school.

THE CFT

This test was given as before but the projection screen was placed only about 1.0 m from the subject. The subject was asked to report what he saw or thought he had glimpsed at each exposure. Sometimes he made drawings of what he had seen

in order to supplement his verbal description. The experimenter also noted the child's behavior.

In addition to previous scoring dimensions the following ones
were used:

1. Subjective additions to the C-phase, C_s, were recorded, with
the exception of drink or food (e.g., "water in the bottle").

2. *Borrowed themes (both PGs)* are themes taken from the immediate surroundings. In these cases the child is either scanning
the room before answering or using its most characteristic features ("a screen," "holes in the walls," "lamps fastened to
shelves," etc.).

3. *Haphazard themes (both PGs)* can be of two kinds. In most
cases the subject answers before the stimulus has been presented
or without looking in the direction of the screen; in a few cases
the subject starts a long harangue of words only loosely con-
nected with the task at hand.

4. *Retention (the straight PG)* implies that, in spite of the fact
that a structure is interpreted differently from before, the old
interpretation is not disqualified. The subject may see a bird
at one exposure but a human being at the next; but he adds
that the person is probably looking at the bird.

5. *More than one-third of the straight presentation series (up to the
end stage) is unstructured,* i.e., these subjects need more time than
other subjects to give the stimulus a name.

Independent scoring of the CFT has shown high inter-rater
agreement. In the present study the raters also agreed for the
most part not only with respect to the old categories, but with
respect to the new ones as well. Occasional differences between
the raters were nearly always due to an oversight by one of
them.

THE MCT

In the MCT we utilized the following gross defensive categories:

External defenses, like eye shutting or sleep behavior, i.e., when
the child shuts its eyes upon glimpsing something new on the
screen or complains about sleepiness, yawns openly, etc. Since

the child might actually be bored by the test, sleep behavior was only noted when accompanied by other signs, e.g., attempts to flee from the situation or seek shelter with the experimenter, a sudden need to go to the toilet, etc.

Internalized defenses of a relatively primitive type, where the percept itself is distorted but the distortions reflect a narcissistic or egocentric perspective. The subject may report that the young person in B closes his eyes or that the new structure appearing in the window is a duplicate of that person (hero duplication).

Internalized defenses of a more mature type, where the threat is seen as a white spot or empty oval (isolation), as a stiff bust or mask or a nonthreatening animal (repression), or where the perception of A is held back and changes in B are reported instead, changes which do not endanger the continuity of the PG (sensitivity projection). Drastic B-changes are considered as signs of a lack of constancy in the child's conception of the world rather than as signs of projective defense (cf. Smith and Danielsson, 1982).

The test protocols were first scored by each of us independent of the other. Disagreements were few. High inter-rater correlations have been reported in other MCT studies (see Almgren, 1971).

THE LANDSCAPE TEST

The cognitive task (Piaget and Inhelder, 1941, 1956) was designed to measure degree of egocentric thinking. A model of a mountain landscape with three (differently shaded) peaks was placed in front of the subject who had four photos of the landscape at his disposal, each taken from a different direction. A doll was then placed in these viewing positions one after the other, starting with the child's own position. The child was asked to choose the photo which represented the doll's perspective.

A child dominated by egocentric thinking prefers the photo showing its own perspective, but a pre-egocentric child would not even understand how to choose when the doll was located in the subject's own position. This was the main reason that the "own" perspective was included in our version of the Landscape. It also should be mentioned that the child was never given the impression that his choices were final. When uncertain whether the child had made an authentic choice, the experimenter asked the child to try again in order to promote optimal performance.

THE INTERVIEW

The experimenter interviewed the child about a number of topics that could be used to construct a creativity-fantasy scale. The central topics are reflected in the following fourteen questions: (1) Can the child imagine itself being a chair in role play? (2) Does he like to dress up? (3) Does he enjoy theatrical play? (4) Can he play alone? (5) Is he capable of improvising play tools? (6) Does he like to draw, paint, mould, build, etc.? (7) Has he composed a song, made up a story, etc., of his own? (8) Has he constructed any of his own toys? (9) Can he tell what happened in one of his dreams? (10) Does he have a fantasy playmate? (11) Does he react positively when asked what he would do if there were no restraining rules? (12) Does he remember any nightmares? (13) Is he sometimes afraid? (14) Does he have a transitional object?

The anxiety variables 12 and 13 were added because imaginative children seem to anticipate danger more easily than unimaginative ones.

All children were given a 1 or 0 in each dimension, except the very central dimensions 7, 9, and 10, where 2 and 0 were used. When analyzing the internal consistency of the scale, we divided the sample in two with respect to age and cognitive maturity and dealt with the high and the low groups (see below) separately. A Likert analysis was performed, with a correction for skewness according to Ekdahl (see Smith and Marke, 1958) included if necessary. A very conservative limit for an acceptable DP (alternatively DP_c) was used: ≥ 0.40.

Five items were deleted in the low groups, and six in the high groups. Omitted in both were items 3, 4, and 6. In addition, 1 and 14 were taken out in the low groups, and 2, 5, and 13 were removed in the high groups. The sum of scores on remaining items was used in each age group (see below), where the best possible median was also drawn. From the way the scale was constructed, it is self-evident that in both combinations it was dominated by items 7, 9, and 10, all of which received very high DP values (0.86, 0.66, 0.86 in the high groups; 0.50, 0.67, 1.00 in the low groups).

ARTISTIC PRODUCTS

Each child was given a piece of clay and was asked to model something for the experimenter. He was also encouraged to draw and paint. Paper, pencils, and colored chalk were within reach during the interview or when the child was waiting to be taken to the testing room.

THE SUBJECTS

The children were taken from four regular nursery schools in Lund. One child with obvious psychiatric problems (confirmed by the nursery teacher) was excluded. Another child was so tense and anxious that the testing was discontinued. Two children refused to accompany the experimenter to the laboratory, two other children were not allowed by their parents to participate. There were 47 children in the remaining group, 11 4-year-olds, 17 5-year-olds, 18 6-year-olds, and one 7-year-old. Twenty-two were girls and 25 boys. Twenty came from homes where at least one parent had studied at a university or similar institution, eleven came from homes where at least one parent had attended high school and perhaps taken some further nonuniversity training, and 16 originated in homes where both parents had less than a high-school education. As expected, in the grouping below, children with academic parents were rated as cognitively mature more often than other children.

When grouping the subjects, our procedure was similar to that used in a previous study of the same age span (Smith and Danielsson, 1982). The number of subjects did not allow more

TABLE 7.1
GROUPING OF SUBJECTS ACCORDING TO AGE
AND COGNITIVE MATURITY

The Landscape Test	Age in years and months					
	5;0	5;0-5;3	5;4-5;7	5;8-5;11	6;0-6;5	6;6-7;0
1. Haphazard responding	1a:3	1a:5	1b:3	2a:2	2b:2	2b:1
2. Tries to choose and understand: A or 1B corr.	1b:2	1b:1	—	—	2b:1	—
3. Makes 2A choices; A or 1B corr.	1b:3	2a:1	—	2a:1	2b:2	2b:2
4. A choice wrong but 2-3 B choices corr. or A and 1B corr.	2a:2	—	2b:1	3a:2	3a:3	3a:1
5. A choice corr. plus 2-3 corr. B-choices	2a:1	—	3b:1	—	3b:3	3b:4

A: doll's and own position coincide.   1a: 3 = 3 children placed in subgroup
B: doll's position other than own.   1a, etc.

than six subgroups: 1a, 1b, 2a, 2b, 3a, and 3b. Since we had to assume that tests with children can be lacking in reliability, it was decided to limit the influence of the Landscape Test relative to the influence of physical age. Therefore we did not mix 4-year-olds and 6-year-olds. Four-year-olds could not be placed higher than group 2a and 6-year-olds not lower than group 2b. Step 2 in the test scale, as illustrated in Table 7.1, was considered to be lower than step 3 because in the latter case the choice pattern was more consistent, even though it was egocentric.

RESULTS

THE MCT

A diagrammatic overview of the types of defenses is given in Figure 7.1. These results confirm previous ones (Smith and Danielsson, 1982). The low-level groups (1a, 1b, 2a) were above all characterized by external defenses. This kind of primitive defense was not altogether absent in the high-level groups (2b,

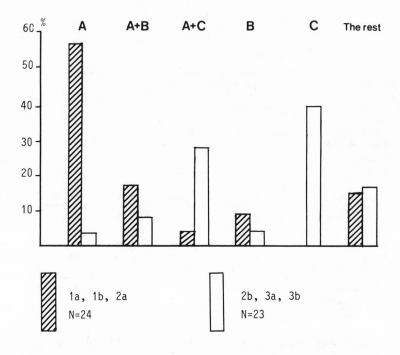

A: External defense, e.g., eye-shutting behavior or
   sleep behavior (if supported; see text).

B: Internalized defense of a relatively primitive type,
   like hero's eye-shutting or shelter-seeking, hero
   duplication, and no other type of defense.

C: Internalized defense of a more advanced type, e.g.,
   repression, isolation, sensitivity-projection (two
   signs of sensitivity required).

The "rest groups" lack clear signs of defense.

FIGURE 7.1
COMPARISON OF MCT DEFENSES BETWEEN THE LOW- AND HIGH-
LEVEL GROUPS.

3a, 3b) but was mixed with internalized defenses. The contrast
with respect to subjects who had only external defenses is almost
total between these groups. The results support the grouping
of our subjects.

Figure 7.2 is less clear but nevertheless implies a cross-vali-

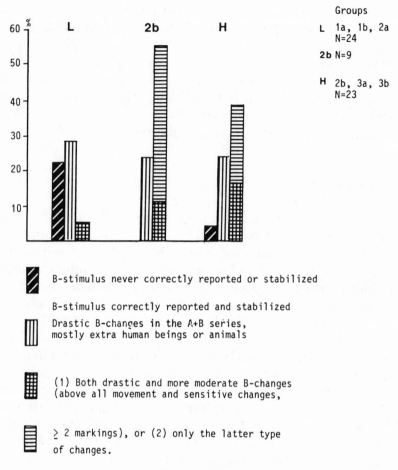

FIGURE 7.2
FORMS OF MCT PROJECTION IN THE LOW- AND HIGH-LEVEL
GROUPS.

dation of results published by Smith and Danielsson (1982). Drastic changes in the perception of the B stimulus were most typical of the low groups. Considering that among these children many could not even stabilize their impression of B, these changes should probably be construed as a lack of stability in the child's conception of reality. In the high groups, changes

were more moderate and were associated with increasing stabilization of the perception of B. What should rather be termed
externalization in the low groups (Novick and Kelly, 1970) becomes more reminiscent of sensitivity projection in the high
groups. As in the previous study, we see a tendency for subjective expansion to reach its peak in group 2b before it abates
in the oldest and most mature children. But these comparisons
admittedly concern rather small subgroups.

The CFT

Figure 7.3 is one of many possible ways to follow what happens in the straight part of the CFT. First of all, it appeared
more difficult for the low groups to stabilize a C-phase; but
even the high groups had difficulties with this nonhuman motif
(dimension A, in the figure). The low groups had less P-phase
themes (the cut made at the high quartile) even though their
protocols often included longer series of presentation (B).
These children did not reconstruct meaningful themes. They
either borrowed themes from the outside, responded in a haphazard manner, or reported that they did not perceive anything
meaningful (C and D). Thus the youngest and most immature
children did not have any PGs in the real meaning of that term.
The P-phase themes began to flow in groups 2b and 3a, where
53% had ≥ 7 themes compared with 9% in the rest of the
material. As in MCT, we trace a dampening of the subjective
expansion at the highest level.

A few more figures should be cited in support of Figure 7.3.
In groups 1a + 1b, no child attained a correct and stable C-
phase (even if some children accepted the experimenter's suggestion); in groups 2a - 3b, 33% of the children succeeded in
stabilizing a C-phase by themselves. Group 1a differed from
the other groups by having fewer themes: 50% placed themselves in the lowest quartile (0–1 themes) as compared with 18%
in the rest of the material. The two lowest groups were also
characterized by what was termed retention in the scoring
scheme: seven, or 41% (only one, or 6%, in groups 2a + 2b,
and none in groups 3a + 3b). This sign has been tentatively

regarded as a sign of creativity. Since we do not find any criterion correlations here, this assumption remains uncertain. The unwillingness to disqualify past themes may be a primitive way of linking together phases that still do not form a coherent PG.

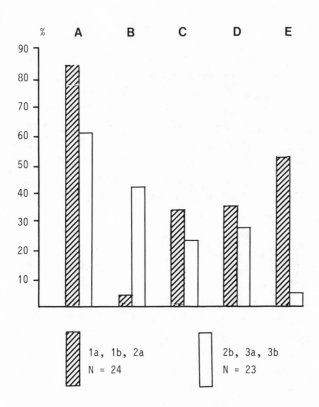

A: Do not reach a correct and stable C-phase.

B: $\geq$ 7 P-phase themes.

C: Themes borrowed from the outside/haphazard reporting ($\geq$ 2 markings).

D: $\geq$ 1/3 of the PG unstructured.

E: A + B + C (or D).

FIGURE 7.3
THE STRAIGHT PG PART OF THE CFT IN THE LOW- AND HIGH-LEVEL GROUPS.

The scoring of the inverted PG runs into difficulties because many subjects, particularly in the low groups, did not reach a stable and correct end stage even when helped by the experimenter. Five children in the high groups received XX or X scores in their inverted PGs, eight if PGs including (but not being entirely dominated by) borrowed themes are accepted. It is clear that inverted PGs in the real meaning of the term—starting from a C-phase and eventually actualizing P-phase themes from the straight PG—were only just beginning to appear in this group of children. Only one child made a vague reference to previous P-phases.

In this situation we have preferred to define the opposite pole—i.e., protocols where the inverted PGs include nothing but reports of either the stable end stage or of uninterpreted impressions. The number of subjects not falling into this category are five (of eight) in 3b, two (of six) in 3a, and four (of nine) in 2b. This scoring category was not used in the low groups, where it had little or no meaning because there were few signs of inverted PGs.

Comparisons between the CFT and the Interview Scale

A comparison between the two kinds of inverted PGs, as just delineated, is made in Table 7.2. Children with inverted PGs which were not merely all-or-none reports (even if these PGs are sometimes mixed with borrowed themes or not clearly defined in other ways) received higher scores on the creativity scale. This outcome was fully in accordance with our predictions.

It was more difficult to make an analogous prediction for the less mature groups. The protocols in these groups were above all characterized by long sequences of unstructured phases (the child could not "interpret" the flash) or by themes borrowed from the outside. Combining these response dimensions, we selected a group of children who did not resort to borrowing themes from the experimental room even though they could not grasp what was being presented to them on the screen. This ability to "wait and see" instead of relying on the well-known

TABLE 7.2
THE INVERTED PG AND THE CREATIVITY SCALE
IN THE HIGH GROUPS

Reports in inverted PG	The scale Above median	Below median
End stage or nothing	2	10
The rest	9	2

P = 0.0028 (Fisher's exact test, one-sided).

may be distantly related to the inclination to entertain deviant interpretations in the inverted PG instead of sticking to the likewise well-known end-stage theme. Nine children belong to the above-mentioned, less stimulus-bound group, and six to the opposite group with borrowed themes and only short, unstructured sequences. All in the former group and two in the latter score above the scale median (P = 0.02, Fisher's exact test, one-sided).

COMPARISONS BETWEEN THE CFT, THE MCT, AND THE INTERVIEW SCALE

As we know from our studies of adults, subjects who were able to reconstruct many themes in their straight PGs were more emotionally involved in their creative endeavors than others. Their rich PGs obviously implied more direct access to an inner, personal world. This was particularly true if some of the themes included live human beings. When looking for a similar correlation in the high groups (2b, 3a, 3b), we excluded six children scored at least twice for borrowed themes or haphazard responses; the presence of such scores in the protocols would throw doubt on the authenticity of the PG. As a criterion we chose the presence of signs of sensitivity projection in the MCT, i.e., signs of flexible change or movement in the reporting of the B-stimulus. We interpret these signs to mean that the viewer feels involved with the hero and his situation. Since the number of themes and the presence of humans in them correlate very highly, we have only tested the latter in Table 7.3. The correlation is obvious.

To further exploit the MCT results in the high groups we compared the defense scoring with the interview scale. Four subjects were excluded because their protocols yielded no defensive scores. Nine children had primitive defenses and ten did not. Among the latter, seven placed themselves above the median, while among the former, two were above it (P = 0.05, Fisher's exact test, one-sided). Children with a more internalized and more differentiated system of defenses thus tend to score higher on the scale, i.e., they more often have a fantasy friend, compose a song of their own, etc. But the correlation is admittedly weak.

TABLE 7.3
THE STRAIGHT PG AND THE MCT IN THE HIGH GROUPS

The MCT	The straight PG Human motifs	No human motifs
Sensitivity-projection	6	1
The rest	0	10

P = 0.0006 (Fisher's exact test, one-sided).

THE ARTISTIC PRODUCTS

Two professional artists appraised the children's artistic products. They were asked to use two dimensions: degree of originality and degree of emotional expressiveness. Products that were judged as clearly more original or more expressive than others were placed in a top category and products at the other end of the scale in a bottom category. Each product thus received four scores, two from each artist. In the low groups, nine clay products were placed in the top category by at least one judge, and six were placed in the bottom category. Corresponding figures for drawings in the low groups were 9/8. In the high groups, the figures for clay products were 8/8, and for drawings, 9/13.

The top category was allotted two points and the bottom zero points. Remaining products received one point. Since our raters seldom differentiated between the two scoring dimensions, we will not treat them separately. The sum of points gave the following inter-rater correlations: low groups, clay products (0.40) and drawings (0.38); high groups, clay products (0.60) and drawings (0.30). Combining the two raters we got the following correlations with the interview scale: low groups, clay products (0.32) and drawings (0.29), high groups, clay products (0.47) and drawings (0.46). It seems to have been more difficult for the raters to work with the products of young and immature children and with drawings. The latter were perhaps more influenced by conventions than were the clay products.

The moderate-to-low correlations with the interview scale could be due to different preferences in our raters, as they seldom discovered traces of creativity in the same product. As a matter of fact, the raters agreed more often about products they considered clearly uncreative.

To test this assumption we performed a simple calculation where ratings for clay products and drawings were used together but where the former were considered more reliable than the latter. We selected a group of creative children in the following way: children who had received at least one top category placement from one rater for their clay products or at least one top placement from each rater for their drawings. This group should have had high scale values.

In the groups of *young* and *immature* children (N = 24) there were seven misplacements (P = 0.036, one-sided, Fisher's exact test, the G-index of agreement being 0.42). In the groups of *older* and *mature* children (N = 23) there were three misplacements (P = 0.006, G = 0.74). We consider this result as supporting the reliability of the interview scale as used in the high groups.

DISCUSSION

Problems of reliability are always involved in studies of children. As we have seen, much of what a young child does and says in a test situation is dependent on momentary whims, a wish to please the experimenter or to tease her, etc. The better the experimenter and the child get to know each other, the more reliable the data are bound to be. Still, it is often necessary to interpret a child's utterances rather than take them literally, a procedure that would appear to decrease the reliability of the data. However, there are two indications that we have mastered the reliability problem: (1) we have managed to demonstrate a series of strong trends in the material, trends that certainly would not have appeared in a haphazard collection of data, and (2) some of these trends are cross-validations of those found in a previous sample (with another experimenter). The interview-based estimates are probably the ones most exposed to uncontrolled influences. Nevertheless, we managed to construct a scale with high inner consistency, correlating both with the test data and the independent criteria.

The developmental ladder constructed on the basis of age and cognitive maturity originally had six steps. In many comparisons we have worked with only two large steps, each including three subgroups. Naturally, subgroup 2a shares many characteristics with 2b, and 2b sometimes tends to differ from 3a and 3b. Since numbers are small, we prefer to play safe most of the time and mainly dwell on a low groups/high groups contrast.

The low groups are characterized by their lack of a correct and stable C-phase, a tendency to borrow themes from the immediate surroundings or give haphazard answers instead of reconstructing impressions given by the stimulus, an associated inability to internalize fears and defenses, an inclination to retain irrelevant material when they see fit, etc. These characteristics may at first look like a self-indulgent disregard for the rules of the experimental game. The child is only seemingly nonchalant, however, since, at the same time, he is highly dependent on the external situation. Because he cannot draw from inner sources or, to express it in Noy's terminology (1969), because he lacks integrated self-nuclei, the child has to rely on what happens to be available close at hand. The central characteristic of this group is its inability to construct a stable relation with outside reality. Not even cognitive egocentricity, which might contribute to stabilizing the group's world, has yet been established, at least not in the youngest subgroups. To summarize the description in another way: these young and immature children still have no real percept-geneses.

In the high groups, traces of stimulus dependence—for instance, borrowing—can still be detected. But these responses more and more often become embedded in true reconstructions. Perhaps these children regress to immature responses when the reconstructive activities are arrested for some reason or other. The growing internalization is accompanied by a subjective expansion visible in both MCT and CFT. At the same time, the stability of the C-phase increases. The balance between the inflationary self and the stabilizing outside world seems to improve as children grow older and more mature. In the highest subgroups these children are on their way out of the egocentric period (cf. an analogous description based on the spiral aftereffect [Andersson, 1984]). The most important conclusion to be drawn is that only after the appearance of PGs originating in their own selves can children construct an independent and stable outside reality.[1]

To the superficial observer, our youngest and most immature children may seem very creative. However, their relation to the outside world does not reflect real freedom but rather instability and dependence on circumstances over which they have little control. They lack permanent anchor points, inwardly as well as outwardly, and lack P-phases growing out of their own private experiences.

In groups 2b and 3a there are, however, children who bristle with fancies, new themes constantly emerging at the spearhead of their PGs. Many people would call them highly creative. We hesitate to concur. After all, we agree with Rothenberg (1979) that intentionality is central in creative activity. These children invest a lot of energy in the prephases of their constructive processes. The process direction is, however, poorly defined and the end product often unstable. It is instructive to observe

---

[1] It is instructive to compare this result in children with the findings reported by Hansson and Rydén (1987) in adults, i.e., if a percept lacks initial anchorage in self referents, as measured in a serial aftereffect task, differentiation in a rod-and-frame test rapidly deteriorates over trials.

how these children are often unable to exploit their fancies in creative products: what they accomplish can be surprisingly conventional and stereotyped.

Because we have defined creativity on the basis of the CFT, it presupposes an established C-phase. To be sure, there are indications of inverted PGs in several children in the high groups, and not only in subgroup 3b. But in the latter group the inverted PGs are most clearly visible. Some of these youngsters have not only acquired a stable relation to the outside world but are able, at the same time, to transgress the confines of their newly established reality context and play with subjective alternatives.

In what specific way, then, has the CFT contributed to enlighten the problems of creativity in our group of children? It is first of all obvious that the inverted PG can be used to detect the first signs of creativity in the older and more mature children, in approximately the same way as in adults. The criteria used for the validation reflect, above all, the child's fantasy life and intimacy with his dreams, but more indirectly also his ability to express himself in artistic products. Even the special character of the straight PG, when including human themes, to reflect the degree of emotional involvement could be validated to some extent in the high groups.

The correlations in the low groups were much more tentative and difficult to penetrate. Part of the reason for this is, naturally, the uncertain reliability of at least some of the measures. A more important reason has been mentioned already: the lack of true creativity in children who can neither uphold a stable contact with reality nor internalize their reactions. It is still interesting to note that children scoring high on the creativity scale preferred to delay their interpretations of the CFT picture rather than succumb to the use of haphazard themes or themes borrowed from the immediate surroundings. This agrees with other findings (Starkweather, 1964; Starkweather and Cowling, 1964) that independence of immediate outer pressure is one prerequisite for creative functioning, which apparently can already be detected in the precreative child.

We would also like to comment very briefly on the use of creativity criteria. It is obvious that a child may show signs of creativity in one dimension but perform in a very stereotyped way in another. Moreover, judges of artistic products are very likely to be sensitive to one kind of creative expression but more or less blind to others. Our best criterion of creativity seems to have been the interview scale, probably for two reasons. First, the child feels relaxed and secure when talking to the experimenter instead of producing a product to be critically judged. Second, the interview scale touches on a broad range of subjects and gives the child ample opportunity to show its colors.

The main conclusions can thus be summarized as follows: the prerequisite condition for a stable conception of reality is a PG emerging from the private inner world of the observer. Or, to put it another way, not until the child can direct his constructive activities toward a well-defined stimulus will he be able to reconstruct the P-phases preceding the C-phase. This developmental period also marks the beginning of true creative activity in which the child not only disregards a reality not yet fully grasped but uses himself to enrich it.

8

CREATIVITY IN EARLY AND MIDDLE
SCHOOL YEARS
(Age 7–11 Years)

Writings about children's creativity abound, even if the search is confined to scientific publications. In spite of the accumulated observations it is still very difficult, on the basis of previous research only, to get a clear view of what really happens during ontogenesis, i.e., whether children are generally more creative than adults or if there are special creative peaks, whether a child's creativity differs from that of an adult's, etc.

Many publications in the field have an essayistic flavor, particularly those appearing in psychoanalytic periodicals. The empirical contributions are generally limited to the age span of 6–10 years and seldom include the preschool period. They rest on a variegated collection of methods and instruments, whose relations to criteria often remain obscure, to say nothing of their mostly unknown intercorrelations. The concept of creativity is either anchored to these not very well-defined methods or in other ways insufficiently elucidated. Considering the purpose of the present study, however, we find some of the previous observations and comments valuable.

The study of preschoolers has shown that the stabilization of an objective perceptual end product requires that the perceptual process become firmly anchored in the perceiver's subjective world of experience. This conclusion is partly supported by Rogolsky (1968) who, using the Rorschach test, found "control" to be an important aspect of child creativity or, translated into our terms, to be truly creative and exploit private associations, children must base these reconstructive operations on a reasonably stabilized C-phase. In other words, creativity is not merely a subjective invasion of reality, such as can be seen in children not yet able to clearly differentiate self and non-self in their fantasies, but is also a dialectic process requiring a separation of these two poles of experience. Our placing of the lower limit of creativity at the five-year-old level is also in agreement with Grippen (1933).

For the present investigation of creativity in school-age children, Torrance's (1962) observations are particularly useful, even if his definition of creativity is not quite congruent with ours. Torrance was, among other things, interested to learn how a child's commitment to creative productivity fluctuates over the school years. According to him, creativity declined when children entered a new school system, i.e., when schoolwork demanded more attention of them than before. At the age of 6–8, children were thus characterized by realistic adaptation to school requirements. When about 8–10 years old, they were able to use their new skills for renewed commitment to creative activity. Since schooling starts relatively late in Sweden, we would have to postpone the beginning of the ebb period to the age of about 7. These observations fit a dialectical model developed by Andersson and his coworkers (1977; Andersson, 1983, 1984). This model is adapted to the five regulatory principles for human development described by Gedo and Goldberg (1973). Two of these principles, regarding reality and creativity, are of special interest here; and two nodal points related to them have been determined by Andersson at ages 5 and 11. According to Andersson's data, obtained in studies of, for instance, the relative importance of intra- and extraceptive tendencies in a spiral aftereffect task, these ages are characterized by subjective expansion. As we have just seen, his observations at the age of five and the years immediately after are supported by our own preschool data: after its first expansive period at around 5 years, subjectivity is checked by an increasingly stabilized and objectivized conception of outside reality (also indicating a more stabilized conception of self). Again, at about age 11, a new expansion of subjectivity occurs. At that time, according to Andersson, it takes the form of a heightened awareness of the individual's own sense of self. This is the starting point and basic requirement for a creative—and later more elaborate—(re)construction of reality. Studies of anxiety and defense against anxiety in childhood and adolescence also agree with this model (Smith and Danielsson, 1982).

In accordance with Andersson's data, our *main hypotheses* are that *signs of creativity will decrease toward the age of approximately 7 years and increase again at 10–11*. If Torrance is correct in his association of diminished commitment to creative activity with the growing demands of schoolwork, the creative output at 7–8 years should be characterized by conventionalization, above all among more immature and dependent children who have just entered the first grade in our school system. One consequence of this would be a deterioration of the test-criterion correlations, which were surprisingly high among preschoolers.

A renewed increase in these correlations could, consequently, be expected among 10–11-year-olds. We will also use the present study to cross-validate a number of previous findings.

Let it be added that Singer (1973) and Weisberg and Springer (1961) have contributed to the field of creativity through their interesting studies of children's play and fantasy life. We like to mention their work, since we have been inspired by many of their findings when constructing our interview scales.

METHOD AND SUBJECTS

Before bringing the children to the laboratory, the experimenter acquainted herself with them at school. At the laboratory, children in groups I and II (the 7–8-years-olds) took the Landscape Test first, followed by the CFT and then the MCT. The testing was interspersed with pauses if necessary. The experimenter met the child at school on another day for an interview. On this occasion the child made clay figures and drawings. Group III (the 10–11-year-old children) did not take the Landscape Test but took the other tests in the same order as the younger subjects took them (see Figure 8.1).

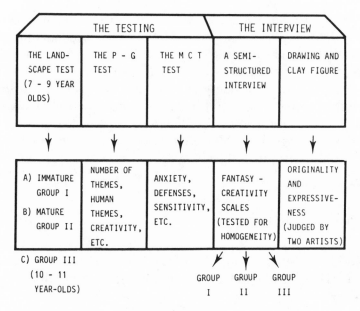

FIGURE 8.1
THE DESIGN.

THE CFT

The scoring dimensions used were the same as those described in Chapter 7. The independent raters agreed for the most part in their scoring. Occasional differences were nearly always due to oversights by one of them.

THE META-CONTRAST TECHNIQUE (MCT)

Most of the scoring dimensions are described in the previous chapter. However, we also scored signs of anxiety. The most *grave signs of anxiety* are *fusion* (the threat enters the room where the hero is sitting or even merges with him), and *leaking defenses* (where something threatening is reported behind the defensive structure, e.g., blackness behind a curtain covering the window in B). *Moderate signs* include *open fright in the test situation* (a severe sign in more adult subjects), *broken structures* (e.g., cracks in the window pane), and *black structures* (stimulus-incongruent or particularly emphasized) reported in the last third of the A + B series. Black structures reported elsewhere in the series plus slight signs of anxiety such as partial structural disintegration were noted but will not be reported here. Total structural disintegration, the so-called zero phases, are considered as ominous signs in adolescents and adults. Single such signs found in the present subjects were not recorded.

THE LANDSCAPE TEST

Here we also refer to Chapter 7. The test was not used in group III, where it was not expected to differentiate the subjects.

THE INTERVIEW

It should be evident by now that our conception of creativity was born of the dynamic tradition or, in PG terms, that we regard creative activity as an interplay between late reality-adapted and early personal-emotional stages in the adaptive process. There seems to be no essential difference in this respect between, for instance, scientists and artists. Another (expected) finding in previous chapters was that creativity correlated with certain other characteristics like interest in dreams and early childhood memories, i.e., interest in one's own inner world of experience. When choosing topics for the interview and subsequent construction of a creativity-fantasy scale, we were guided by these presumptions and findings but had to adapt our choice to the age of the children. Thus the topics used for preschool children could not be transferred directly to the 7–8-year-olds. Some topics were excluded because they did not seem relevant any longer, as, for instance, interest in make-believe games; others were excluded because they lacked dispersion, e.g., interest in drawing, painting, sculpture, and building. Topics added to the original preschool scale are 1, 3, 4, 9, 12, and 13 below.

GROUPS I AND II

The following questions (dimensions) were addressed in the creativity-fantasy scale of 7- to 8-year-olds, where 1–7 were included in the final scale for group I and 4–9 in the final scale for group II: (1) Does the child collect things (not stamps, coins, etc.) that may be used for unexpected purposes? (2) Does he react positively when asked what he would do if there were no restrictions for one day? (3) Does he have color dreams? (4) How far back in life does he remember? (5) Has he constructed at least some of his own play tools? (6) Has he composed a song, made up a story, written a poem, etc., of his own? (7) Does he have a fantasy playmate? (8) Does he enjoy theatrical play? (9) Does he keep a diary? (10) Does the child like to be alone sometimes? (11) Can he describe what happened in a dream? (12) Does he enjoy dreaming? (13) Does he often indulge in fantasies?

These children were given a 1 or 0 score in each dimension except the very crucial dimensions (6 and 7), and in 11. In 6 we scored 2 or 0 and in 7 we used three grades, 2-1-0, where 1 represents relatively unspecific cases. In dimension 11 we added ½ as an intermediate value when the child could not describe a recent dream but referred to previous dreams or seemed to talk about dreaming in a rather general way. A Likert analysis was then performed in each of the 7- to 8-year-old groups, with a correction for skewness. A very conservative limit for an acceptable coefficient of discriminatory power (DP, alt. DP_c) was used: >0.40. After deletion of dimensions with unacceptable DP values in group I, the following dimensions remained: 1, 2, 3, 4, 5, 6, 7. We also constructed a *small scale* made up of items previously found to correlate with creativity: 3, 4, 11. In group II, dimensions 1 and 11 had to be deleted because they lacked dispersion (less than 10% minority responses). After the homogeneity analysis, the scale was left with the following items: 4, 5, 6, 7, 8, 9. A small scale included two items and was only used in the factor analysis below.

GROUP III

Three questions addressed to the 10- to 11-year-old group III were borrowed from groups I and II (1, 2, and 11 below), while others were new or reformulated (e.g., 3, 4, 5, 7, 10, and 12 below). These were the original dimensions, where 1–7 were included in the final small scale and 1–10 in the large scale: (1) Does the child write or compose musical pieces at home? (2) Does he collect things (not stamps, coins, etc.) which may be used for unexpected purposes? (3) Does he often indulge in daydreaming? (4) Does he have, or has he had, a fantasy playmate? (5) Does he like to be alone sometimes? (6) Does he dislike imitating other people's ideas when drawing, or dislike being imitated? (7) Does he have memories from the age of 4–5 years? (8) Does he invent or build his own models? (9) Does he have fantasy fears of thieves, darkness, etc.? (10) Does he have memories from the age of 3? (11) Does he enjoy theatrical play? (12) Can he distinguish between a color dream and a black-and-white dream? (13) Is the child able to admit fears? (14) Does he know how it feels to be an outsider? (15) Does he prefer having dreams, even if these are nightmares, over not having dreams? (16) Does he enjoy writing letters more than receiving them?

Since we expected signs of creativity to become more diversified with age, we not only chose to include more dimensions but also refrained from emphasizing certain items as more central than others. Only scores 1 and 0 were therefore used. Dimensions 13 and 16 were deleted because they lacked dispersion. After the homogeneity analysis, the following items remained when the lower limit of DP was set at about 0.40 (>0.37): 1, 2, 3, 4, 5, 6, 7, 8, 9, and 10. A more conservative DP limit of >0.50 further reduced the scale so that only 1, 2, 3, 4, 5, 6, and 7 were left. Thus for group III we have two scales: the *large scale* and the *small scale*, the latter being more homogeneous.

It should be emphasized that the scales do not reflect the experimenter's subjective impression of the child but are based on the child's actual answers to the concrete questions.

ARTISTIC CRITERIA

Two artists judged the children's artistic products with respect to *originality* and *emotional expression*. Drawings and clay figures were judged separately and the artists worked independently of each other. The ranking system will be described later. The same artists worked with groups I and II. Since one of them left town, another artist was appointed to work with group III.

SUBJECTS

The subjects were taken from the public-school system in Lund, one group of fifty-five 7- to 8-year-olds from grades 1 and 2 and another group of thirty-one 10- to 11-year-olds from grades 4 and 5. To begin with, all children in a class were asked to participate. Later, to balance children from academic and nonacademic homes, certain criteria were used for selection in another class. Three 10- to 11-year-olds, two boys and one girl, the latter from an academic home, were not permitted to participate by their parents.

The 7- to 8-year-olds were divided in one younger and/or cognitively less mature group (I) and another older and/or cognitively more mature group (II). The 10- to 11-year-olds were labeled group III. Group I included (a) all who did not understand the Landscape Test, irrespective of age (five children); (b) basically cognitively egocentric children (i.e., those who made the correct A choice plus another incorrect A choice and not more than one correct B choice) within the age span of 6:10 (6 years, 10 months)–8:6 years (thirteen children); (c) relatively mature children (i.e., those who made the correct A choice plus at least two correct B choices) within the youngest age span of 6:10–7:6 years (eight children). All the other children were referred to group II; (d) children performing as defined above but belonging to the age span of 8:7–9:2 years (three children); (e) the relatively mature children as defined above, except those belonging to the age span of 6:10–7:6 years (twenty-six children). Thus age and cognitive maturity determined the group composition, but age was somewhat more influential.

The prerequisites for scoring the CFT was that the subject could stabilize a C phase, with or without the experimenter's assistance, and that he refrained from using more than one borrowed theme. Four children in group I and seven children in group II could not do so. When the CFT was included, only twenty-two children in each group qualified for additional analysis. Group III was not differentiated according to cognitive maturity. There were originally thirty-one subjects and two were excluded for the reasons just given. Comparing the excluded children with the remaining ones, we could not find any significant differences in the MCT and creativity scales.

Group I originally included 42% of the children from homes where at least one parent held a college or university degree; in the reduced group there were 41% from such homes. The corresponding percentages were 57 and 50 for group II and 48 and 45 for group III. It was hardly surprising to find more academic children in group II. However, these cognitively more sophisticated children did not apparently have any more stable a conception of reality than their less sophisticated classmates: relatively more of the former had unstable C-phases and borrowed themes in the CFT. This could perhaps, from the point of view of creativity, be a positive sign of "delayed closure."

RESULTS

The number of themes in the straight PG increases from group I to group III (Table 8.1). The contrast between groups I + II and group III (the two left columns against the two right ones) is significant ($\chi^2 = 6.64$, df = 1, P = 0.01). At the same time the tendency to transgress the stable C-phase also increased (Table 8.2). There is a significant difference ($\chi^2 = 8.52$, df = 1, P < 0.01) between the same constellation of groups (median cut, i.e., the right column against the other ones). Most of the change toward recovering clear subjective themes [categories XX, X, (X)] was found in children with academic parents.

TABLE 8.1
NUMBER OF P-PHASE THEMES IN tHE STRAIGHT PG

	≥ 4.0	2.0-3.5	1.0-1.5	0-0.5
Group I	3	8	4	11
Group II	4	10	11	4
Group III	9	14	4	4

TABLE 8.2
SCORING CATEGORIES IN THE INVERTED PG

	XX	X	(X)	0	≥ 2S	The rest
Group I						
Acad.	1	0	0	0	0	8
Nonacad.	1	0	2	1	1	8
	2	0	2	1	1	16
Group II						
Acad.	0	2	1	2	0	6
Nonacad.	1	0	1	0	2	7
	1	2	2	2	2	13
Group III						
Acad.	3	3	2	0	1	4
Nonacad.	1	2	0	2	6	5
	4	5	2	2	7	9

The within-group difference is modestly significant ($P = 0.023$, Fisher's exact test, two-sided).

Table 8.3 presents anxiety signs in MCT, while Table 8.4 gives signs of primitive defenses. As the number of children with anxiety signs increases from I to II + III the number of primitive defenses decreases. It is particularly typical of group III that the narcissistic signs of hero duplication (the threat described as a young person) have been drastically reduced. The overall difference between groups I and III is clearly significant ($P = 0.001$, Fisher's exact test, one-sided).

The intercorrelational pattern was analyzed by factor analysis. Only a few correlations were dealt with separately, particularly correlations between the inverted PG in the CFT and key

TABLE 8.3
ANXIETY SIGNS IN MCT

	Late black struct.	Open fear	Fusion	Leaking mech.	Some sign	No sign
Group I	2	4	0	1	6	16
Group II	4	4	1	2	11	11
Group III	9	3	2	3	14	15

signs in MCT, on the one hand, and the creativity scale and artistic criteria, on the other. We mostly used the G-index of agreement (Holley and Guilford, 1964; Starvig, 1981) and sometimes also r to estimate the size of the covariation between two variables.

In groups I and II there were relatively few signs scored in the inverted PG. We therefore had to distinguish between children with at least one sign of any kind and those without any sign at all. When signs became more numerous in group III we were able to separate children with signs XX, X, (X) (referring to tangible, subjective themes) and children with no such signs. With respect to the interview scales, children were grouped above or below the best possible median. After transforming the inverted PG test into a scale with six equidistant steps (a somewhat doubtful transformation, to be sure), we were able to use r as a measure of the PG/scale correlation. The difference between G and r was usually small.

In group I we found no correlation between the inverted PG and the interview scale. Using the small scale, consisting of three items selected on the basis of previous results, we obtained a G of 0.45 (P = 0.04, Fisher's exact test, one-sided). The PG/scale correlation in group II was 0.55 (P = 0.02). In group III it was 0.52 for the original scale (P = 0.006) and 0.59 for the smaller, more homogeneous scale (P = 0.002).

It has been shown that moderate anxiety tends to enhance a subject's inclination toward subjective reporting in the inverted PG (Chapter 5) but that excess anxiety or low anxiety tolerance can have the opposite effect (Chapter 6). Fusion and

TABLE 8.4
PRIMITIVE SIGNS IN MCT

	Eye-shutting behavior	Sleep behavior	Eye-shutting hero's	Open fear	Wants to quit	Hero dupl.	Some sign	No sign
Group I	5	1	3	4	3	13	18	4
Group II	0	0	1	2	2	12	13	9
Group III	3	4	2	3	0	4	14	15

TABLE 8.5
THE ARTISTIC PRODUCTS AND ANXIETY IN MCT

Artistic products High placements	Signs of anxiety in MCT		
	Excessive anxiety	Moderate anxiety	Slight or no anxiety
Group II			
High placement	0	9[a]	3
The rest	1	1[a]	8[a]
Group III			
High placement	2[b]	7[b]	9
The rest	5[b]	0[b]	6

Note: High placement implies 1 H and no L or 2 H irrespective of the number of Ls.
[a] P = 0.004 (Fisher's exact test, one-sided)
[b] P = 0.01 (Fisher's exact test, one-sided)

leaking mechanisms are grave signs of anxiety, the latter signs being judged as more severe when found in older children. Primitive defenses (defensive regression) triggered by these grave or by medium signs of anxiety (late dark structures, broken structures, open fright) can be interpreted in group III as indicating low anxiety tolerance. Since it was relatively difficult to detect low anxiety tolerance in the younger subjects, we confined our calculations to group III, where seven cases of severe anxiety or low anxiety tolerance were excluded. The correlations increased drastically in the remaining group; for the original scale, $G = 0.73$ ($P = 0.001$, Fisher's exact test, one-sided), and for the small scale, $G = 0.82$ ($P = 0.0002$). What happened most often in cases of excessive anxiety or low anxiety tolerance was that they did not score XX, X or (X) in the inverted PG (six of seven cases). Contrasting excessive anxiety and little anxiety with moderate anxiety (cf. Table 8.5), we find some association between XX, X and (X) signs and moderate anxiety ($G = 0.45$, $P = 0.05$, one-sided).

THE ARTISTIC PRODUCTS

As previously described, two professional artists judged the children's artistic products (drawings and clay figures) in two dimensions (A = originality, B = emotional expression), independently of each other. About 25% of the children were placed in a high group and 25% in a low group. The artists were not required to use these rules rigidly but were encouraged to consider natural "gaps" in the distribution. When quantifying the results we used 2, 1, and 0 for placements in the high, the two middle, and the low quartiles, respectively. In groups I and II the correlations (r) between judges varied from -0.12 to 0.52. Correlations between dimensions were 0.43 and 0.72 for one judge and 0.65 and 0.68 for the other. The judges, who had also worked with our preschool children, complained that the products were more stereotyped and difficult to judge. In group III, interjudge correlations varied between 0.40 and 0.63. Interdimensional correlations were 0.79 and 0.78 for one judge and 0.40 and 0.56 for the other.

To enhance reliability we collapsed results over judges and dimensions. We then distinguished between children obtaining one high placement (H) and no low placement (L) plus children obtaining at least two H's and any number of L's and the remaining children. The inverted PG and the scales correlate positively but most often nonsignificantly with this criterion scale in all groups. In group II there is a slightly significant correlation with the scale (G = 0.45, P = 0.03, Fisher's exact test, one-sided). The artistic products of the young children were apparently difficult to differentiate. One possible explanation could be that the older the children, the more likely it is that their creative activities are canalized along several dimensions—of which the artistic ones may no longer be the most important. A young poet in group III recovered many themes in the inverted PG but was not considered for high placements by the artists.

Even if the artistic criteria do not correlate with the inverted PG or the creativity scale, there is an interesting correlation with MCT anxiety, in groups II and III, where signs of anxiety were relatively numerous. In Table 8.5 we distinguish among excessive anxiety (and intolerance for anxiety), moderate anxiety, and the remaining subjects (most of whom had signs of slight anxiety in group III). Only one subject (with fusion) was placed in the excessive anxiety column in group II. It is quite clear that our judges reacted most positively to artistic products of children with moderate anxiety. Excessive anxiety (in group III) and lack of anxiety (in group II) seemed to obstruct genuine artistic production. Right columns in groups II and III differed from each other in that the latter had more children with signs of slight anxiety, while the former had more children apparently free from anxiety.

THE INVERTED FACTOR ANALYSIS

As before, the inverted factor analysis was based on the G-index of agreement. In all groups there were ≥3 markings for presence or absence. Varimax rotation was used down to Eigenvalues ≥1. In group III the first rotation gave eight factors. The next time we set a limit of five. In groups I and II the original factor rotations, yielding five and six factors, respectively, are presented together with brief accounts of four-factor rotations. The inverted factor analysis produces factors of persons. The factor solutions were guided by the rule that only loadings of ≥0.50 were acceptable. For a subject to be assigned to a factor, the difference between his two largest (positive) loadings had to be ≥0.10.

On the basis of a factor solution, a D-index of discrimination was calculated. That estimated the degree to which an item discriminated between the representatives of one factor and the rest of the subjects. Items with D-values of <0.50 were not considered. D-values are presented with decimal points omitted in the factor descriptions.

Special emphasis will be put on the inverted PG (a weight of 5).

FACTOR STRUCTURE, GROUP I

I,1: Eight Children

All characteristics are negative. The highest D-values (−71) concern the small scale including the interview dimensions "telling a dream," "color dreams," and "early memories." The differentiating power of the scale is not enhanced in combination with artistic criteria. Incidentally, D for the inverted PG is −43. This seems to be a group of typically uncreative children.

I,2: Three Children

H-placements in the B-dimension by one or both artists received high D-values (84) which were, however, deflated when combined with interview scales. The D for the comprehensive scale is 58 and that for the small scale is 63. The single item with the highest D (68) is "make up a story, etc." D is 58 for human themes in the straight PG. The last finding should be considered as a corollary to the high D-values for the emotional B-dimension; previous studies have shown an association between human themes and emotional involvement.

I,4: Three Children

The inverted PG produced high D-values. These were highest (95) when XX, X, and (X) were separated from the rest of the PG scale. The small interview scale was also important (74 for the upper quartile). Reference to the straight PG in the inverted one received a D of 61, and human themes a value of 58. A combination of at least one H-placement by an artistic judge with the upper quartile in the comprehensive scale resulted in a D of 63. The projective signs in MCT (drastic and/or moderate B-change) are also worthy of notice (74).

There were two additional factors with two children each. When we rotated the results in group I, setting a limit of four factors, nineteen of twenty-two children were able to be placed in factors. Those children most closely corresponding to the uncreative factor I,1 became still more dominating (eleven children, seven of them girls). Some of the negative D-values increased: including scores in the inverted PG (-55), above-median values in the small interview scale (-91), and at least one H-placement in a B-dimension by each artist (-55). Another factor, the approximate counterpart of I,4, included four instead of three children, a change that did not appreciably affect the D-values.

FACTOR STRUCTURE, GROUP II

II,1: Seven Children

This factor corresponds to I,1 but is more strongly determined by the inverted PG (-60). Both criteria correlate with the inverted PG, i.e., at least one high placement by each artist in some dimension and/or placements in the upper quartile in the comprehensive scale (-73). All children in the factor are girls.

II,2: Three Children

This factor corresponds to I,4 and was strongly colored by the inverted PG: *XX, X,* and *(X)* versus the rest gave a D of 90. Reference to the straight PG in the inverted one or to human themes in the former also produced high D's of 90 and 63, respectively. D is 84 for "make up a story, etc.," for "fantasy playmate," and for placement in the upper quartile in the comprehensive scale. Artistic judgments did not inflate these values. Repression in MCT (reports of objects) resulted in a D of 74. This clearly creative group was not fully appreciated by the artists.

There were four additional factors with two children each. When we again restricted the rotated factor solution to four factors, nineteen of twenty-two children were placed. The factor corresponding to the uncreative factor II,1 increased to include eleven children (eight of them girls). The contribution of the artistic judgments to the formation of this factor are more obvious here: at least one H-placement in any dimension by each artist received a D of −82. These children showed no signs of anxiety late in the MCT series (−55). There are two "creativity" factors: the stronger one is reminiscent of II,2 and includes three children; the weaker one includes two children. Both factors received H placements by each artist (68, 65). The strong factor is closely associated with high scores on the interview scale, while the weak factor reflects the presence of MCT signs. The remaining three-children factor corresponds to a two-person factor in the first solution because it was determined by positive artistic judgments and positive scores on "early memories" and "telling a dream."

FACTOR STRUCTURE, GROUP III

III,1: Six Children

All D-values are negative. These children did not receive above-median scores on either the large scale (−61) or the small scale (−57) and received zero scores for such items as "theatrical play" (-52) and "dislikes imitating other people's ideas, etc." (-61). They tended not to come from academic homes (-57). A combination of at least one H-placement in a B-dimension by each judge and upper-quartile scores on the large scale also produces negative scores (-52). All in all, this seems to be a rather ordinary group of children with little fantasy.

III,2: Six Children

These children received bottom scores in the inverted PG (-87). They do not "write or make compositions at home" (-53). MCT is characterized by the narcissistic hero duplication (62). They were not given H-placements by either judge (-57). Combinations of artistic judgments and upper-quartile scores on the large scale resulted in similarly negative values (-52). This interesting association between low creativity, negative judgments by the artists, and relatively primitive defenses will be taken up in the discussion.

III,3: Six Children

This factor was determined mainly by *XX*, *X*, or *(X)* in the inverted PG (78). Less than one-third of the straight PG is unstructured (52). The following scale variables are characteristic: "to write or make compositions at home" (52), "to collect things which can be used for unexpected purposes" (57), "dislikes imitating other people's ideas, etc." (65). Various scale values are above median (65) or in the upper quartile (75) on the large scale as well as on the small scale (70 and 58). This factor is equivalent to I,4 and II,2 but stands out more prominently among the factors. The artists did not really note any creative qualities in the drawings or clay figures, but the CFT and the scales are closely interwoven.

III,4: Three Children

Although these children have more than two themes (above median values) in the straight PG (50), they still reach their C-phase comparatively early (50). They like theatrical play (65). Their MCT protocols are characterized by signs of sensitivity (65) or sensitivity movement (62). The artistic judgments dominate the factor: H-placement of drawings in the B-dimension by one judge (81) or the other (77), at least one H-placement in some scale by both judges (62), some H- but no L-placement of drawings by both judges (89), and a number of less powerful variations. Here we find a combination of interest in theatrical play, sensitivity to marginal cues, and, above all, emotional qualities in the drawings as noted by the artists.

A fifth, rather vague residual factor included three children.

CONCLUSIONS

MAIN HYPOTHESES

Our main hypotheses were at least partly confirmed. After entering regular school there is an obvious low tide in the child's creativity, most conspicuous in the youngest and most immature group, I. A stabilized C-phase is the prerequisite condition for analyzing the inverted part of the CFT. Since many preschool children did not attain such a C-phase, and, moreover, since they were not inclined to reconstruct real P-phase themes, a comparison including these children could easily be misleading. Let it just be noted that among eight children in the oldest and/or cognitively most mature preschool subgroup, five received XX or X scores (with or without an admixture of occasional borrowed themes) as compared with only two of twenty-three schoolchildren in group I. The younger and/or cognitively less mature subgroups were particularly inclined to mix their stimulus descriptions with accidental impressions from the testing room, memories of TV programs, etc., in a seemingly haphazard fashion. This irreverent treatment of information from the outside was superseded among the "high" subgroups by increasingly frequent signs of true creativity, i.e., an interplay between private material and a correct conception of stimulus, without corrupting the latter. The results in group I differed from those of the preschoolers, and even more from the results in group III.

We also predicted an increase in the correlation between the inverted PG and the independent criteria. This seems to be true as far as the creativity scale is concerned, at least if we assume that excessive anxiety or low anxiety tolerance can restrain either the flow of reconstructions in the inverted PG or the play of fantasy as reflected in the scale, or both. Correlations with artistic criteria did not increase, however, but seemed to have reached their optimum among the oldest preschoolers. As we said previously, the artists complained about the stereotypization of the children's artistic products in groups I and II, which made the differentiation rather difficult and unreliable. In addition to this explanation for the diminishing correlations, another one may also be applicable, especially for group III, where we had expected a renewed increase: older children may have more differentiated outlets for their creative activities than younger or more immature ones—i.e., drawings and clay figures may no longer be capable of canalizing the creative urge of all children, some of whom may prefer to write poems, compose songs, make inventions, etc. It is consonant with this reasoning that artistic judgments correlate with the CFT and creativity scale on the "negative" side more often than on the positive.

What happens when children enter regular school? It is tempting to agree with Torrance (1962) that they become absorbed in the new world confronting them with novel and often overwhelming requirements. Once the children have assimilated new cognitive skills—assimilation occurring faster in the more mature children—they can again indulge in creative activities, as the children in group II and especially those from academic homes in group III are doing. This explanation is probably not sufficient, however. First of all, the decision that children should start regular school between the ages of 6.5–7.5 years was certainly not made at random but took into account the increasing reality orientation of children at that approximate age. Secondly, if we accept dialectic discontinuity as a basic principle of development (Andersson, 1984; see also the focus on discontinuity in Brim and Kagan, 1980) it would seem reasonable to assume that the subjective expansion characterizing 5- to 6-year-olds should be followed by a contraction one or two years later. Langer (1969) used the model of a spiral to describe ontogenesis. Although the model is more tentative than Andersson's, the picture of a spiral is attractive. As we follow the spiral upwards from the age of 5 we again encounter a phase of subjective expansion around the age of 10–11; but this expansion is at a higher level of cognitive sophistication, being less dependent on accidental impressions and more dependent on material incorporated into the child's private self. Considering the attempts at creative activity in preschoolers as more or less premature and accidental, even if charmingly disrespectful of adult conventions, we can conclude that at age 10–11 we enter the first stage of true creativity.

PRIMITIVE SIGNS AND RETENTION

A few things should be mentioned about the MCT results before we examine the factor solutions more closely. It is obvious that the MCT results agree with the general trends observed in previous studies (Smith and Danielsson, 1982): those characteristics that we believe to be signs of early anxiety or primitive-narcissistic defense mechanisms were shown to diminish rapidly with increasing age and maturity. In the same studies of children aged about 7 to 11 we observed an MCT sign, called *retention*, implying that one interpretation of the threat (stimulus A) was retained even though the subject had ventured to replace it with another. Retention was tentatively associated with creativity because we thought, along with Niederland (1976) and others, that such a juxtaposition of alternative meanings could probably be useful in creative work (cf. "homospatial imagery" as described by Rothenberg, 1979). In the present study, however, we have not only found retention in one of the small factors in group II, where high scores on the creativity scale also abound, but we have also found it in the residual factor in group III, where signs of creativity seem more marginal. We defer our conclusions until more data have been collected.

ANXIETY

MCT anxiety is another group of signs of considerable interest here. Signs of moderate anxiety were particularly associated with creativity as defined by the artistic criteria in groups II and III. The artistic judges apparently reacted to a special expressive quality in the drawings and clay figures. Even performance in the inverted PG test in group III was slightly associated with moderate anxiety and was clearly blocked when anxiety threatened to become intolerable. Children in factor I,3, whose MCT protocols showed signs of anxiety and strong defensive reactions, were characterized by lack of creativity at the same time. The uncreative children in factor III,2 should also be mentioned here because their use of relatively primitive defenses signified that more mature defenses could not be trusted to ward off anxiety. Anxiety did not appear as an item in this factor apparently because it also appeared in other factors—without hero duplication.

Moderate anxiety was found to be a constituent part of the creativity syndrome in adults (Chapters 5 and 6). Even if the correlation between creativity and moderate anxiety is not very impressive as far as the CFT is concerned, the fact remains that the number of moderate anxiety signs in MCT sharply increases with the number of inverted PG signs, from group I to group III. It is customary among dynamic psychologists to denote anxiety as a signal announcing that a threshold is about to be crossed—e.g., between secondary and primary modes of functioning. This signal could be a warning to the person not to cross the line. But it might also be taken as a startle response in the face of something novel and breathtaking or, to paraphrase Kierkegaard, as a presage of liberation from the dullness of everyday existence. Even if anxiety functions as more than just a warning signal of inner dangers, there is undoubtedly an intimate connection between anxiety and conflict. In children,

as in adults, inner contradictions (or chaos, as Vladimir Na-
bokov would have said), often projected into the outside world,
are probably important incitements to creative activity. Anxiety
would, then, be an indication that a contradiction about to reach
awareness needed to be dealt with in a constructive way by the
creative subject. If the anxiety is about to become intolerable,
however, all constructive activity becomes dangerous and is restrained.

SENSITIVITY

Sensitivity in the MCT refers to a plastic perception of reality,
a susceptibility to what is marginal, just liminal, or even subliminal. This characteristic has been shown to correlate with susceptibility to nuances in subject-subject relations and even with
tendencies to projective perceiving (Smith, Sjöholm, and Nielzén,
1974). An inclination to perceive objects as symbols rather than
signs is one characteristic of creative functioning, closely related
to dream appreciation. We see a connection between sensitivity
and symbolic functioning because the sensitive person registers
not only a word or a gesture, but a whole spectrum of nuances
that can give the word or gesture a surplus meaning. MCT
sensitivity-projection appears together with signs of creativity
in factor I,4, with H-placements in the B-dimension and with
interest in theatrical play in factor III,4. Apparently it is inti-
mately bound up with some aspects of creativity. Sensitivity to
nuances in subject-subject relations and an inclination to emotional display may very well fecundate certain forms of artistic
productivity. Greenacre (1957) regards sensitivity as a crucial
quality of the artist as a child (see Chapter 13).

FACTOR SOLUTIONS

Since the factor solutions refer to groups of persons and not
to groups of items, one cannot use them to draw any conclusions
regarding the single- or multifactor nature of creativity. What
they show is rather that creativity need not be associated with

the same set of characteristics in different individuals. It should also be kept in mind that the factor solutions are determined by the most common variables—i.e., the CFT signs, scale values, and artistic judgments. Since the three solutions rest on similar combinations of variables, however, it is possible to compare them with each other. Groups I and II are each dominated by "uncreativity" factors—even more so when the number of factors is restricted—with small creativity factors in addition. In group III the creativity factor is far more prominent. In all groups there is a factor focused on the inverted PG test and on other signs of creativity. There are also additional, more complicated, often small factors. Factor III,4 is of special interest because it combines high appreciation by the artists (the B-dimension) with interest in theatrical play and many themes in the straight PG. An adult factor characterized by similar results in the CFT and also by an ability to make swift but shallow associations was labeled "pseudocreativity." It would perhaps be unfair to bind III,4 too closely to such a designation. But the absence of human themes in the straight PG (such themes are indicative of emotional involvement, as observed in previous studies, and cross-validated by factors like I,2) and the inclination for extroverted, emotional display points in that direction.

REGRESSIVE FUNCTIONING

In our operational definition of creativity, construction of a stable C-phase was considered to be a necessary condition. Creative children are not subjective in the careless and ignorant manner of cognitively egocentric preschoolers. But nothing could prevent them, in principle, from occasional regressions to primitive functioning. Previous studies (Smith and Danielsson, 1982) have demonstrated a clear correlation between regressive tendencies, on the one hand, and weak defenses and low anxiety tolerance, on the other. In factor III,2, immature defense mechanisms are even negatively associated with various signs of creativity. Considering these findings, it would be rash to conclude that close proximity to primitive modes of functioning is a *sine qua non* for the subject in order to work creatively. Instead we believe that it is rather more important for him to be able to exploit all kinds of functions, even atavistic ones, from a certain, reality-adapted distance. As argued elsewhere (Kragh and Smith, 1974; Smith, 1981; cf. Rothenberg, 1979), we prefer to define this activity as a kind of reconstruction rather than as regression or even "adaptive regression," in the meaning of Kris (1952).

THE UNCREATIVE CHILD

Although we have discussed creative children and those with creative urges blocked by defensive operations, little attention has been given to the appearance of the ordinary uncreative child. The youngest children in this category are often girls well adapted to school and eager to do the right things. Among the 10- to 11-year-olds interest in extroverted activities, like sports, is prominent. Factors I,1, II,1, and III,1 are typical. The first two are more decidedly uncreative than the third. This is in line with our assumption that the early school milieu has a negative influence on creativity. An insensitivity to inner contradictions capable of leading the child to engage in constructive work is typical for children placed in these factors. Likewise, an associated lack of emotional involvement in such activities is another characteristic. As in the CFT, these uncreative children are dominated by that which is obvious and manifest in their C-phases; they are not prone to reconstruct subjective experiences or to revive such P-phase themes when left to their inner resources, i.e., when exposure times are shortened.

9

CREATIVITY IN MIDDLE AND LATE SCHOOL YEARS
(Age 12–16 Years)

As we see it, the motivational force behind creative functioning originates in the experience of conflict; why else should anxiety, even at moderate levels, be a typical companion of creative activity! People with a creative set do not suppress conflict-laden material but introject the contradictions as part of their own self, the accompanying anxiety and discomfort notwithstanding. This personalization also applies to scientific problems formulated at abstract-symbolic levels (Székély, 1976). When faced with an unsolved problem the creative person thus feels forced to assume responsibility for it.

The previous two chapters have shown that after their first creative phase at late preschool age (around 5–6 years in Sweden), children's creativity subsequently decreases after entering school. This decline is probably reinforced by demands made by the school and in the home. A few years later, at the age of 10–11, these children use their new cognitive skills when entering a more inward-directed period, which is foreboded by richer straight PGs. This change increases their possibilities of creative functioning. Typically, the creative 10- to 11-year-old phase is most accentuated in children from academic homes. Other children are content with more cautious interpretations in the inverted PGs.

For children 12–16 years of age in the present study there were three general predictions:

1. Developmental studies of anxiety and defensive strategies (Smith and Danielsson, 1982) have shown that prepuberty is characterized by compulsive tendencies. Since such tendencies are probably detrimental to creative functioning, we predict prepuberty (12–13.5 years) to be a period of low creativity.

2. Popular opinion holds that creativity reaches its height during puberty. Thus it would be reasonable to expect some positive change in children entering this phase. On the other hand, this period of a second individuation (Mahler, 1971) is, among other things, characterized by confusion, low self-reliance, peer group dependence, etc. (cf. Erikson's [1963] description of the period as one of "identity versus confusion"). Since we associate creative functioning with high self-reliance, our expectations were that the recovery of creative function would occur after puberty, if at all.

3. Children from academic homes were favored by what we thought to be their self-confidence. Since their home background is also likely to favor rationalism, we expected their change from a creative period at 10–11 to a non-creative one at 12–13 to be more abrupt than in children from non-academic homes.

METHODS

We used the CFT, the MCT, and an interview.

The core interview topics used for the 10 to 11-years-olds (Chapter 8) were also used here with the addition of some new topics believed to be relevant for the older age groups. The most important of these topics appear in the text below.

Scores 1 and 0 denoted presence and absence respectively. After a homogeneity analysis *ad modum* Likert, items with DP values (corrected for skewed distributions) > 0.40 were kept within the creativity-fantasy scale. The number of items in the scale did vary somewhat between the age groups, but not much as far as central creativity items were concerned (dreaming, early memories, creative activities). Usually, 2–4 items were excluded for lacking dispersion in each age group (less than 10% scored as 1 or 0).

It should be emphasized that the scales do not reflect the experimenter's interpretations but are based on the subject's actual answers to the concrete questions.

Subjects

The subjects were taken from 6th to 10th grade classes in the Lund public school system. Generally, whole classes participated. The home background was defined as academic if one parent had a college or university degree. This was usually not determined until afterwards. Therefore, the proportion of academic children was not constant from one age level to the next. In the preceding study of 7- to 11-year-olds it varied between 41% and 49%. Since we generally divide age levels according to home background in order to test its influence on data, differences in these proportions should not markedly influence our conclusions. Youngsters seldom declined to participate, probably because they were motivated not only by curiosity but also by a small sum of money.

In Table 9.1, the age, number of subjects, sex ratio (percentage males), and proportion of subjects from academic homes are presented.

TABLE 9.1
SUBJECTS (N TOTAL = 142)

Age	N	% boys	% subjects from academic homes
12	26	53	53
12 + young 13	37	54	54
13	24	54	42
14	29	48	59
15	30	50	50
old 13 + 14 + 15	72	50	50
16	33	52	52

RESULTS

In analyzing most of the data, age groups 12, 13, 14, 15, and 16 were used. We know from previous studies (Smith and Danielsson, 1982), however, that—in Sweden at least—prepuberty also encompasses part of the age of 13. Therefore we have sometimes endeavored to combine the 12-year-olds with the younger half of the 13-year-olds.

THE CFT

In the preceding chapter it was shown that the 10- to 11-year-olds had significantly more signs in the inverted PG than did the 7- to 8-year-olds. The 10- to 11-year-olds from academic homes had relatively stronger signs—XX, X, (X)—than those from nonacademic homes.

There was no clear tendency for the ratio signs/no signs to change thereafter. However, the number of very strong signs (i.e., XX, X) decreased significantly with an increase in age from 10–11 to 12 years ($\chi^2 = 4.66$, P <0.05), which was somewhat more accentuated in academic children. The proportion of strong signs was higher in 10–11-year-old academic youngsters

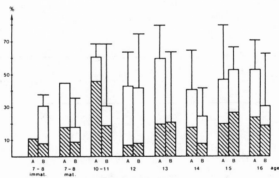

A: Children from academic homes. B: Children from non-academic homes
⊠ Strong signs: XX, X. ☐ Medium signs: (X), 0. ⊤ Weak signs: S.

FIGURE 9.1
SCORES IN THE CFT.

than in all 12–15-year-old counterparts taken together (χ^2 = 5.73, P <0.02). Irrespective of home background, there were relatively more *XX, X*, and *(X)* signs in 10- to 11- and 16-year-olds than in the 12- to 15-year-olds (χ^2 = 4.13, P<0.05).

The number of themes in the straight PG was high in both ages 10–11 and 12. Among twenty-six 12-year-olds, twenty-one had at least two themes, while among one hundred and seventeen, 13- to 16-year-olds this figure was 57 (χ^2 = 8.81, P<0.01). All 12-year-olds from academic homes had human themes. The percentages were generally lower among 13- to 15-year-olds but rose again at the age of 16 (82% for academic youngsters, 69% for the others).

ANXIETY

At the age of 10–11 years, signs of anxiety in the MCT were often mixed with signs of primitive defenses or were characterized as fusion, a rather severe but mostly childish form of anxiety. As expected, the number of primitive signs diminished as age increased. So as not to confuse immaturity and degree of pathology, we have only concerned ourselves with one all-encompassing category of "late" signs (see the previous description of MCT scoring). With respect to these signs the age span of older 13-year-olds together with those age 14 to 15—a period we would like to call "high puberty"—stands out against the preceding and following age levels. Of the high puberty subjects, forty-six were scored for signs of anxiety and twenty-seven were not; the corresponding figures for the before-and-after subjects were twenty-one and forty-eight (χ^2 = 14.19, P<0.001).

ISOLATION AND KINDRED STRATEGIES

In this category of compulsive and compulsive-like strategies for dealing with the provocation in the MCT we have included isolation, tendencies toward isolation, negation ("it's not something dangerous"), reports of the back-of-the-head instead of the face of the threatening figure, and intellectualization. The young 13-year-olds differed sharply from the older adolescents of 13: eight of eleven young subjects were scored for compulsive strategies compared with one of thirteen older ones (P = 0.0016, Fisher's exact test, one-tailed). A comparison of 12-year-olds plus young 13-year-olds with all older subjects yielded a χ^2 of 5.33 (P<0.05). In the academic group the difference was slightly more pronounced (χ^2 = 5.78, P <0.02).

THE CREATIVITY-FANTASY SCALE

Because the various scales were constructed *within* the age groups, the group of 13-year-olds was kept intact in most comparisons. The exception was our attempt to delineate prepuberty.

The standard deviation of subjects' agreement with interview questions was almost exactly alike in boys and girls. Still, girls appeared less inclined to be negative than boys. This difference tended to become most pronounced at the age of 16, even with respect to central creativity items (write, compose, invent, collect things to be used for unexpected purposes, fantasy playmate, remembering a recent dream, longing for creative solitude, very early childhood memories). It is therefore of particular interest to note a substantial correlation between the scale and the CFT for the 16-year-old girls. We used three equidistant steps at each axis and got an r = 0.83 (P<0.001).

Three items on the scale were assumed to represent childish trust: no mistrust of parents, no keeping of a (secret) diary, confiding in parents. These items correlated positively with the CFT in the group of 12- and young 13-year-olds (χ^2 = 16.21, df = 2, P<0.001). In other words, those who were still like 10- to 11-year-olds—i.e., trustful and open—scored higher than the less trustful on the inverted PG test.

THE INVERTED FACTOR ANALYSIS

An inverted factor analysis was used to group subjects at each age level. The technique was described previously (see Chapter 4 for details).

The factor picture was sometimes vague: the factors seemed to have been determined by a few prominent items, above all the CFT, plus an assortment of items with relatively modest D-values. Some trends were discernible, however.

In the previous study, 10- to 11-year-olds were above all characterized by a creative factor where the creativity-fantasy scale and the judgments by professional artists of the children's drawing and clay figures were also decisive. At 12 and 13 the creative factors appeared to shrink. What seemed to be a growing extraversion made children at 12—even relatively creative ones—reject daydreaming (factor I). Moreover, clearly creative ones reported difficulties in recalling dreams (IV). At the same time, the influence of the scale could still be seen in small creativity factors.

Among the 14 and 15-year-olds, creative functioning seemed to be making a slow recovery. Typically, however, the positive association between creativity and the creativity-fantasy scale was no longer apparent at this age. At 16, when the most mature youngsters should be on their way out of puberty, creativity was found to be back at the center of the factor stage. We had expected the creativity-fantasy scale to appear again in the creativity factor. The generally low scoring of boys on the scale, however, explains why creativity scores and scale values are so poorly associated when both sexes are present in one creative factor (I). It also should be noted that repression in MCT was found to become gradually more tied to creativity at the ages of 15 and 16.

The creativity factors are presented below: The first in a solution is designed as I, the second as II, etc.

12 years, 26 subjects: Twenty-two subjects placed in four factors.

IV: Three subjects. The only really creative factor in the age group: strong signs in the inverted PG (D = 54), many themes in the straight one (57), daydreaming (61), yearning to be alone (83), memories from the age of 1–2 years (78), above median values on the creativity-fantasy scale (78), drawing judged as original (74) and expressive (74), etc.

13 years, 24 subjects: Eighteen subjects placed in four factors.

III and IV: Two and four subjects. Both factors strongly creative. Factor IV above all characterized by strong signs in the inverted PG (90). These individuals collect things that can be used for unexpected purposes (80), yearn to be alone sometimes (60), score above the median on the creativity-fantasy scale (65), show signs of repression in the MCT (55), etc.

14 years, 29 subjects: Twenty-eight subjects placed in four factors.

III and IV: Five and four subjects. Both factors include creative subjects (strong signs in the inverted PG, 68 and 59, respectively). III is also characterized by isolation and isolation tendencies in the MCT (63), IV by late anxiety in the same test (60) but lack of repression (-56), low values on the creativity-fantasy scale (-60), reluctance to confide in other people (-64), etc.

15 years, 30 subjects: Twenty-seven subjects placed in four factors.

III: Seven subjects. A creative factor (inverted PG, strong signs, D = 91), somewhat stronger than the corresponding factors in previous age groups.

16 years, 33 subjects: Twenty-seven subjects placed in four factors.

I: Eight subjects. A clearly creative first factor (strong, inverted PG signs, D = 84). Repression in the MCT also obvious (elaborate interpretations, 76; all signs, 68).

III: Six subjects. Scoring above the median on the creativity-fantasy scale (63) and with signs of sensitivity in the MCT (54).

DISCUSSION

In the previous chapter we found a great deal of anxiety in the 10- to 11-year-olds but also a great deal of creativity, particularly pronounced in children from academic homes. These children are obviously able to handle the anxiety-arousing uncertainties of their experience by means of creative construction. Greater capacity to handle symbols might be a contributing factor (cf. Gardner, 1973).

We expected an increase in compulsive and compulsivelike strategies around the age of 12–13 years (Smith and Danielsson, 1982), and this prediction was substantiated. The change is accompanied by a decrease in strong creativity signs, particularly in academic children, and by a decrease in signs of anxiety. There is no clear tendency, however, for protocols devoid of creativity signs to become more numerous. The "low tide" at the age of 7–8 years remains unique.

These compulsive strategies probably serve an adaptive purpose in prepuberty, directing the youngsters toward a consolidation of knowledge and cognitive skills before the tumultuous event of puberty. The fact that the straight PG remains rich in themes, particularly human themes in the academic subgroup, supports our assumption that the compulsive strategies are not solely defensive in character (cf. Hartmann, 1939). Since the presence of human themes has previously attested to emotional involvement (Chapter 4) prepuberty youngsters could perhaps be described as potentially rather than manifestly creative. The openly creative ones are those who have remained "young in heart," open and full of trust.

The correlation between the CFT and the creativity-fantasy scale breaks down in prepuberty (except the "trust" items) and continues to be low throughout puberty. One reason seems to be that many of these youngsters are unwilling to confide in an interviewer, another that they do not really know what they want but depend on the opinions of peer groups. Signs of anxiety increase and signs of compulsion cease to be dominant. Creativity scores, however, increase only slightly, though visibly, as attested by the factor solutions. Among the reasons for the slow recovery, formulated in the second prediction, we particularly want to emphasize lack of self-reliance (see Chapters 10 and 11). On the whole, inward-outward communication remains deficient in many youngsters at puberty.

As the pubertal negativism recedes in 16-year-old girls, the high criterion correlation from the age of 10–11 years reappears. At this age, generally, signs of anxiety in the MCT recede. A similar change at the beginning of prepuberty is accompanied by an increase of compulsive strategies and a decrease of strong signs of creativity. The number of compulsive signs remains relatively low at the age of 16 years, however; instead, creativity scores tend to become more numerous. It still seems as if youngsters from academic homes receive stronger scores in the CFT. Is this because they have remained more trustful of their own inner realities?

The present study of children and youngsters started out with the assumption that in childhood and adolescence, creative periods alternate with less creative, consolidating ones. On the whole, however, this periodicity seems to be moderated after age 12. Neither prepuberty nor puberty are so lacking in creativity as the age of 7–8 years; consequently, the subsequent recovery is not as dramatic as it was at 10–11. As development gradually slows down at the threshold of adulthood its periodic rhythm is tempered.

The fluctuations between low- and high-creative periods are probably necessary for growth to continue. There has been much discussion about continuity versus discontinuity in behavioral development (Brim and Kagan, 1980). Often, continuity has been regarded as more genetically determined and discontinuity regarded as more influenced by changes in the child's environment. If one was to regard discontinuity as part of nature's dialectical way of functioning, the polarization would seem superfluous (cf. Hinde and Bateson, 1984). This does not mean, however, that we dismiss outside factors as being of little importance in determining the degree and timing of the periodicity.

We have presumed that the compulsive or compulsivelike strategies at prepuberty also serve an adaptive purpose. Nevertheless, by separating the youngster from his emotional self, these strategies reduce the strength of his creative impulses. In a clinical study (Chapter 6) we found compulsive defenses together with depressive stereotypy, both in the MCT, to be particularly detrimental to creative functioning. A separate study of the 16-year-olds has repeated that finding (Chapter 10).

We will now try to summarize creativity development from preschool age to the year just beyond puberty. When about 5–6 years old, children enter a period of subjective expansion accompanied by a consolidation of their reality contact (stable final phase in the CFT). This double-directed communication or duality of inwardness and the outside world apparently facilitates their first attempts at creative functioning. A few years later, at age 7–8, the subjective channel is blocked and creativity constricted. However, a gradual enrichment of the perceptgeneses at this stage precedes a new subjective expansion at 10–11 when, in spite of increasing anxiety, the trustful inward-outward balance is obviously preserved. Creativity flowers until preoccupation with the subjective side diminishes a year or two later, as evidenced by an abrupt reduction of anxiety and the strengthening of isolation and kindred avoidance strategies. Even if the prepuberty youngster remains potentially open to his own subjective world, he seems more inclined to trust outside reality. The next step, into the period of mounting anxiety and confusion at puberty, does not imply a clear revival of creativity, probably because no new inward-outward balance can be reached until about 16 years of age. By then, anxiety can be better controlled by means of flexible, adult strategies, and self-reliance is restored.

A note of caution before the discussion is concluded: much of the periodicity detected in this cohort has been most typical of academic youngsters. The creative peak at age 10–11, and the decline in creativity at 12 may therefore tend to be smoothed out in a more representative sample, explaining why these age periods are not clearly differentiated in most developmental theories. Rather than admit that our difference is a social artifact, however, we suggest that the fertile climate in many academic homes allows the manifestation of important developmental trends otherwise restrained by a lack of appreciation of the child's true nature.

10

CREATIVITY AND AGGRESSION IN 16-YEAR-OLDS

Interest in the relation of creativity to aggression originated in a study of creativity where the subjects were thirty-one psychiatric patients (Chapter 6). Here we demonstrated that grave anxiety and dominating defenses of a depressive or compulsive character, as defined by the MCT, were detrimental to creative activity. A subsequent study of creative development in children (Chapters 7–9) showed that a creative peak at 10–11 years is followed by a relatively uncreative period in 12 and early 13-year-olds, the change being particularly abrupt in children with an intellectual home background. Simultaneously, the amount of compulsive defenses increased in the MCT, and signs of anxiety decreased.

Depressive and compulsive reactions both appear to imply that the perceiver blocks the reconstruction of early, subjectively colored stages in his percept-genesis, thus making them inaccessible. In psychoanalytic conceptions of creativity, this could be formulated as a thwarted communication between primary- and secondary-process modes of functioning. This agrees with Deri's (1984, p. 283) thoughts about creative artists who "have a special openness to their psychic organization, from the perceptual apparatus to the preconscious, and 'down' into the energy reservoir of the id." In the depressives or compulsives there are simply no subjective, "symbolic" interpretations of the provocative picture in the MCT. As shown by Hentschel (1980), moreover, the defense of isolation is correlated with a poor ability to associate.

There is apparently reason to ask what depressive retardation and compulsive isolation have in common. In both cases, obviously, emotion is barred from the focus of experience. This would be one way to explain the lack of creative impetus in these people. In the present project, however, we are more interested in how depression and compulsion are associated with aggression. Introaggression is one of the most conspicuous features of depressive states. Instead of acknowledging their own aggressive impulses, depressive people turn them inwards, feeling dejected, worthless, and guilty. In classic psychoanalytic theory (Fenichel, 1945) it has been taken for granted that aggressive impulses are countered by the postoedipal (compulsive) defense mechanism of isolation; supporting experimental evidence has been presented by, among others, Rutstein and Goldberger (1973). In a series of experiments testing psychoanalytic propositions, Westerlundh and Sjöbäck (1986) have been able to substantiate this assumption very convincingly. Using a test situation similar to the MCT, they demonstrated that while sexual provocations tended to increase the amount of repressive defenses, aggressive provocations affected the compulsive ones. The definitions of repressive and compulsive defenses entertained by these investigators agree with the ones described for the MCT.

Since depressive and compulsive subjects both seem to avoid conscious recognition of their own aggressive impulses and since, moreover, they tend to receive low scores in the CFT, we were led to presume some sort of association between aggressive impulses and creativity. We do not mean to suggest, as MacKinnon (1962, 1965) and Barron (1968) have done, that creative people are more openly aggressive, power-seeking, or ruthless than others. This was definitely not the case in a sample of suggestors in a Swedish industry (Ekvall, 1971). Agreeing with Rothenberg (1979), we have already claimed that when engaged in creative work an individual tries to actively master and exploit more and more unconscious material. We had also observed in our developmental studies that youngsters with an academic background tended to score higher on the CFT than contemporaries from nonacademic homes, the latter being more guarded and conventional when describing the tachistoscopic flashes. We interpreted this difference as depending, at least in part, on a difference of trust in the value and reality of one's own inner world. Hence we were tempted to see a relation between creativity and self-reliance.

Part of our predictions are directed at the new Identification Test or IT (Smith, Carlsson, and Danielsson, 1985), where the subject is manipulated to identify with an aggressor or with his victim. We expect creative people to identify more openly with an aggressive person than noncreative ones, the latter being more evasive or outright denying. We also predict that creative subjects will show fewer signs of depression and compulsive defenses in the MCT. The last finding would be a cross-validation not only of results arrived at in the study of psychiatric patients just mentioned but also in a study of professional artists (Chapter 14). Let it also be added that subjects may react with signs of depressive stereotypy or compulsive isolation, or with any of the signs we have chosen to score in the MCT in the present investigation, without necessarily being characterized as mentally ill or severely neurotic.

As described in Chapter 9, a group of 16-year-olds was tested as part of a developmental project. According to our test and interview data, these youngsters had left most of their puberty problems behind them. When we also found that the group included subjects with high as well as low scores in the CFT we decided that it was suitable for the present study.

METHOD

The three test instruments were the CFT, the MCT, and the Identification Test.

The CFT was administered as before.

The MCT was also administered as before. We did, however, make the choice of scoring dimensions more explicit.

Stereotypy. A stereotyped repetition over at least five, and often many more, consecutive phases of the same interpretation of

A or, of a noninterpreted A ("something in the window"). A sign of depression.

Empty protocols. Except for one or another detail the picture appeared similar to the subject and there was no mention of the A-stimulus until he recognized the correct A. Here, the category also included protocols with no scorable signs at all and should thus be considered less strict. Empty protocols were found in compulsive subjects; many of these showed depressive symptoms at the same time.

Isolation. The threatening A-stimulus was seen as a harmless white spot, such as curtains covering the window in the B-stimulus, etc. This "isolating" response is typical of compulsive subjects.

Repression. The subject reported A as a lifeless bust or a mask instead of a live, threatening face. This kind of stimulus-proximal report is particularly common in primitive-hysterics but was rare in the present group of subjects who were, instead, inclined to give more elaborated answers: a tree, a house, an object, etc.

Sensitivity movement. Instead of reporting A as a new structure within B, the subject suppressed A and reported change in B: another perspective, enlargement, movement, etc. This response category has been interpreted as a mild form of projection, lacking the rigidity typical of paranoid subjects but still sensitive to marginal cues.

THE IDENTIFICATION TEST

The basic assumption underlying the test design was that on a picture depicting an "aggressor" and a "victim" face to face, subliminal projection of the word "I" (Swedish "jag") on one figure or the other should affect a subject's impression of or attitude toward the contrasting roles they represent.

The picture was drawn by Dr. Bert Westerlundh. The aggressor and the victim, both male, stand half facing each other, the aggressor to the left. The victim is holding his arms stretched downwards in an open gesture, the aggressor's arms are bent at the elbows and his fists clenched. The mouths of both figures are half open as if they are talking, and that of the aggressor is twisted in a snarl.

The picture and the word "I" were presented tachistoscopically by the same apparatus as used for the MCT. Exposure times began at 0.01 sec. and were prolonged step by step with a quotient of $\sqrt{2}$. When subliminal stimuli were used they were flashed immediately before the picture.

The letter B_1 was used to represent the aggressor-victim picture, while the letters Aa and Av stood for the word "I" when flashed on the aggressor and victim, respectively. Starting with an exposure value of 0.01 sec., B_1 was then presented in the series of increasing exposure times. This series continued until the subject had correctly recognized the aggressor and the victim. Thereafter, the following four series were presented, the exposure for the A-stimuli being 0.014 sec. and for the B_1 stimulus 0.057 sec.:

1.	B_1 alone	5 times	3. Av + B_1	5 times
2.	Aa + B_1	5 times	4. B_1 alone	5 times

The presentation order of 2 and 3 was randomized and unknown to the experimenter. The manipulation made by the experimenter to switch from Aa to Av or vice versa was camouflaged by several faked manipulations.

The subject received the following instructions:

> I'm going to show brief flashes of pictures on the screen and will say NOW before each flash. On these pictures you'll see persons; I want you to describe them, but also to tell me your impressions of them—what kind of people you think they are, whether you like them, what you believe they could be thinking and feeling. Also try to describe the atmosphere in the picture. Sometimes you may think that the pictures we show are very much alike, sometimes that they change from one exposure to the next. Please note such changes.

SCORING OF THE IT

The protocols were divided into three main categories: (1) Clear aggression or gradually increasing aggression reported in the series where "I" was presented behind the aggressor; (2) no aggression in any series; (3) evasive or no reports of aggression in the "aggressor" series, but at least some indication of aggression when "I" was presented behind the victim.

VALIDITY OF THE IT

The IT in its present form was validated in a group of psychiatric patients, part of them characterized as borderline, others as paranoid. The borderline subjects encountered perceptual difficulties when manipulated to identify with the aggressor and even resisted identification with the victim. Paranoid subjects had similar problems with the aggressor but easily identified with the victim, reporting the aggressor's aggression (Smith, Carlsson, and Danielsson, 1985). The IT testing principle was also validated with another picture in the same publication.

RELIABILITY OF THE TESTS

The CFT and the MCT were scored by two judges independently of each other. One of the judges had tested the subjects with both tests on one occasion but scored them several months later, never knowing to whom a protocol belonged, thus being unable to pair protocols emanating from the same subject. The second judge was totally naive. At the most there were one or two disagreements per test, none of which could not be resolved in joint discussions.

Then IT was also scored by a third judge who disagreed with the former judges in one of twenty-eight cases. The opinion of the third judge prevailed.

SUBJECTS

The subjects were the thirty-three 16-year-olds mentioned in Chapter 9 from the 10th grade of the public school system in Lund. In five cases, however, there were technical problems when they came back to take the IT, leaving twenty-eight acceptable protocols from that testing.

RESULTS

Table 10.1 shows the correlation between creativity and identification with the aggressor. As predicted, clear aggression in the IT differs from no aggression and evasion. By dividing the CFT signs according to the best possible median, we produced a four-field table yielding a P (Fisher's exact test, two-sided) of 0.005. The G-index of agreement (Holley and Guilford, 1964), corresponding to a correlation coefficient, is 0.71.

Next we compared the CFT with the MCT dimensions: isolation-depression and repression-sensitivity (Table 10.2). The main reason for combining isolation and depression was, as the reader may remember, that these "rigid" defenses had both previously proved detrimental to creative activity. Sensitive reactions and the kind of "symbolic" repressive transformations of stimulus A seen here were regarded as more flexible defenses and have also been registered in our study of creative artists (Chapter 14). In this table, all thirty-three subjects were able to be used. Contrasting I:A with the other categories and dividing the PG signs according to the best possible median resulted in

TABLE 10.1
COMPARISON OF THE IT AND THE CFT

| | | The Inverted PG test | | |
		XX/X	(X)/0	S/-
The	Clear aggression	3	5	1
IT	No aggression	2	0	5
test	Evasion	0	1	11

TABLE 10.2
COMPARISON OF THE MCT AND THE CFT

| | | The Inverted PG test | | |
		XX/X	(X)/0	S/-
The	I:A	7	5	4
	B	0	0	3
MCT	II:A	0	1	5
	B	0	1	7

I: Not isolation/tendencies to isolation/depressive stereotypy/empty protocols.
II: Isolation, etc.
A: Repression/tendencies to repression/sensitivity movement.
B: Not repression, etc.

TABLE 10.3
COMPARISON OF THE IT AND THE MCT

| | | The MCT | | |
		Depressive stereotypy/ Clear isolation	Empty protocols Tendencies to isolation	The rest
The	Clear aggression	0	2	7
IT	No aggression	2	2	3
test	Evasion	7	0	5

a fourfold table yielding a P of 0.0006 (Fisher's exact test, two-sided). The G-index of agreement is 0.64.

Finally, MCT was compared with IT (Table 10.3). Here we have tried to differentiate the MCT results by distinguishing depressive stereotypy and clear isolation from empty protocols and isolation tendencies, respectively. As far as the IT is concerned, we have considered evasive answers as being more defensive than answers included in the category "no aggression" (which often reflect more active involvement). The correlation coefficient for the two dimensions is 0.44 (P = 0.02).

DISCUSSION

As already mentioned, interest in the subject of creativity and aggression is not entirely new. Whereas MacKinnon (1962, 1965), Barron (1968), and others found more signs of open aggression and self-assertion in creative subjects, Ekvall (1971) did not comply. These conflicting results can partly be explained by cultural differences and partly by the amalgamation of social success and creativity in the criteria used by the American investigators. In this connection it is interesting to note that Götz and Götz (1979a, 1979b), using Eysenck's Personality Questionnaire, found male artists to be higher on psychoticism than male and female nonartists. This result could be taken to mean that the male artists were more ready to accept their aggressive impulses, more autonomous, and less inclined to conform, an interpretation in some agreement with our findings and with those recently presented by Hentschel and Schneider (1986).

The main results of the present study were as follows: Subjects scoring above the median on the CFT, receiving the most reliable signs of creativity, according to previous studies, were more open to identification with an aggressive role—i.e., reporting the aggressor's aggression when manipulated to identify with him—than subjects scoring below the median. This result was cross-validated in our study of thirty-three 10- to 12-year-olds (Chapter 11). At the same time, the MCT protocols of the 16-year-olds were characterized by the defense strategies of repression and light projection (sensitivity) rather than by depressive stereotypy and compulsive isolation. As expected, the relation between the propensity to report aggression when manipulated to see oneself as aggressive and type of defense was less obvious. However, clear signs of isolation together with depressive stereotypy were associated with resistance to aggressive identification. This last association supports the basis for our main hypothesis.

Our creative subjects are probably not more aggressive than others, at least not in the acting-out meaning of the term. Instead, we propose that they are less neurotic in their dealings with aggressive impulses. It seems tempting to describe them as more actively "dealing with" the preconscious material constituting the source of their anxiety. As a matter of fact, there was a tendency (≤ 0.10) for these creative youngsters to show more signs of anxiety in their MCT tests than less creative ones. We know from previous studies (Chapter 5; cf. Sjöberg, 1984) that creative people are not free from symptoms of anxiety but seem more tolerant of them, more ready to accept them as unavoidable companions of creative functioning. One reason for their tolerance might be that they do not feel themselves to be passive victims of anxiety but active masters of it (in their creative work).

We have also suggested that open identification with the aggressive role is a sign of self-reliance. Let us, as a support for this speculation, repeat that in our developmental studies (Chapters 8 and 9), especially at the age around 10–11 years—when creativity peaked—but even in the present group of 16-year-olds, youngsters from academic homes seemed to be more openly creative than children from nonacademic backgrounds. They did not hesitate to report strong signs in the inverted PG. It could reasonably be argued that these children were more sure of themselves, feeling less dubious about their private impressions and more inclined to believe in their own whims and ideas. At the same time, the home background favors their development of intellectualizing and compulsive defenses for use at prepuberty (12- and early 13-year-olds in our material) when they briefly turn to the outside world and deny the inner dimension.

The use of repression and slight projection (mostly combined) as defensive strategies obviously goes together with creativity. This should not be interpreted as pathological behavior, since the repressive strategies were not indicative of primitive-hysteria, nor were the sensitive strategies typical of reality-distorting projection. It would be more appropriate to venture that creative subjects intermittently exploit analogues of repression at a high level of stimulus transformation, combined with a plastic but reality-adapted restructuring of the information. In fact, upon reading the protocols, the impression is not one of a rigid warding-off of the threatening message but of an active, diversified gestalting of it, being coherent and rich in contrasts at the same time.

The signs of sensitivity specifically disclose that these subjects are open to preconscious influences (operationalized in the test as the subliminal stimulus A in MCT). By comparison, depressive-compulsive protocols seem empty, rigid, and devoid of affect.

11

CREATIVITY AND AGGRESSION IN 10- TO 12-YEAR-OLDS

This chapter deals with the relation between creativity and aggression in 10- to 12-year-olds using a research design similar in all respects to that in the previous chapter, except for the MCT. The predictions for this group of subjects had to be slightly reformulated, however, for the following reasons.

A recent developmental study (Smith and Danielsson, 1982) demonstrated that children around age 12 exhibit a large amount of isolating defenses. This prepubertal period can be considered as a time when aggressive impulses are actively warded off in order to promote adaptation to external realities. Moreover, in our study on creative development (Chapters 8 and 9), we found a marked decrease in strong creative signs beginning around the age of 12.

Even if most subjects in the present study had not yet reached the age of 12, it seems reasonable to presume that open identification with an aggressor would be less acceptable to them than to the 16-year-olds in the previous chapter. We thus expected that these 10- to 12-year-olds would exhibit various avoidance strategies in their dealings with the aggressive theme, although the relation with creativity would remain. The more creative children should still have less problems with aggressive identification in the IT than the less creative ones.

METHOD

The two tests used were the IT and the CFT.

THE IT

This test was given as before but the following, slightly elaborated scoring dimensions were used.

1. More aggression is seen by the subject when "I" is shown on the Aggressor than when shown on the Victim. $+1$ is scored if the aggression is judged to be clear or getting stronger during the series; $+0.5$ if vague aggression is reported or diminishing during the Aggressor series.

2. More signs of anxiety (reports of increasing darkness in the picture, or the picture is said to become diffuse or to disappear) or of perceptual distortions (the picture obviously changes) when "I" is presented on the Victim than on the Aggressor. Small changes, for instance, when the position of a figure slightly changes from one exposure to the next, are not counted. Each sign of anxiety or distortion is allowed $+1$.

3. More aggression is seen by the subject when "I" is shown on the Victim than on the Aggressor. A -1 is given if aggression is clear or increasing, and reports of vague or diminishing aggression during the Victim series (and no aggression in the Aggressor series) are given a -0.5 score.

4. More signs of anxiety or perceptual distortions (corresponding to [2]) when "I" is shown on the Aggressor than on the Victim. Score $= -1$.

5. The subject shows signs of fatigue (yawns). A -1 is given if the subject yawns only in the Aggressor series, -0.5 if only in the Victim series or in both series. This sign is considered to be a primitive form of passive defensive behavior (as scored in the MCT).

A scoring category including the same degree of aggression in both series was omitted in the calculations. The stereotyped character of these protocols gave the impression that the child tried to evade the whole problem by answering in a fixed manner.

RELIABILITY OF THE IT

All IT protocols were scored independently by two judges. One had tested the subjects several months earlier, and the other judge had no knowledge of the subjects. An additional outside judge also scored the subjects and the interreliability between the two sets of judges was measured as follows. For each protocol the sum of scores given by the first set of judges was compared with that of the outside judge. The range of scores comprised nine steps between -2 and $+2$. A product-moment correlation between the two sets of data yielded $r = 0.83$. We did not compute correlations between judges in every column, since one set of judges seemed more sensitive to the aggression and the other to anxiety or defensive distortions.

THE CFT

In the present study a newly constructed (Carlsson and Smith, 1985) parallel version of the CFT was used (CFT II). This picture depicts an old-fashioned armchair with a round small table beside it. In the background is the vague image of a drape.

RELIABILITY OF THE CFT II

The two independent judges found it slightly more difficult to score the CFT II than to score CFT I. Some small differences were easily resolved. As regards the parallelism between the two tests, previous correlational analyses yielded r values between 0.71 and 0.91.

SUBJECTS

The subjects were thirty-three children (nineteen boys and fourteen girls), 10:2 to 12:0 years old. Mean age was 11:1 for boys and 11:4 for girls. Twenty-one of the children were taking part in a follow-up study of preschool children and their creativity development (Chapter 12).

RESULTS

When comparing the results on the CFT with the scores in the IT, we divided the subjects into three groups: Group A with plus scores in the IT, group B with zero scores, and group C with minus scores. In terms of the score, it made no difference whether there was consensus between judges or if only one set of judges had discerned the sign. As mentioned above, there was a slight difference in sensitivity between judges with respect to the different categories. In the creativity test the group was divided into two subgroups, one with signs (XX–S) and the other without signs. This was also the best median cut (Table 11.1). Group A contrasted with C yielded a P = 0.0008 (Fisher's exact test). Calculating a χ^2 (2 × 3 table), resulted in a value of 14.04 (df = 2), P = 0.001. The contingency coefficient (C) based on the χ^2 value is 0.54. Maximum C in a 2 × 3 table is approximately 0.77 and C_{max} is 0.70.

As described in Chapter 10, the IT was also used in a group of 16-year-olds. These adolescents were more open to identification with the aggressor. Only three categories were needed in the scoring of their IT protocols: (1) Clear or gradually increasing aggression, in the aggressor series, with or without clear aggression in the victim series; (2) vague or no aggression in any series; and (3) vague or no reports of aggression in the

TABLE 11.1
RESULTS IN THE IT TEST COMPARED
WITH CFT SCORES

Inverted PG	IT		
	A (+ scores)	B (0 scores)	C (− scores)
XX - S	11	4	3
	1	4	10

aggressor series, but at least some indication that the subject saw aggression when "I" was projected on the victim. If these categories had been applied in the present group, there would have been no correlation whatever with the CFT results. This is in part due to the character of eight protocols where clear aggression was reported in both series. In five of them the subject scored "−" in the CFT, and in the IT the subliminal series were often just stereotyped repetitions of the control series. This was the reason that we considered only *differences* between the two series and gave no points to protocols with clear aggression in both. In the 16-year-olds there were only few such instances of aggression in both series; two if we count those where both sets of judges agreed. This might indicate less stereotyped reactions in the adolescents.

In twenty of the protocols we were able to differentiate anxious from defensive distortions in the subliminal IT series. The most prominent features were black structures and so-called zero-phases, where no picture motif was seen (both signs scored as anxiety in the MCT). Furthermore, the persons in the picture were perceived as statues (a sign of repression) or just as white spots (isolation in the MCT). In the previous study of 16-year-olds, no scoring of anxiety and defense was made, since the aggressive theme was obviously better tolerated and thus better perceived.

When we created one table for anxiety and defense (Table 11.2a) and another for aggression (Table 11.2b), we found that creative children showed more signs of anxiety and defense

TABLE 11.2A
RESULTS IN CREATIVITY COMPARED WITH ANXIETY
AND DEFENSE IN THE IT

Inverted PG	IT Less anxiety and defense in Aggr.	No differen- tiation	Less anxiety and defense in Vict.
XX - (X)	6	4	0
O - S	5	2	1
—	2	7	6

TABLE 11.2B
RESULTS IN CFT COMPARED WITH MORE
AGGRESSION IN A SERIES IN THE IT

Inverted PG	IT More aggression in Aggressor series	No differen-tiation	More aggression in Victim series
XX - (X)	4	4	2
O - S	3	5	0
—	4	7	4

when forced to identify with the victim of aggression. The un-creative ones exhibited just the opposite reaction, namely, a disinclination to identify with the active, aggressive party (Table 11.2a). When we based the table on "more aggression" in the aggressor series compared with more aggression in the victim series, most of this tendency disappeared (Table 11.2b).

The sleep behavior registered during the testing is also worthy of notice. Of thirteen children who yawned in one or both of the IT series, nine scored "−", one scored "S", and three received a "O" in the CFT.

Certain other possible correlations were also tested. There was a slight tendency for girls to get lower scores on the CFT than boys: 21% of the girls got strong scores (XX–(X)) compared with 37% of the boys. Interestingly, only one girl got a score of 1 in the "more aggression" columns, and four girls scored 0.5. The corresponding figures for boys were 8 and 4. Both sexes had about the same distribution of scores in the IT, but the variation for girls was mostly based on scores of anxiety and defense.

Finally, we compared age with anxiety and defense and divided the group into three age levels: 11 years and under; above 11 up to and including 11:6; and above 11:6 years. A χ^2 analysis (2 × 3 table) showed an increase of anxiety and defense over age ($\chi^2 = 6.40$; df = 2; P < 0.05). When we excluded the girls, who seemed more prone to react with anxiety and defense, and divided the boys into a young and an old group, a similar tendency was observed (P < 0.05, Fisher's exact test, one-sided).

DISCUSSION

The expected difference in aggressor-victim identification between uncreative and creative children was found in these 10- to 12-year-olds, even if it was not as straightforward as with the 16-year-olds. The creative children had fewer problems in identifying with an aggressor than the uncreative ones. Although they seemed rather reluctant to recognize themselves as aggressive, they avoided the role of a passive "victim" even more strongly, thereby arousing anxiety and defensive reactions.

The uncreative group showed less resistance to the surrendering role while shying away from the active aggressor. Their preference for a passive role was also revealed by their frequent yawning in the series where the subliminal "I" was projected. In the MCT this kind of reaction has been interpreted as a passive-avertive behavior, most common among children (Smith and Danielsson, 1982).

The influence of prepuberty in these children is somewhat unclear. The fact that the girls were more cautious in the creativity test and more unwilling to discern any aggression in the subliminal series might indicate that they had reached the compulsive, relatively low-creative period of prepuberty. There might also have been an influence of gender—seventeen of the nineteen boys saw aggression in the subliminal series (if stereotyped reactions are included) compared with only six of the fourteen girls (P = 0.001, Fisher's exact test, two-sided).

Although girls and boys differed in their perception of the aggressive theme in the IT, the creative ones of both sexes had the same preference for the aggressor, who was also being more active than the victim. An active disposition is probably decisive for creative endeavors, implying a willingness to reshape one's reality.

12

PREDICTING CREATIVITY IN CHILDREN

Although longitudinal studies of creativity development should be important for illuminating the subject of creativity, such studies are difficult to trace in the literature. Articles describing studies in which early childhood (before the age of 7) is made the starting point for predictions over a period of more than one year are extremely scarce (according to Harrington, Block, and Block, 1983; confirmed by our own search).

The just-mentioned authors have made such a study. Even though they defined creativity in the Binet tradition, i.e., as divergent thinking (DT), their study is of considerable interest to our own work in the field.

Harrington et al. ask: "Do regression equations involving intelligence *and* DT measures account for more variance in creativity than regression equations involving only intelligence scores?" A total of seventy-five children were tested at the age of 4–5 years and rated by teachers for creativity six to seven years later. This creativity criterion was judged to possess a good construct and high discriminant validity. The conclusion was "that DT high-quality scores in early childhood carry information related to teacher-evaluated creativity in adolescence that is not captured by sex, tested intelligence and DT fluency scores in early childhood." The correlation between high-quality scores and the criterion was 0.45, supporting the authors' assumption of continuities in the development of these personality characteristics.

There is no reason to contradict this conclusion, which is in line with our own previous findings (Chapter 9) even if continuities may be obscured by developmental periodicity with regard to creativity.

When predicting creativity we had to test children at points in their development where it supposedly showed great variation. Otherwise we would have risked confounding a temporary developmental low in creativity with permanent loss. We chose the age periods of 5–6 and 10–11 years. In spite of all precautions, we included a few children in the first testing who were still too young to be genuinely creative and included some others in the second testing who were well on their way into the low-creative prepuberty. We will deal with this problem in more detail when presenting the subjects.

To broaden the basis for predictions we also employed a number of other instruments (see below). Our general prediction was that degree of creativity at 5–6 would correspond to degree of creativity at 10–11. We also expected, however, that the defensive profile revealed by the MCT at 5–6 would be predictive of creativity at 10–11. This expectation was based on correlations between the differential use of defenses, and degree of creativity, in the groups of 16- and 10- to 12-year-old youngsters (Chapters 10 and 11) and a group of professional artists (Chapter 14).

METHODS AND SUBJECTS

At the age of 5–6 years the children were tested with the original version of the percept-genetic, creative functioning test (CFT I) and with the Meta-Contrast Technique (MCT). They were also interviewed regarding creative interests, etc. (All this is described in Chapter 7). Later, at age 10–11, they were again interviewed and were then tested only with the parallel version of the CF test (CFT II). In addition, at age 5–6 they produced paintings and clay figures that were evaluated by two professional artists.

The CF Tests (Administered on both Occasions)

There was one stimulus for the 5- to 6-year-olds (CFT I, a bottle and a bowl) and another for the 10–11-year-olds (CFT

II, an easy-chair and a table with a drape). Correlations between the two pictures were reported in Chapter 11.

Raters of the CFT protocols easily agreed for the most part. An occasional difference between the raters was nearly always due to an oversight by one of them.

THE MCT (GIVEN AT THE FIRST OCCASION)

The most important scoring dimensions have been presented in Chapter 7.

As mentioned previously, they concern *external defenses*, like eye-shutting behavior or sleep behavior, and *internalized defenses of a relatively primitive type*, where the percept itself is distorted but the distortions reflect a narcissistic or egocentric perspective. We also noted *internalized defenses of a more mature type*, where the threat was perceived as a white spot or empty oval (isolation); as a stiff bust or mask; or (typical of our group) as an inanimate object with a more distant relation to the threatening stimulus but still immobilized (repression). In some instances, the perception of A was also held back, and changes in B of a type not endangering the continuity of the PG were reported instead. (This is called sensitivity movement, a mild variant of projection.)

Another scoring dimension of interest in the present study is *anxiety*, which was scored when the subject reported fusion between the person in B and the threatening A, when structures in B were perceived as broken, or when blackness was over-emphasized in the last third of the A + B series (close to the C-phase).

INTERVIEW 1 (5-TO 6-YEAR-OLDS)

The interview items were presented in Chapter 7. On the basis of a Likert analysis a scale was constructed, including eight of the fourteen items. A smaller, more homogeneous scale included three items (Has the child composed a song, made up a story, etc., of his own? Can he describe what happened in one of his dreams? Does he have a fantasy playmate?).

Interview 2 (10-to 11-Year-olds)

The items in this interview were presented in Chapter 8. On the basis of a Likert analysis a scale was constructed, including nine of twenty-four items. The small, more homogeneous scale was made up of four items (Does the child often indulge in daydreaming with constructive fantasy components? Does she have or has she had a fantasy playmate? Does she have fantasy fears? Does she trust her parents—e.g., does she believe that they actually say what they really think when praising her drawings?).

It ought to be emphasized that neither this nor the foregoing scale reflects the experimenter's subjective interpretations of the subject. Instead, they are based on the child's actual answers to the concrete questions.

Artistic Products (Created on the First Occasion)

Each child was given a piece of clay and asked to model something for the experimenter. He was also encouraged to draw and paint anything he liked. Paper, pencils, and colored chalk were within reach during the interview.

Two professional artists appraised the drawings and clay models. They were asked to use two dimensions: degree of *originality* and degree of *emotional expressiveness*. Products that were clearly more original or more expressive than others were placed in a top category. Children receiving at least one top placement from each artist were placed in one category, the other children in another.

Subjects

The children were described in Chapter 7. There were originally forty-seven children, eleven aged 4 years, seventeen aged 5 years, eighteen aged 6 years, and one aged 7 years. The twenty-one oldest and cognitively most mature among these participated in the follow-up study. These subjects were also part of the cohort in Chapter 11.

As said in the introduction, the CFT I results may have been unreliable in some of the youngest and most immature subjects because of their inability to reconstruct phases in their PG series preceding the (generally unstable) C-phase. To delete subjects at this end of the age-maturity continuum, we had to either take out only one or five, aged 5:4–6:4 years (because four of them were all 6:4 years old and could hardly be differentiated). Conversely, some of the oldest and most mature subjects on the second test occasion may have had reached prepuberty, at which time CFT results are known to deteriorate. We thus created a separate group comprising three subjects who were older than the others (at the follow-up, above 11:6 years). There was no need to restrict the sample at the immature end when MCT, the interview items, and artistic products were used as predictors. Although, for instance, immature children were not able to report defensive perceptual distortions in the MCT, they might have still *behaved* defensively. At the other end of the continuum, we will present two sets of results, one set including the three oldest subjects and another set excluding them.

PREDICTIONS

Generally, we expected a correlation between creativity at 5–6 and at 10–11. This prediction was based partly on the fact that creativity seems to peak at both these ages. Predictions based on an earlier age, before children have yet become truly creative, or on an age at which creativity seems to abate—i.e., at age 7–8 or on the age of late 11 onwards—would probably be less successful.

Most predictions to be presented later are obvious, except the one based on the MCT. In studies of 10- to 12- and 16-year-olds we found a positive correlation between the willingness to take the role of an aggressor rather than that of a victim (when manipulated by subliminal stimulation to do so) and creativity as measured by the CFT. We have also found that creative subjects showed signs of repression and sensitivity movement more often than of isolation and depressive stereotypy. Based on our assumption that identification with an aggressor reflects an inclination toward active role taking, we predicted that sleep behavior (regarded as a passive way of reacting to a threat) in MCT would be contraindicative of creativity. Thus the absence of sleep behavior combined with the presence of repression and sensitivity movement was considered to be a positive sign of creativity in our predictive study.

RESULTS

POINTWISE PREDICTIONS

Most of the comparisons between occasion 1 and occasion 2 are based on 2 × 2 contingency tables. Significance levels were estimated by means of a two-sided Fisher's exact test. To measure the degree of association between data, we computed G indexes of agreement (Holley and Guilford, 1964; Starvig, 1981) that correspond approximately to correlation coefficients. C-coefficients were calculated for the 2 × 3 tables, and a Pearson correlation coefficient was calculated for the one 3 × 4 table.

When comparing creativity scores in CFT I with CFT II (involving thirteen subjects; see above), we distinguished XX, X, (X) scores from the remaining scores (G = 0.69, P = 0.029).

Cutting results along the medians based on the interview scale produced a nonsignificant correlation between the two sets of data (G = 0.24, N = 21). The small scales correlated significantly, however (G = 0.71, P = 0.003).

In MCT our interest was centered around the absence of sleep behavior and the presence of signs of (distant) repression and sensitivity movement. Subjects were placed along a four-step scale, including subjects scoring for all three signs to those scoring for none. CFT II results were divided into three steps: XX, X, and (X) and O, S, and "–". For twenty-one subjects, r = 0.66 (P < .01). Deleting the three oldest subjects produced a marginal increase of the coefficient, and a G-index based on a 2 × 2 table also reached a slightly higher value (0.71).

Evaluations by artists on the first occasion are not significantly correlated with CFT II values (G = 0.52, N = 21). When the three oldest subjects were removed from the group, G increased to 0.67 (P = 0.02). The artists' evaluations correlated with scale values based on interview 2 (G = 0.62, P < 0.05, N = 21; G = 0.67, P = 0.015, N = 18). By combining CFT II and scale 2 and constructing three steps (high scores in both, high scores in one, and low scores in both) we arrived at a substantial correlation with the artists' evaluations (C = 0.58, P < 0.01, N = 21; C = 0.64, P < 0.01, N = 18; C_{max} = 0.77; C/C_{max} = 0.75 resp. 0.83).

FACTOR ANALYSIS

An inverted factor analysis involving uniformly weighted data from both test occasions (seventy-three bits altogether) was used to group the subjects. (For a methods description refer to Chapter 4.) D-indexes of discrimination were also calculated. In their presentation below, the decimal points have been omitted.

The number of factors was limited to four. Ordinarily, we demanded a factor loading of at least 0.50 and a distance between the highest loading and the next highest of ⩾0.10 for a subject to be counted as a member of a factor. In this case we have also regarded three marginal subjects with loadings of 0.45–0.48. We were then able to place all but two in factors. The uniqueness of these factors is illustrated by the fact that only three differences between the highest and next highest loading for a subject were <0.20. Among the highest factor loadings, eleven were higher than 0.60 and four higher than 0.70.

When interpreting the factors by means of D-indexes, we kept in mind that D is not independent of the size of a factor, usually being lower in large factors than in small ones. D-values < 0.50 were disregarded in all cases.

The first factor includes nearly half of the subjects (N = 9). They showed no signs of creativity on any of the test occasions.

In the second factor (N = 4) creativity is represented by strong CFT signs, by a single interview item on the first test occasion, and by the interview scale and several additional items on the second occasion. Factor 3 is comprised of only two subjects, both belonging to the youngest and most immature subgroup when tested the first time. Note the positive MCT signs and the creativity signs in CFT II. In factor 4 (N = 4) MCT is ambiguous, with positive as well as negative signs, but the interview results and the artists' evaluations seem clearly positive. On the second test occasion, a number of items outside the scale gain prominence, most of them associated with creativity but one of them pointing to creativity as something belonging to the past.

Before contemplating the more detailed account of the factor analysis presented below, the reader should keep in mind that the CFT items could not successfully compete with the interview items for two obvious reasons: the former were few in comparison with the latter, and, as mentioned before, CFT items were probably not representative of the children's potential at the low and high ends of the age-maturity continuum.

Factor 1 (N = 9)

First Test Occasion

MCT. Sleep behavior (D = 61), no sensitivity (50), no sensitivity or movement (58).

Interview, Scale 1. Sum of scores below median (56), no fantasy playmate (64), does not remember nightmares (56).

Interview, Small Scale 1. Sum of scores below median (72).

Artists' evaluations. One (75) or no top placements (70).

Second Test Occasion

CFT II. No creativity signs (53).

Interview, Scale 2. Sum of scores below median (72), does not write at home (50), does not indulge in daydreaming with fantasy components (53), does not trust parents (72).

Interview, Small Scale 2. Sum of scores below median (83).

Factor 2 (N = 4)

First Test Occasion

CFT I. Strong creativity signs (52).
MCT. Extra people or animals (57).
Interview, Item outside Scale 1. Likes to play alone (71).

Second Test Occasion

Interview, Scale 2. Sum of scores high—upper quartile (94), indulges in daydreaming with fantasy components (59), remembers a fantasy playmate (75), dreams at least once a week (53), has fantasy fears (65), trusts parents (59).
Interview, Small Scale 2. Sum of scores above median (65).
Interview, Item outside Scale 2. Likes to compose music (63).

Factor 3 (N = 2)

First Test Occasion

Youngest in the immature subgroup 2b (84).
CFT I. Human interpretations (53).
MCT. No primitive signs (68), sensitivity (79), at least two of the following signs: repression, sensitivity movement, no sleep behavior (68).
Interview, Item outside Scale 1. Does not like to draw, etc. (79).

Second Test Occasion

Interview, Scale 2. Does not indulge in daydreaming with fantasy components (58), trusts parents (53).
Interview, Items outside Scale 2. Can tell what happened in a recent dream (58), has friends of the opposite sex (68).

Factor 4 (N = 4)

First Test Occasion

Dominated by girls (52).

MCT. Sensitivity (57), sensitivity or movement (52), isolation or tendencies toward isolation (82).

Interview, Scale 1. Sum of scores high (upper quartile) (63) or above median (71), reports transitional objects (59).

Artists' evaluations. At least one top placement by both (71).

Second Test Occasion

Interview, Items outside Scale 2. Keeps a diary (52), can tell what happened in a recent dream (65), was creative in the past (52).

DISCUSSION

Even though only twenty-one subjects took part in this investigation, the number of instruments used, and the consistent data generated allow us to draw conclusions with a relatively high degree of certainty.

Thus it was possible to detect the 5- to 6-year-olds in the 10- to 11-year-olds. The creative preschoolers generally remained creative, while the uncreative ones remained in the shadows. This finding is of particular interest since results of our previous studies suggest that creativity is more or less dormant during the interjacent years. Those who were creative on the first test occasion may very well have lost interest in creative activities after a few years, to regain it later.

This result should also caution us against blaming the school system for destroying a child's natural creativity as suggested by our research—i.e., that, creativity seems to abate just when the child begins regular school. The result is also important for our understanding of developmental continuity. In spite of the fact that the child at 7–8 differs considerably from the child at 5–6 and the youngster at 10–11, together these age periods form a developmental continuity, the condition during one period being the prerequisite for the full blooming during later ones. Periodicity in development should not be mistaken for discontinuity (see Hinde and Bateson, 1984).

How, then, does the creative child appear at the age of 5–6

years and again five years later at 10–11. The two highly intercorrelated small scales provide a good basis for these descriptions. Young children like to compose their own poems,
stories, songs, etc.; they are able to describe their dreams, and
they usually have a fantasy playmate. They obviously feel free
to use their inner life as a point of departure and as a play-
ground. At age 10–11, similar items are central: the youngster
likes to indulge in daydreams, not passive ones but with active,
constructive fantasy components; he entertains fantasy fears,
and even if he does not keep a fantasy playmate any longer he
remembers a former one. There is one item, however, seemingly unrelated to this cluster: trust in the opinion of one's
parents. We have previously interpreted such trust as indicating
that the young person has not yet entered the pseudorational
period of prepuberty but remains open to his own need for
close emotional contacts and experiences. Furthermore, this
trust is a sign of the child's opinion of himself and his products.
If he does not like what he creates, he cannot believe that another (authoritative) person really likes them.

In making full use of the high correlation between the small
scales, we should also note that, according to the factor analysis,
the association between the two age periods is more accentuated
on the negative side than on the positive one. The way the study
was designed, however, the positive side leaves more room for
variation, as we have also learned in our study of artists (Chapter
14). In factor 2, MCT and CFT I represent early signs of creativity while the interview items represent the late ones. In factor
4, the creative bent in the children was spotted by the artists
and was also pronounced in the interview. But MCT presents
a double message because signs of sensitivity are also associated
with prominent signs of compulsive isolation, or tendencies toward such a defensive style. The profile at age 10–11 is also
ambiguous because creative interview items combine with an
item describing creativity as something of the past. The interviewer found these youngsters rather reserved. The early signs
of isolation may perhaps be seen as a presage of an early en-
trance into the compulsive and relatively uncreative period of
prepuberty.

One type of item, i.e., memories from early childhood years, has remained in the background. It is conceivable that these items have not been able to compete with other, more frequently appearing ones in the factor analysis. Moreover, youngsters at the age of 10–11 years may be particularly reluctant to recall experiences during early childhood. It can be instructive to note that these items are not closely associated with scale 2. Without speculating further, we still want to point out that early childhood memories seem to be typical of true creative adults' readiness to communicate with their subjective past.

The artists' evaluations require some comments. Since the two artists often disagreed, it is surprising to find that combined, their evaluations have a solid predictive value. Thus each of them was probably sensitive to different manifestations of creativity in the children's artistic products. We believe that predictions based on a later age phase would have been less successful, partly because children's products—particularly their drawings—tend to become more stereotyped with increasing age and partly because some children abandon artistic products as an outlet for their urge to create, turning instead to writing, musical composition, invention, etc.

One of the most interesting results concerns the MCT. Those who became creative at age 10–11 were sensitive to marginal cues at the age of 5–6 and used what we have called distant repression—i.e., they were able to transform a threatening stimulus into something only remotely resembling the original. We have interpreted the latter to mean that they can handle their impressions more freely than others at the level of symbolic transformations. This picture of the dynamics of the creative 5- to 6-year-old child seems to make sense. But to this picture, absence of passive defenses, manifested at this early age as sleep behavior, must be added. We have previously found that in 11-12- and 16-year-olds (Chapters 10 and 11) the willingness to identify openly with an active-aggressive role (when manipulated by subliminal stimulation) correlates with creativity. Passive-evasive defenses are just the opposite of such role taking and are probably also associated with the low self-esteem and distrust in the value of one's own subjective whims and ideas.

Only by identifying with the aggressor can the subject dare to call the object into question, in order ultimately to replace it (cf. Chasseguet-Smirgel, 1984).

To identify the 5- to 6-year-old children most likely to develop into creative 10- to 11-year-olds, one should search after those willing and able actively and freely to transform their experiences into manageable forms, sensitive to internal cues, even vague ones, enjoying their inner life including dreams and ready to exploit their inner life as they please. Such children may indulge in fantasy play, but not necessarily in group play organized according to fixed roles.

13

GENDER DIFFERENCES IN DEFENSE MECHANISMS COMPARED WITH CREATIVITY

Upon entering the world, we meet with partly different realities, caused by the sole fact of our biological gender. As the child develops, inborn tendencies combine in a many-faceted way with environmental forces. One of the endeavors of psychoanalytic theory is to describe the differential psychosexual development of girls and boys. A crucial point, according to this theory, is the oedipal phase. At this stage the child begins to have sexual wishes for the parent of the opposite sex, while he jealously wants to get rid of the same-sexed parent.

The boy continues to love his first love object, the mother, and wishes his father dead. This leads the boy to fear revenge from his rival, and what is named castration anxiety develops as a result.

As theory has it, the girl normally has increasing problems with her mother, whom she loves at the same time. Since she begins to have sexual wishes for her father, part of her love is deflected away from the mother. Consequently, she fears rebuke from her mother. For obvious reasons she does not experience the pure castration anxiety of the boy; instead she fears that mother will no longer give her the love that she, as a little girl, still needs. These outlines are naturally a simplification of much more complex developmental phenomena; nevertheless they increase our understanding of "the prevalent

177

roles of castration fear or fear over loss of love in man and woman respectively" (Fenichel, 1945, p. 100).

The young boy develops problems in handling both his own and his father's aggressive impulses, and he therefore reactivates the anal-sadistic modes of reaction. If the boy's phallic love for his mother is not accepted, it gets mingled with and distorted by aggressiveness, and he may regress more definitely, in extreme cases developing a compulsion neurosis, in which "people are generally and obviously concerned about conflicts between aggressiveness and submissiveness, cruelty and gentleness, dirtiness and cleanliness, disorder and order" (ibid., p. 273).

Initially, the girl does not mobilize defenses against her aggression, but rather tries to hide her sexual wishes from herself (and from her mother). If the parents are too strict with their daughter, this may cause a fixation in the oedipal stage and provide the basis for symptoms of conversion. As Fenichel argues, the mechanism of repression (to make something nonexistent or lifeless) would be the preferred one in a family (or a society) where the whole area of sexuality—especially female sexuality—is more or less taboo. Aggression in males, on the other hand, is usually not altogether forbidden; it is often enough for the little boy to divide his aggression into "good" and "bad" parts. This is the basic function of isolation—to keep things safely apart (ibid., pp. 150, 155). Thus the personality of women would dwell more in the vicinity of hysteria, with an overweight of repressionlike defenses, while men would tend to use strategies of (compulsive) isolation. In this context it must be stressed that psychoanalytic theory does not ignore other aspects of the reality and fantasy world of the child. Both sexes have mixed feelings toward both parents, and from birth have to cope with the dual drive derivatives of aggression and sexuality.

Psychoanalytic theorizers from Freud onward have based their theories primarily on observations of patients under analysis. Recently, experimental studies have been used to test psychodynamic hypotheses. For instance, Westerlundh and Sjöbäck (1986) tested the assumption, by means of subliminal thematic pictures, that aggressive and sexual stimuli provoke different defensive strategies. Their overall conclusions were supportive of the theory outlined above, namely, that aggressive pictures tend to activate isolation mechanisms, while sexual pictures are inclined to activate repressive ones.

Group studies of gender differences in defense mechanisms are sparse. This sparsity may be due to the difficulty in finding subject groups in which the sexes are equally representative of the larger population, as well as the lack of proper test instruments. In certain studies, carried out with a specially designed questionnaire, the answers to multiple-choice questions are supposed to indicate a preferred defensive style (the Defense Mechanisms Inventory, Gleser and Ihilevich, 1969). Such studies have revealed differences between male and female adolescents. In one study, male youngsters were found to use strategies for externalizing conflict, while females were more likely to deal with the conflict internally (Cramer, 1979). However, as Dudley (1978) points out, this inventory is sensitive to social desirability factors; thus it may often mirror attitudes and roles rather than mechanisms for dealing with conflict. In contrast, percept-genetic techniques, like the one used by Westerlundh and Sjöbäck in the above-mentioned study, are minimally sensitive to attitudinal aspects.

As already mentioned, the present study employed the MCT, which has, to a large extent, been validated in psychiatric groups (where the distribution of gender is already skewed). Recently it was used in a visual half-field design in a group of architectural students, where a significant difference was found between males and females. In part this difference was due to the almost exclusive occurrence of signs of psychoticlike regression in the right hemisphere of a group of females, while the males showed weak signs of sensitivity to marginal cues (Carlsson, 1986). Students of architecture are, admittedly, a rather select group. In the present study a more randomly chosen group of youngsters, from the creativity project, were investigated, especially with regard to gender differences.

Based on existing theories and knowledge, we propose that the subjects will show different patterns of defense, depending on sex, i.e., boys will show a preponderance of isolationlike defenses, while girls will tend to exhibit relatively more repressive and projective mechanisms. Furthermore, since we had already found that a creative person is more tolerant of aggressive impulses—when forced to identify with an aggressive role (Chapters 10 and 11)—we also tested the assumption that highly creative subjects are less liable to rely exclusively on isolating defenses and more likely to have a variable defensive structure compared to less creative subjects.

METHOD

DESIGN

In the original study all children were first tested with the CFT and immediately thereafter with the MCT. The testing was followed by an interview, at which time the children also made a drawing and a clay figure. The results from the interview are not considered here.

THE META CONTRAST TECHNIQUE (MCT)

The following scoring categories, taken from the MCT manual (Smith, Johnson, and Almgren, 1982), will be used:

Anxiety. Three levels of anxiety are described. In this group of subjects, slight signs were omitted in the scoring of the protocols, and only medium and grave signs were counted (see previous descriptions).

Repression implies efforts of decathecting the threat, and in the manual it is divided into several categories: (1) Reactions more typical for children (the subject gets sleepy and yawns heavily or reports that the boy in B is sleeping); (2) immature, stimulus-dependent signs (the threat is perceived as a loose limb or interpreted as the window in B but coming before the rest of the B-picture; (3) the threat is perceived as a lifeless bust or statue; (4) more distant transformations of the threat (a tree, a flowerpot, etc.). A small category comprising "tendencies" toward repression was also included.

Answers under the heading of *isolation* varied from (1) primitive denial ("the man in the window is not a monster") to (2) attempts to separate the threat from the boy by means of whitening the window or covering it with a curtain. Another kind of isolation was typified by the so-called (3) empty protocol, which contains no reactions at all before the threat is suddenly seen correctly. In the present group of youngsters, empty protocols were scored together with protocols where no scorable signs were found, even if the latter did not quite belong to the empty protocol category. Signs of intellectualization were also put under this heading, as were tendencies toward isolation.

Sensitivity and projection. Early in the subliminal series, before the threat has yet been perceived as a separate structure, the sensitive subject reacts by noticing small changes in the B-picture instead (the position of the boy is seen as changing, or the perspective in the picture varies from one picture to the next). When these changes get stronger (for instance, when the subject perceives clear movements in the picture), they turn into more projective maneuvers. Other categories in the MCT manual, for instance, depression or regression, occurred only occasionally in these youngsters and will not be considered.

The Creative Functioning Test (CFT)

In this study we were interested only in creativity per se, and therefore only scored the *inverted series*. An abbreviated scale was used to characterize this series—S (strong); L (light), and "–" (no sign of creativity):

S: Strong signs of creative functioning corresponding to *XX*, *X*, and (*X*) in previous chapters.

L: This category corresponds to *O* and *S*.

"–": Here the subject sees no changes, except that the picture gets hazy, darker, disappears, etc.

Subjects

The subjects were the 171 youngsters in our previous studies, aged 10 to 16 years. All subjects in this age group that had been

TABLE 13.1
OVERVIEW OF THE SUBJECTS

Age	n:	Females %	Academic %
10-11	29	48	45
12	26	46	54
13	24	46	42
14	29	52	59
15	30	50	50
16	33	48	52
	171	49	49

part of the project were reexamined in the present study. Table 13.1 shows an overview of the cohort.

RESULTS

OVERVIEW OF THE DEFENSE MECHANISMS

The distribution of defensive categories and of anxiety level in each age group is shown in Figure 13.1, together with the means for both sexes. There was a marked variation between age groups. For instance, already shown, at the age of 12, isolation was at its highest and anxiety at its lowest. We also found an ebb in creativity among the 12-year-olds. The combination of low creativity, low anxiety, and high isolation typifies the compulsive, prepubertal period. Moreover, isolation was predominant among boys, while girls tended to show more sensitive-projective strategies and also tended toward more repression, although this difference was small. Chi-square tests showed significant differences in the distribution between the sexes (Table 13.2)—i.e., 4.9 (P < 0.05) for isolation, and 4.1 (P < 0.05) for sensitivity projection, while for repression, there was a tendency only ($\chi^2 = 1.61$, P = 0.2).

The children in this study most often made use of combinations of defense strategies, and the sexes did not differ when combinations were considered. But as can be seen in Table 13.3,

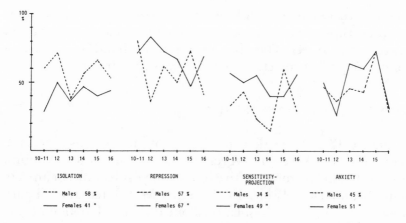

FIGURE 13.1

SIGNS OF ANXIETY AND DEFENSIVE STRATEGIES IN THE AGE GROUPS
AND IN MALES AND FEMALES.

TABLE 13.2

ISOLATION AND SENSITIVITY-PROJECTION IN
MALES AND FEMALES

	Isolation		Sensitivity-projection	
	+	−	+	−
Males	51	37	30	58
Females	34	49	41	42

+ = signs of the defense
− = no sign of the defense

TABLE 13.3

OVERVIEW OF THE COMBINATIONS OF
DEFENSE MECHANISMS

	Isolation only	+ repr. or + sens. or + both	Repression only	Sensit.-proj. + repr. only		No sign
Males	19	32	15	8	4	10
Females	3	31	16	15	12	6

boys were much more often characterized by isolation only, with no repressive or projective interspersions (a binomial test gave P < 0.0004). The girls, on the other hand, had more of only sensitivity projection than the boys (P < 0.04).

ANXIETY AND DEFENSE MECHANISMS

Figure 13.1 shows that the degree of anxiety was about the same for both sexes. However, in earlier studies it was found that isolation is often effective in warding off feelings of anxiety (Smith and Danielsson, 1982). Thus we wanted to compare degree of anxiety with isolation alone or in combination (Table 13.4). This comparison gave a chi-square of 13.1 (df = 2, P < 0.01). Table 13.4 also shows that subjects in which isolation predominates have almost no signs of anxiety in the MCT. As already shown, boys characteristically exhibit more isolation than girls; therefore boys ought to show less anxiety. However, this difference was small (6%). Table 13.4 shows that only boys in the category of isolation alone were able to shield themselves efficiently from anxiety, while isolation helped shield girls from anxiety when combined with repression and/or sensitivity-projection (the contrast 19–13/11–20 yielded a P < 0.07, Fisher's exact test, two-tailed).

PERFORMANCE IN CREATIVE FUNCTIONING

The two sexes in this group differed slightly in their strength of creativity. The boys received somewhat higher scores: 32%

TABLE 13.4

ISOLATION ALONE, OR IN COMBINATION, OR ONLY OTHER
DEFENSES, COMPARED TO ANXIETY OR NO ANXIETY

	Isolation		Repression only	Sensit.-proj.		No sign
	only	+ repr. or + sens. or + both		+ repr.	only	
Anxiety	3(0)	30(11)	18(10)	13(9)	7(6)	11(6)
No anxiety	19(3)	33(20)	13(6)	10(6)	9(6)	5(0)

Numbers in parentheses = females

with strong signs, 40% with light signs, and 28% with no sign of creativity. Percentages for the girls were 27%, 35%, and 38%, respectively.

Percentages also differed among age groups. Strong signs were most common in the 10- to 11-year-olds and least common in the 12-year-olds. For the entire group, strong signs of creativity were found in 29% of the individuals.

CREATIVITY AND DEFENSE MECHANISMS

Does the defensive makeup of an individual differ depending on the strength of his creative functioning? To address this question, we tested whether the three creativity groups differed with respect to defensive strategies. In Table 13.5 we see that the "creative" defense mechanism par excellence was repression ($\chi^2 = 12.5$, df $= 2$, P < 0.01). This trend was the same for both sexes. Here we find that in creative subjects repression very often occurs in association with isolation and sensitivity-projection (Table 13.6).

These latter two strategies alone, on the other hand, were mostly found in subjects with few or no signs of creativity in the CFT ($\chi^2 = 22.1$, df $= 10$, P < 0.02). It is interesting to note that in creative subjects repression occurs significantly more often in combination with both isolation and sensitivity-projection than alone or in combination with either isolation or sensitivity ($\chi^2 = 11.5$, df $= 2$, P < 0.01).

TABLE 13.5
DEFENSE MECHANISMS COMPARED TO DEGREE
OF CREATIVITY

CFT	Repression		Isolation		Sensit.-proj.	
	+	−	+	−	+	−
Strong	39	11	25	25	21	29
Light	41	23	38	26	32	32
No sign	26	31	22	35	20	37

+ = signs of the defense
− = no sign of the defense

TABLE 13.6
COMBINATIONS OF THE DEFENSES COMPARED
TO CREATIVITY

CFT	Repression + isolation + sensit.-proj.	Repression + isolation	Repression +/− sensit.-proj.	Isolation +/− sensit-proj.	Sensit. -proj.	No sign
Strong	8(1)	12(7)	19(11)	5(1)	3(1)	3(1)
Light	13(6)	10(5)	18(11)	15(3)	4(3)	4(1)
No sign	1(1)	8(5)	17(9)	13(5)	10(8)	8(4)

Numbers in parentheses = females

CREATIVITY AND ANXIETY

Since the level of anxiety was previously shown to be of importance in creative endeavors (Chapter 5), we compared the various creativity groups in terms of their anxiety signs (MCT). The comparison revealed a slight tendency for creativity to be positively associated with anxiety ($P < 0.2$).

DISCUSSION

To a large extent our initial hypotheses were confirmed. The sexes differed considerably in preferred defensive style. Boys reacted as predicted with a significantly higher degree of compulsive, isolating defenses than girls. As was predicted, the predominant defense for the girls was repression, but they did not, however, differ significantly from the boys in this respect, since the boys also had much repression. Instead, the "girl-specific" defense was a sensitive, slightly projective way of perceiving.[1]

[1] Here we would like to quote the wording of Kogan (1973): "To the extent that women are highly sensitized to the social context in which they are working, the possibility of being distracted from strictly cognitive involvements is high. It appears that men are more capable of screening out the interpersonal context, and hence can pursue their work in a more single-minded, persistent and non-distractable fashion."

The high anxiety level during the pubertal period may be the cause of the relatively high amount of defensive reactions in this age class compared with older individuals. It is possible that reactions to high anxiety have also accentuated gender specificity, but nevertheless there are very consistent trends in this group. Furthermore, some of the subjects have not yet reached high puberty, while others have just left it.

In previous studies we found that a moderate degree of anxiety was often associated with creative functioning. In the present group however, we found only a weak tendency in this direction. But these youngsters, many at midpuberty, generally had more anxiety than the average youngster, so the positive tie with creative functioning could well have become blurred.

In this connection it is intriguing to note that for the boys it was only the category of single isolation that correlated negatively with anxiety, while for girls isolation kept away anxiety also when working in combination with other defenses. Our theoretical basis was that isolation is a method to particularly handle aggressive feelings. In the young boy, the gender-specific greater degree of aggressive threats (in connection with castration anxiety), can be assumed to cause a stronger emphasis on isolating mechanisms, compared to the girl. When in the MCT an angry, grimacing monster is shown, the boy immediately puts on his armor; and those who are least tolerant react with a single, inflexible defensive style, allowing little or no conscious anxiety. More tolerant boys, on the other hand, can react to the threat with a more flexible attitude, i.e. they can shift between different defenses. Since isolation in girls is less gender-specific and less common, it is often blended with other defenses, but of course it still retains some of its capacity to keep anxiety out of awareness.

How do the results in girls fit with the psychoanalytic theory regarding loss of love? Girls did not differ considerably from the boys in repression, as had been expected; instead, they differed in sensitivity-projection. Since society's views toward sexuality have changed from the days of Freud and Fenichel, it is probable that parents nowadays place fewer restrictions on the sexual behavior of their daughters; thus the difference between the sexes should have diminished.

The predominance of sensitivity-projection in girls is not incompatible with the "loss of love" hypothesis, namely, when the child becomes afraid to lose her mother's love, she becomes sensitized, as it were, to small cues provided by her mother. To understand her mother's inner feelings becomes very important, and as a result sensitive "antennae" spring up to further a good relationship.

The results in this young cohort support the hypothesis that each sex views the world in a slightly different light. We believe that this is true not only in youth but also in adulthood. Whether the oedipal stage is the sole contributor to this difference is an open question. To the extent that this period has left its mark on mature men and women, it is probable that when they become parents, they will tend to treat boys and girls differently already from birth.

Nevertheless the majority of these youngsters were characterized by a mixed defensive picture. When the various combinations were compared with the results in the CFT, this mixture showed a particularly positive correlation with creativity. Although repression alone was positively associated with creativity, subjects deemed as having all three defense categories were significantly more creative than subjects with repression alone or together with either isolation or sensitivity-projection. Uncreative subjects often made use of either isolation or sensitivity. These strategies were also the most gender-specific.

In line with this are the findings of Milgram et al. (1977) in a study of creativity. They conclude that "cross-sex-typing or the simultaneous endorsement of masculine and feminine sex-role characteristics confers an advantage to children making such endorsements." It is perhaps not farfetched to assume that functions of reality-oriented logic (related to isolation), sensitivity to apparently insignificant nuances, and a symbolic gestalting of inner conflicts contribute positively to the creation of an original product.

Actually, the special subcategory of immature hysteric signs in the repressive category was altogether *negatively* correlated with the CFT (in highly creative subjects only one had single hysteric signs of this kind compared with ten in subjects considered to have slight or no creativity; P <. 0.05). Thus, although the category of repression in the MCT generally showed a highly positive correlation with creative acceptance of subjective content, it seemed nevertheless to consist of different subcategories. In clinical practice, immature, stimulus-dependent signs are often found in patients with a histrionic personality. The category of more stimulus-distant, symbolic repression, on the other hand, indicates better neutralization and hence a cognitively more mature defensive function.[2]

In some respects these results may seem slightly at odds with previous results in adults where creativity was more clearly correlated with sensitivity. Sensitivity in these groups was not, however, strictly analogous with the defense scored in the MCT but rather reflected the general flexibility of the C-phase conception in the CFT. In other comparisons, e.g., the 16-year-olds in Chapter 10 and the artists in Chapter 14, sensitivity was scored mostly in combination with repression. MCT sensitivity was associated with creativity as scored by the CFT in children younger than the ones tested here (factor I.4 in Chapter 8).

---

[2]This type of repression seems to correspond with what Fenichel (1945) called "successful repression" or sublimation. He writes: "Sublimated impulses find their outlet, though drained via an artificial route, whereas the others (defenses that use counter cathexes) do not" (p. 141).

14

ARTISTS AND ARTISTIC CREATIVITY

The artist as a person has been an immensely popular topic among psychologists and psychiatrists. More comprehensive studies in this area are, however, relatively sparse and generally outdated. Roe's analysis of the personalities of a broad selection of well-known American artists (1946a, 1946b) has provided many important modifications to the romantic conception of the typical artist. Her study covered the spectrum from profuse imagination in some artists to almost no signs of inventiveness other than "efficient form" in others. Kris (1952), as we know, coined a household phrase for the discussion up to the present. In the general perspective of creativity, artistic inventiveness has been studied in recent years by, among others, Arieti (1976), Rothenberg (1979), Rose (1980), and Deri (1984). Initially, these were all in some respect dependent on the key idea of Kris, being fascinated with the role of unconscious processes in the production of art. They have, however, become increasingly interested in the purposeful and conscious side of creative work.

Most students of creativity in artists focus their attention upon well-known individuals from the elite of the Western art world. Their methods of research have been historical-biographical. Sometimes one feels tempted to agree with Perkins (1981) in his doubt of the popular illustrative approach toward creativity. There is at least an apparent danger in the commonly reiterated historical patterns and romantic clichés appearing in many art monographs, etc., even those based on serious scholarly research.

A few students have used a more direct approach by referring to artists in therapy (e.g., Niederland, 1976). To be sure, much has been collected from biographical and clinical studies that might be of interest for an understanding of the creative mind. But there are also reasons for skepticism, not the least with regard to the generalization of the proposals from this tradition. The experimentalist would most of all criticize the lack of systematic and well-controlled data. The art researcher might not endorse those psychologizing students claiming to be informed in matters of art. Moreover, one might have reservations as to the representativeness of very famous more or less neurotic artists in terms of production as well as personality types.

For various reasons we decided, in spite of all, to enter into this well-trodden field. Our most immediate reason for this undertaking was the following: after applying the CFT in samples of researchers and amateur artists and also in psychiatric patients, where creativity was often stifled, we believed it might be possible to elucidate the complex connections between some psychological dimensions in the creative professional artist and various qualities in his artistic work.

In many studies of creativity there has been no clear conceptualization of the term. The CFT makes an operational definition possible that comes reasonably close to the common-sense understanding of the word. Thus in our view, creativity has as a constituent quality the ability to transgress a conventional conception of reality.

With the CFT we were able systematically to study a relatively broad selection of regionally active artists, unknown ones as well as "celebrities." To obtain a multifaceted view of the artist, we used additional test methods to illuminate aspects of personality functioning other than creativity. We also arranged for an independent, formalized characterization of the individual artist's production.

It was the artist as a person, his anxieties and defense strategies, his ego identity—to borrow a term from Erikson (1968)—his emotional involvement in his work, his memories and dreams, and of course his creativity, that was our primary focus of interest. But we also wanted to ensure that the artistic qualities of the individuals were genuine in the sense that there was real inventiveness in the work. This was accomplished by internal comparisons among artistic products. The evaluation of products was made by the art specialist (SS) while interviewing and testing of the subjects was planned and performed by the psychologists (GS and IC).

Obviously, we expected to find many creative persons in the present group. However, a habile artist is not necessarily creative. His accomplishments may mainly be an act of "generative intelligence," to use a wording of Chomsky's. Even such a traditional artist, by definition, might to some viewers seem creative, if he follows the modernist tradition.

We must also assume that a creative artist is not necessarily an important artist. He might, for instance, work within a relatively narrow thematic and formal sphere, relying upon limited personal experience, but without compensating for this in intensity or frenzy, as is sometimes relevant in such cases. Still, he or she might be willing to cross the boundary between a conventional and a more original conception of the world.

METHODS

The choice of methodology was partly motivated by our previous studies. Since we found that anxiety is an unavoidable companion of creative activity and that certain types of defense are likely to arrest the creative impetus, we decided to use the MCT. In a recent study (Smith, Carlsson, and Danielsson, 1985), an analysis of the present group of artists according to the so-called Identification Test (IT) were presented. In this test the viewer's identification with either of two otherwise similar figures appearing in different environments was manipulated. We found the results of that study highly relevant to our present investigation and will include them here. Our central instrument was, of course, the CFT. In addition to using these laboratory methods, we interviewed the artists and evaluated their artistic productions according to certain dimensions. Among the laboratory methods, only the IT will be described in some detail here.

THE IDENTIFICATON TEST (IT)

The basic methodology was described in Chapter 10. Here we used a different B-picture drawn by one of the present authors (IC). Two human figures stand half-facing each other. Except for minor differences in hair and dress they are quite similar, wearing trousers and lacking obvious sex attributes. They are separated by a partition with a glass pane. The crucial difference between the two sides concerns the background: the left figure is standing against an open, diffusely structured background and the right figure inside a small room.

The subjects were instructed as follows:

> We are going to present pictures on the screen in front of you. First of all I want you to describe what you saw. But I would also like you to tell me your impression of the figures in the picture, what kind of people they are, what you believe they are thinking and feeling. Also try to describe the atmosphere in the picture. Sometimes you may think that the pictures are alike, sometimes that they change from one exposure to the next. Please notice any such change.

After each exposure the experimenter asked the subject to give a general description of the picture, a characterization of the two persons and of the mood in the picture.

The main picture, B, was always exposed with the open background to the left. Starting with an exposure value of 0.01 sec., the picture was then presented alone in an increasing time series until the subject had recognized the figures and their backgrounds as correctly as possible. Thereafter, the following four series were given with constant times: 0.057 sec. for the B-picture and 0.014 sec. for the subliminal "I". The "I" was shown immediately before the B-picture:

1. B alone 5 times

   2. "I" toward the open background 5 times ("I" open + B)
   3. "I" toward the closed room 5 times ("I" closed + B)
   4. B alone 5 times

Series 3 might also be presented before series 2, the order being randomized so that the experimenter herself was unaware of it. The manipulation that the experimenter had to make to switch from open to closed, or vice versa, was camouflaged by several faked manipulations.

SCORING OF THE IT

   The symbols +, −, +/−, and 0 were used to characterize the tendencies registered in the two manipulated series. The control series was meant to serve as a baseline. The latter three presentations in a manipulated series of five were considered to be more decisive than the first two for the overall characterization.

   A "+" is given for any of the following: the picture is described in clearly positive words; the environment and the sex (if attributed) of the figures are more clearly perceived than before; the subject's interest in the picture is increasing; more contact is reported between the two figures.

   A "−" is given for any of the following: the picture is described in negative words that express aggressive or anxious feelings or the subject finds the picture artificial; the subject tries to depreciate the picture; the subject becomes irritated, tired, or loses interest; the sex of the figures is changed (within the same series) or the environment is concealed or transfigured; other defensive strategies are used and the subject's attention is centered on the side of the picture where the subliminal "I" is not presented.

   A "+/−" is given when both the above-mentioned alternatives can be applied to the same series (even sometimes to the same single exposure).

   A "0" is given when the above alternatives do not apply, i.e., when the subliminal stimulation seems to have no noticeable effect.

RELIABILITY OF THE IT

Since this test was recently developed and the scoring may still be sensitive to judges' idiosyncrasies, we let two of the authors (GS and IC), on the one hand, and an extra outside judge, on the other, score the protocols independently of each other.

Each subject was scored for two series: "I" open + B and "I" closed + B. Since there were few outright positive reactions, we grouped + together with +/−. The two independent sets of judges agreed in twenty-five of thirty-two cases. In four of the seven cases of disagreement, the extra judge hesitated between one alternative, implying full agreement with the other judges, and another slightly different alternative—finally settling on the latter. The three remaining disagreements were also slight.

GROUPING

When grouping subjects to test predictions, we took both agreements and disagreements between the judges into consideration. We designated groups 1b and 3 to contain the disagreeing cases.

Group 1. All subjects in this group differentiated between the alternatives by reacting positively (ambivalently) to one alternative and negatively to the other.

1a Positive (or ambivalent) in the "I" open series (all judges agreed)—14 subjects.

1b Positive (or ambivalent) in the "I" open series (according to one set of judges) and more negative in the "I" closed series (consensus)—2 subjects.

1c Negative in the "I" open series and more positive in the "I" closed series (consensus)—2 subjects. A transitional group.

—*Group 2.* No positive scores in this group, negative scores at least in the "I" closed series.

2a Negative in the "I" closed series (consensus)—2 subjects.

2b Negative in both series (consensus)—3 subjects.

Group 3. Slight disagreement between judges in all cases because of the indeterminate character of the reports, close to "0" score line. In 4 subjects nothing but "0" scores according to one set of judges, in the remaining subject very similar, vague reactions—5 subjects.

Group 4. Only "0" scores (consensus)—4 subjects.

The B-stimulus depicted the figures as indeterminate with respect to gender and, not surprisingly, the male/female-attribution varied considerably among the subjects, and for some subjects also varied from one exposure to the next. We used three classes to characterize this variation: *no shift*—early attribution and no subsequent change (11 subjects); *shift*—sex attribution not later than the control series, thereafter shifting with the subliminal stimulation (15 subjects); and finally *indeterminate*—6 subjects who were indeterminate about the sex of the figures in the picture.

THE INTERVIEW

The interviews were carried out by one of the authors (GS) who knew nothing about the test results at the time. The interview was half-structured and dealt with anamnestic milestones. Topics taken up were education, positive and negative sides of the professional life, the artist's own characterization of his production. We also inquired into such topics as early childhood memories, dream life, oceanic feelings, symptoms of anxiety, depressive periods, neurotic symptoms, relations with other people, and the like. Those topics had shown to be of particular relevance in the experiences of other creative individuals.

ART DIMENSIONS

The art specialist among us (SS) worked independently of the others and used eleven dimensions to describe the artistic production of twenty-nine of the thirty-two subjects. He did not feel familiar enough with the work of the other three artists to characterize or evaluate.

The dimensions were: *form* (emphasis on formal matters,

even when indistinct); *content* (emphasis on thematic matters); *articulation* (structure, even without emphasis on formal matters); *renewal* (i.e., the artist changes his way of creating); *originality; expression; static quality* (as opposed to dynamic quality, which was accounted for by the negation); *message* (social and political pamphleteering), *aestheticism* (special emphasis on beauty and harmony); *authenticity* (the works really represent the artist); *level* (drawing upon different sides of life and art experiences, exposing depth, manifoldness, complexity, etc.).

These dimensions are further discussed in the results section. First, however, we present a few simple calculations made to ascertain the level of independence between dimensions. To denote the certain presence of one of the mentioned qualities in a subject, the judge used a plus (+), while the certain absence of a quality was denoted by a minus (−). A zero denoted uncertainty, i.e., the judge lacked sufficient knowledge or the subject was not distinctly pro or con. The scores for three of the dimensions—namely, form, estheticism, and authenticity—showed a skewed distribution with less than 15% of the scores being negative. To estimate correlations between dimensions, G-indices of agreement (see below) were calculated based upon plus and minus scores while excluding zero scores.

The three highest correlations are between originality and expression (0.77); originality and dynamic quality (0.58), and expression and dynamic quality (0.48). The first two should be considered as highly significant and the third as suggestive.

STATISTICAL METHODS

In the statistics we have made use of *Fisher's exact test for 2 × 2 tables* when testing differences between proportions. To get a more complete picture, two different multivariate techniques were also applied: a *cluster analysis* based on the Clustan program (Lund University Computer Center) and an *inverted factor analysis* based on the G-index of agreement (Holley and Guilford, 1964) approximating a correlation coefficient.

All scoring dimensions were dichotomized (as already demonstrated in the case of "static quality" above). Altogether there were seventy-five dimensions including the tests, the interview, and the art dimensions.

The purpose of the *cluster analysis* was to group intercorrelated items. The grouping was achieved gradually, resulting in many groups during the first stages of the analysis and fewer groups during later stages. There was no differential weighting of items in the cluster program.

The *factor analysis* implied a grouping of subjects instead of items. Varimax rotation was used. When selecting typical representatives of a factor (for the computation of the D-index), we chose individuals with loadings of at least 0.50 in that factor and loadings at least 0.10 smaller in the other factors. The difference was, however, usually much more pronounced. The discriminating power of individual items was tested by means of the D-index (Holley and Risberg, 1972). The factor analysis was run twice. In the first analysis two CFT test variables (presence of *XX, X, (X)* or of *XX, X, (X), O, S*) were each given a weight of 5. In the second analysis, the evaluations by the art specialist were each given a weight of 2, whereas the above-mentioned CFT variables were not given any extra weight.

SUBJECTS

The subjects were professional artists living in the southwestern part of Sweden, not too far from the laboratory. A list of artists compiled by the local employment agency served as a basis for selection, and our art specialist deleted those he considered to be "nonserious" and added others instead. Altogether, thirty-three subjects participated in the investigation and were paid a nominal fee. Twelve other artists did not want to participate, for various reasons. One of the thirty-three subjects was excluded because of suspected brain dysfunction. Of the rest, twenty-three were men and nine were women. Seven were younger than 40 years of age and thirteen older than 49. As mentioned above, the art specialist evaluated only the twenty-nine subjects known by him.

RESULTS

DISTRIBUTIONS OF CREATIVITY SCORES

As an introduction it may be instructive to learn how creativity scores were distributed among the subjects in the present group. The scale steps are XX, X, (X), O, S, and " − ". There were 4 XX scores, 7 X, 4 (X), 6 O, 1 S and 10 " − " scores. The small number of subjects designated as S depends on our use of the scoring system as a scale. For example, subjects with both X and S scores received a final X designation. Comparing the outcome for the artists with that in our previous study of researchers, the proportion between XX and X was 4/7 in the present group and 0/5 in the scientists' group (Chapter 4). The same relation in the group of amateur painters and poets was 6/2 (Chapter 5). In this respect, the professional artists seem to hold a position somewhere in between the two previously investigated groups—a fact that may be interpreted as reflecting their dialectic use of fantasy and craftsmanship. While amateurs are inclined to indulge in subjective fancies, researchers were anxious not to lose sight of the world of facts.

CREATIVITY AND DEFENSIVE STRATEGIES

In Table 14.1 creativity, as judged by the CFT, is related to results of the MCT. The table shows that tendencies toward depression and compulsive isolation are likely to obstruct creative processes, while tendencies toward repression and sensitivity are positively associated with creativity. The G-index of agreement, as applied to median cuts in the distributions, is 0.63. It should be made clear that, in our case, repression does not refer to the kind of defense used by primitive-hysterics, but to transformation at a (symbolic) distance from the stimulus. The sign of sensitivity in the MCT is only remotely related to the projecting defense of paranoid patients, and should rather be understood as sensitivity to marginal cues. An analogous result was found in the group of 16-year-olds (Chapter 10). This results may be an illustration of the dual roles of defense.

TABLE 14.1
CREATIVITY AND DEFENSIVE STRATEGIES

	MCT				
	Isol., isol. tend. or depr. stereotypy			Not isol., isol. tend. or depr. stereotypy	
CFT	Not sens./movement or repr./repr. tend.	Only one of them	Both of them	One or both of them	None of them
XX, X, (X)	2	1	4	7	1
0, S, -	6	8	0	1	2

$X^2 = 12.44$ P>0.001

A defensive strategy which protects the creator from too direct a confrontation with menacing aspects of his own self may, at the same time, allow a symbolic "gestalting" of these aspects.

CREATIVITY AND ART DIMENSIONS

Creativity scores correlate with the art dimensions of originality, expressiveness, and authenticity, as will also be shown by the cluster analysis. Two of them, originality and expressiveness, have just been mentioned as tending to correlate significantly with each other. Evaluations of authenticity were particularly delicate to make and were tentative in outcome.

An extended and more reliable evaluation scale for measuring correlations between art dimensions and creativity can be constructed by including still more art dimensions (see Smith, Carlsson, and Danielsson, 1985, regarding the rationale guiding this construction)—i.e., originality (plus), expression (plus), level (plus and zero), form and articulation (plus for not more than one of them), dynamic quality (i.e., minus for static quality), renewal (plus). Authenticity was excluded here, because of its skewed distribution. A plus for both form and articulation in the same artist was regarded as an indication of formalized and tightly structured art production, at least partly the opposite of expressiveness, for example. The distribution of scores for "level" was statistically improved by placing zero scores on the plus side. This gave us a scale comprising six steps.

The CFT scores were divided in three. To accomplish this, the (X) category was split in two: $(X)+$ including subjects who returned to abstract themes in their inverted PGs, and $(X)-$ for the remaining subjects. The three steps were thus as follows: (a) = $XX, X, (X)+$; (b) = $(X)-, O, S;$ (c) = " $-$ ". The product-moment correlation between art dimensions and PG scores is 0.72 (P < 0.01).

HUMAN MOTIFS IN THE CFT

In the study of researchers (Chapter 4), subjects reporting human presence (H) in the virtually inanimate CFT picture tended to be those that were emotionally involved in their own creative endeavors. The present sample represents a considerable variation with respect to such interpretations. When dividing the sample into subgroups either *with* or *without* human themes, however, we had to take into account the fact that the presence of H-signs in the straight series of PG projections increases the likelihood of creativity indices in the inverted series. When comparing subgroups differing with respect to H-signs, therefore, we had to make sure that the results were not merely dependent on differences in degree of creativity.

Accordingly, we have constructed four subgroups with respect to the presence of human themes in the reactions to the straight PG projections: A, B, C, D (see Table 14.2). An additional but marginal group of two persons seeming to fit in somewhere between C and D was excluded in the first comparisons. One person whose results did not fit in at all was excluded.

According to the outcome of the CFT, the subjects in subgroup A should be characterized by having open access to their emotional life—a characteristic that we assume they use fully in their creative work. They all show signs of high creativity. And they all, with just one exception, represent an art form which is not abstract and not constructivist, even if not representational in a realistic sense. Among the remaining

TABLE 14.2
GROUPING WITH RESPECT TO PRESENCE OF HUMAN THEMES

Group	Straight PG	Inverted PG	MCT, IT, Interview
A (n = 9)	H	H, *X* or higher	Work and childhood memories seen in both negative and positive light
B (n = 5)	H	no H, *(X)* or higher	Work and childhood memories seen in both negative and positive light
C (n = 9)	H	no H, *0* or lower	Troubled relations with others. Shift category in IT
D (n = 6)		no H, one *(X)*, the rest 0 or lower	Isolation or stereotypy, no sensitivity in MCT

twenty subjects in groups B to D, there are thirteen abstract artists (P = 0.02).

Subgroups B and C both show H-signs in the straight PG series, but not in the inverted one. The most conspicuous difference between them concerns the strength of signs for creativity: there are stronger creativity scores in the B subgroup. The B subjects apparently maintain a creative relation to their experiences even if this relation is not allowed to be permeated by emotions (represented by H-signs). Instead, emotions are kept at a certain distance once the stimulus has been discerned. Four out of the five subjects in subgroup B reported that they produce more or less abstract art. In the interview, the C-subgroup, with its more limited creative ability, all reported difficulties in communicating with other people or troubled relations with the opposite sex. Hence, we propose that lack of creativity also restricts their possibilities for solving personal problems in their art. Instead, their conflicts tend to surface in real life. To express it in another way, the subjects in B might be able to express their tensions and resolve their conflicts in creative work to a greater extent than those in C.

The persons forming subgroup C differ from the subjects in

A and B in that they show no signs of high creativity in the inverted series in spite of reporting human themes in the straight PG series. When comparing the nine C-subjects with all the other subgroups, including the two persons initially omitted in these comparisons, we found that the group stood out in one distinct respect. As mentioned above, they are all characterized by troubled human relations. The same was true for only five of the remaining twenty-two subjects of the present study (P = 0.0001). An analogous difference, although less pronounced, was found with regard to sex attribution in the IT. All nine C-subjects fall into the category "shift," which means that they shift with the shift of subliminal stimulation, thus avoiding the risk of identifying themselves with both sexes. In the other subgroups only nine subjects fall into the same category in the IT (P = 0.005).

Groups A, B, and C differ from group D in that D persons used isolation in MCT to master the threat or showed depressive stereotypy with no "emollient" signs of sensitivity movement. As mentioned before, the latter type of defense implies that the threatening A picture is kept outside awareness, while changes in the B picture are reported instead.[1] Among twenty-three persons accounted for under A–C, only two have protocols showing such tendencies, while all persons in subgroup D have such protocols. The probability of this contrast occurring by chance is as low as 0.0001.

Even when we only compare subgroup C with subgroup D, both showing few signs of creativity in the inverted PG series, the significant difference remains: there is only one subject among the nine in subgroup C who resembles the six subjects in D (P = 0.003). Subgroup D is thus characterized in this context by a lack of signs for emotional involvement. This lack is associated with compulsive and depressive tendencies that are not softened by sensitivity.

Two further aspects may highlight the differences between subgroups. The way persons in A and B speak about their work

[1] In essence, the way the MCT is constructed with a subliminal stimulus impinging the stabilized perception of B, this implies sensitivity to subliminal cues, a right hemisphere characteristic according to Sackeim, Packer, and Gur (1977).

is characteristically distinct from that of persons in C and D: among the former pair it was common in the interview to describe work in positive as well as negative terms, while in the latter only one aspect was emphasized, positive or negative. In their reminiscences of early days, moreover, the persons in A and B reported happy as well as unhappy childhood memories, while the tendency among people in C and D was to withhold one of those aspects. The P in the former case is 0.014, and in the latter case 0.027.

The subjects in A and B thus seem to be more open to all sides of their work and life experiences, while the subjects in C and D maintain an attitude of either/or. This, of course, has to be considered in relation to the just-mentioned fact that creativity signs were far more frequent in the A and B subgroups. The creative attitude, as assessed by indirect methods, is thus consistent with attitudes to life and work openly displayed in the interview and probably also in the social life of the artist.

Independent Assessments of the A–D Subgroups and the *XX* Group

The list of the subgroups as such, but not the results just related, served as a starting point for a further evaluation by the art specialist among us, who attempted a characterization of the subjects' artistic personalities. There is a certain disproportion between the results above, based on thirty-two protocols, and the following considerations referring to seventeen artists known to him. But the main interest is naturally the extent to which the indications given for those seventeen fall into the patterns of the respective subgroups and possibly complement them.

In the following, six persons in A, four in B, four in C, and three in D have been considered. In subgroup A all except one were described as totally absorbed by their artistic work, and even the B subjects seemed mainly to be so engaged. The C-subjects showed a more complicated relation to their role as artists, and subjects in D clearly had other roles besides the artistic one.

Four of the subjects under study received XX-scores in the CFT, implying that during the inverted part of the projection series they totally abandoned their contact with the "correct" meaning of the picture, indulging instead in subjective interpretations. The three of these XX-subjects known to the art specialist were described by him as follows: "For all of them art is their life, the 'real' reality."

THE UNCREATIVE ARTISTS

Aspects of Uncreativity, Results of the Factor Analysis

In the factor analysis, of which two solutions were obtained under slightly different conditions, creative signs and their correlates appeared to be distributed over a variety of combinations. On the other hand, characteristics indicating low creativity or total lack of creativity were mainly accumulated in one or two factors.

The first factors coming up in a factor analysis are bound to represent most of the variance (about 20% in both cases here). When characterizing subjects constituting a factor as compared with all other subjects, we only considered D-indices of 0.50 or more, as mentioned before.

In the first solution, based on material where special emphasis was put on the CFT scores, the first factor contained four artists. They had low creativity scores on the CFT and are, according to their own descriptions, representational-realistic in their art. They were free from signs of anxiety, extroverted, and on the whole well adapted. None of them preferred the open alternative in the IT. Their products were evaluated as unoriginal, unexpressive, static and unconvincing with regard to authenticity.

In the second solution the art dimensions had been given more relative weight. In this analysis, one more person was added to the first, just-discussed factor. The description of the group encompassed by the new factor can now be supple-

mented with the following characteristics: none of the artists
were acquainted with oceanic feelings (which implies merging
with something greater than oneself); none reported color
dreams; on the whole they seemed to lack interest in dreams.
In their artistic work they were mainly inclined to stick to a few
established methods.

Besides the major factor in the first solution, there was also
another low creative factor including three artists. These subjects had severe anxiety and signs of depression; they worked
irregularly, were inflexible in their identification with the
male/female role, and their works were evaluated as static and
without renewal.

As indicated here, lack of creativity appears both in association with good and poor adaptation to life and work. Both
ends of the continuum are thus represented.

Disturbance Signs

The cluster analysis resulted in two main clusters, in which
the occurrence of several previously identified signs of creativity
or disturbance permitted the use of two general labels, "creativity signs" and "disturbance signs," respectively.

The following items were part of the "disturbance cluster":

> Inconsistency in interpretations of the straight PG in CFT
>   (inability to stick to one interpretation).
> Reports of seeing movement in the CFT.
> Reports of seeing color in the (black-and-white) CFT.
> Severe anxiety reported in the interview.
> Signs of severe anxiety in the MCT.
> Sleep disturbances.
> Engagement in other creative activities besides pictorial art.
> Signs of depressive stereotypy in the MCT results.

In this cluster, the first three items may be interpreted very
generally as indicating disturbance. Any further analysis should
not be carried too far since our knowledge of the matter is still
limited. However, we know from MCT studies that color reports
indicate regressive tendencies. (It is here a question of colors

added to a concrete sense impression; not, as in dreams, just part of the dreamer's own imagery.) Reports of movement in the presentation of a single stimulus are clearly unmotivated by the test situation. All three features may thus represent a basic instability. On quite another level, the same can be said for the tendency to engage in alternative activities, implying that the temptation to identify with something other than art work is near at hand. The rest of the disturbance signs have regularly proved to be detrimental to creative activity—e.g., severe anxiety, depressive retardation, and compulsive defense (Smith and Carlsson, 1983a, Chapter 6).

Further illustrating aspects of uncreativity is a correlation in the present sample, already reported in a previous paper (Smith, Carlsson, and Danielsson, 1985), regarding art dimensions and the IT. Most conspicuously, there is a consistent relation between results in the IT and the artistic dimensions of concentration on form, articulation, and a tendency toward renewal. When a subject has received a positive marking for both "form" and "articulation," but a negative one for "renewal," this description already indicates static production, dependent on a rigid internal order. The correlation with a preference for the "closed" alternative in the IT justifies further speculation about this formal restriction and rigidity as an expression of a basically noncommitted type of personality.

THE CREATIVE ARTISTS

We will concentrate on the cluster analysis, since the factor analyses resulted in small, variegated factors.

Creativity Signs

CFT scores *XX/X/(X)* versus the other signs, or all CFT scores versus the noncreative " – ."

Color dreams.

Positive evaluations for art dimensions "originality," "expressiveness," and "authenticity."

Mainly positive identification with the open alternative in

the IT and/or more negative identification with the closed one.

Reports memories from early childhood, at least from the age of three.

In the creative cluster, two items have been shown to correlate with creativity in previous studies: dreams in color and access to early memories. A person who readily affirms that he dreams in colors (as opposed to noncolor—not black-and-white) is likely to have close contact with his dream life. Access to early childhood memories probably reflects a general openness to past experiences (which also includes later periods in life). Both characteristics thus imply that the individual's conscious present is not cut off from its inner and early roots.

THE IMPORTANT ARTISTS

Five artists received "level" scores in the art historian's evaluation of their works, implying that a certain depth and mobility was seen in their products. They could all be regarded as our most "important" artists in the region, important even on a national scale. Another subject, close to the others in many respects, was added to increase the number for the sake of comparisons. These six are all discussed below.

In the MCT all six reacted with repression on a very high order of transformation. This mechanism allowed them to address the threatening stimulus well away from its "real" meaning (the angry face does not just become a stiff bust, but is instead seen as a tree or the like). In the IT they showed no tendency to shift identification so as to stay with their own gender, but were open to alternative identifications, even with the opposite sex. In the CFT, all except one (who got a *0*) received *XX–(X)+* scores. Taken together, these characteristics attest to a flexibility and freedom of expression on a very high level of mental functioning.

DISCUSSION

The technical problems related to the methods used have already been dealt with. Most of the results imply cross-validations. We would rather like to discuss topics specific to the present study, i.e., the relation between the artistic personality and aspects of genuineness and importance in art—as well as in everyday life.

In the outcome of the tests, evaluations, and interviews, some features traditionally ascribed to the typical artistic personality appear with reassuring emphasis. The individual outcomes, however, direct our attention to the fact that art is not just an area of traditional and unified activities, but a field for constant initiation and diverging ambitions. Making the selection on the basis of a regional art life was probably advantageous in the sense that it spared the researchers the trouble of addressing numerous deviations from "the mainstream." Perhaps even the apparent fact that there is a mainstream is the result of a regional focus. It is probably fair to characterize the group as an organic cross-section of a reasonably developed regional body of artists. And in that body, judged importance seems to be closely related to freedom from conventions, attained by means of authentic personal experiences, as well as versatility.

There is, however, a crucial point to be noted: The existence of art that is clearly formal in its intentions but which, due to its formality, is also highly regarded, makes it impossible to maintain any deprecating relation between "formal" and "restricted artistry." Should there be a skewed tendency in that direction here, it just has to be accepted as one of those irregularities associated with most samples restricted in time and place. When comparing our artists with those in the classical study of major American artists by Ann Roe (1946a, 1946b), we find, however, that the present sample is far less eccentric relative to the classical image of the artist, even in individual cases.

To the general reader and to the artist or art historian, the most impressive outcome of this study might be the affirmation that real creativity is dependent on a fair level of harmony—by no means complete but sufficient for control and efficacy.

Moreover, creativity does not seem to function without a certain measure of anxiety which the artist must tolerate so as not to dodge crucial steps in the artistic process. Severe mental burdens can inhibit creativity—there is no reason to uphold the old romantic notion of extremely fruitful creation on the verge of despair and madness. On the other hand, a lack of conflict-laden or deep experiences may result in tame art products, even if they are "genuine." Beyond these general conclusions, which are not particular to the present material—even if they receive unusually good support from it—there are many other indications of interest. For instance, the results may make it easier to comprehend why the dynamics found behind an everyday creative attitude to the world are similar to those found in works of high artistic originality.

Among the many different combinations of personal qualities discussed here, some constantly reappear in combination with high creativity (e.g., preference for the open alternative in the IT) and others in combination with low or blocked creativity (e.g., dread of ambiguity). Other qualities, however, combine more individually, as is evidenced by the numerous one-two person factors in the inverted factor analyses, for example. Among the persons included in factors or groups of some size, there are several who, while certainly enjoying general esteem for real artistry, are still not counted among the regionally or nationally famous artists and often do not seem to strive in that direction either. But even if not considered important at present by most judges (obviously, opinions may differ in this respect and may change over time), they seem to be genuine; and their combinations of qualities also tend to form descriptions of *genuine* artistic personalities with creativity, freedom, and originality or expressiveness, etc.

It is interesting to note that creativity and productivity are not necessarily positively associated with each other (as was also shown in the previous study of researchers, Chapter 4), and in some of our cases the productivity of highly creative artists seems surprisingly low. Even if this can sometimes be ascribed to life conditions, there is still a residual group of people who apparently just produce much less than most and may be satisfied with their performance. It is certainly important to pay as much attention to genuineness as to productivity in the study of artistic creativity—but it is also difficult methodologically and uncertain in the end. Artistic performance, in spite of everything, is measured primarily as the ability to be creatively *productive* in a specific area.

The use of human motifs in the CFT was an important factor associated with our art specialist's estimate of the degree to which various artists were absorbed by their artistic work. In partial analogy with the Rorschach test, where reports of human movement are signs of introversive tendencies and emotional intensity, we showed in Chapter 4 that human motifs are indicative of emotional engagement in creative endeavors. Obviously, the world for people thus engaged cannot be dehumanized without affecting the very roots of creative motivation. Or to express it differently, creativity thrives through projections of basically human needs and problems even if, as in many of the present cases, the projections may be difficult to discern and decipher. Looking at our results in this way we find it understandable that creativity can be associated with very diverse items in the factor analysis.

As already mentioned, the processes emphasized in this chapter are not specific to any group of people, and the ways in which our artists reacted to the stimuli can be observed repeatedly in nonartists. Many of the latter may function very much in the same way as the most important artists here, without having either an artistic personality, artistic ambitions, or resources for artistic creativity. For example, the creative treatment of sense impressions and experiences may be a common everyday phenomenon in many individuals—i.e., seeing things very differently or in a new light. Certainly, we can learn much about the resources for attaining life quality and resolving personal conflicts by more closely examining the genuine artists' ways of handling their impressions.

15

DISCUSSION

Summary of a Model for Creative Functioning

We have operationally defined creativity by the percept-genetic, creative functioning test (CFT). The straight genesis in that test appears to mirror slightly different aspects of creative functioning than the inverted one. The straight PG represents the subject's appreciation of his visual world and more or less flexible representation of it. Once the subject has accepted the correct meaning, however, the crucial matter becomes his inclination to free himself from this objective reality and to return to more uncertain, imaginative interpretations. The straight genesis can thus be said to reflect more of the motivational-emotional side of creativity while the inverted PG represents more of the intentional side.

One of the presumptions of the present series of investigations was that the individual cannot function creatively without open communication between the distant and proximal poles of constructive processing, or to paraphrase Kris (1952), without access to ways of thinking other than the usual logical ones—namely, egocentric thinking, condensation, symbolization, etc. In spite of our criticism of some facets of the psychodynamic tradition, in particular its sole use of the *Leitmotif* regression in the service of the ego and its heavy reliance on clinical case material, we have accepted its emphasis on irrational, subjective material as indispensable sources for the creative individual.

It is not enough, however, to discuss open communication between our so-called P-phases and C-phases without specifying the kind of P-phase contents the individual is willing to exploit. First of all, reconstruction of P-phases at a "middle distance" from the C-phase may often be as important as reconstruction of very early P-phases. It could, for instance, imply actualization of dormant ideas stemming from some point in the individual's youth or early adult life. Moreover, according to our results, creative people are ready to confront very diverse aspects of their private world, dark as well as bright, frightening as well as soothing, primitive, incomprehensible, demonic, etc. Obviously, these people are tolerant of the anxiety likely to be aroused by such confrontations. Without this tolerance their freedom to exploit new and paradoxical aspects would be impeded.

Persons open to the ambiguities in their inner world apparently feel more at ease with the contradictions of human existence. It is not surprising, then, that they willingly identify themselves with various kinds of problems, concrete as well as abstract, and make them part of their personal life, in spite of the inconvenience and even anxiety caused by such identifications. What apparently motivates the creative person not to give up his search for a good solution is that the problem does not remain a matter outside himself but has become incorporated into his own private world of problems. By working on the incorporated problem he is also working to enlighten his own problem landscape.

Why are creative people tolerant of anxiety and discomfort? There may be several explanations. One of them is their particular way of confronting threatening messages. Many creative people are characterized by sensitivity to marginal, even subliminal cues. To be sensitive to subtle nuances in one's world of experience can obviously be an asset for the creative individual. The sensitivity, at least as scored by the MCT, can also imply a tendency toward projection, to make threats part of the outside world instead of the intimate, personal one. In this way the sensitive person becomes less vulnerable. He can also use a defense implying that threats are transformed to manageable forms at a symbolic level, a sophisticated variant of repression.

In these various ways creative people may allow themselves to confront and manipulate threatening material (sometimes threatening merely because of its incomprehensiveness)—in a way, to play with it.

Other defensive strategies function quite differently. When curbing anxiety, these strategies also throttle the communication between the roots and end stage of the perceptual process. Such is the case with compulsive isolation—which in some instances, though, may be only partial—and with depressive retardation. In these cases anxiety is often completely suppressed. On the other hand, states of excessive anxiety and insufficient defenses are detrimental to creative functioning.

However, we have to go beyond phrases like tolerance of anxiety and strategies designed to increase that tolerance. Many uncreative people are at least seemingly healthy and generally free from both symptoms of anxiety and neurotic strategies to suppress it. It seems as if anxiety were a necessary companion of creativity. Let us venture the speculation that only a person ready to try unusual and provoking solutions to the problems incorporated by him, thereby raising his emotional temperature, will be able to follow his creative endeavors to the very end.

Not surprisingly, we found that creative people were more inclined to face threats in an active manner, to identify with an aggressor rather than a victim, and to pay attention even to subtle whims of their own, not ignoring them in the face of more established truths. Such attitudes are bound to increase these people's tolerance of anxiety (which, at least, they do not have to endure as passive victims). At the same time they are necessary ingredients in the creative person's efforts to question established truths and paradigms. Creative acts are basically revolutionary (although revolutionary acts are not necessarily creative).

These characteristics of creative people seem to have their roots far back in ontogeny. It was possible for us to use results obtained with 5–6-year-olds to predict degree of creativity in these same children when they had reached the age of 10–11. The results of the very first study, however, where we influenced the scores in the CFT by means of placebo pills and instructions, suggest that it is not impossible to make a person more susceptible to his own latent creative possibilities. This may also account for the difference between children from academic homes and other children. They appear to differ with respect to self-reliance.

Creative potentialities, as defined here, cannot be fully exploited until the age of 5–6 years when the child's representational world has become clearly distinct from the surrounding real world. As the child grows older, its creative efforts become more differentiated. Still, this development is interrupted by low-creative periods when the child's reality contact is consolidated and its cognitive instrumentation improved. The creative periods are characterized by open inside-outside communication and some degree of anxiety. During the uncreative periods, with their extroverted attention and compulsivelike defense strategies, anxiety is effectively suppressed. It is of particular interest to note that our investigation cannot support the myth of puberty as a time of high creativity. Instead, the necessary reconstruction of early P-phases is often rendered difficult during these years.

Creativity and talent do not necessarily go together, nor do creativity and exceptional life experiences. It is not unusual to find uncreative but versatile artists, or creative artists who are not particularly deep or complicated. What creative people have in common are not their accomplishments but a certain generative attitude toward living. This attitude makes continuous renewal possible, at various levels of work and experience. The generative attitude appears to be combined with a particular form of ego identity, partly demonstrated by their identification with an active aggressor rather than the aggressor's victim, or with a "free" figure rather than one enclosed in narrow safety.

THE METHOD DEFINING THE MODEL

To some, the CFT may seem too narrow and with too perception-oriented a basis on which to build a model of creative functioning. Throughout the present series of experiments, however, we have tried to establish a network of criterion correlations. Let us mention only a few: originality and emotional involvement in researchers and professional artists; an urge to create in amateur artists and poets; drawings and clay products in preschool children; creative interests in all children and youngsters except during high puberty; etc. Correlations have usually been high, particularly if compared with the correlations usually attained in personality research. Inter-rater reliabilities have also been consistently satisfactory.

In addition to all this, the CFT results have proved to be closely related to various forms of mental functioning, as reflected in dreaming, recall of early childhood memories, defensive reactions, identification with the role of an aggressor, etc. Taken together, these relations contribute to a broadening of the empirical foundation of our model by placing creative functioning within the scope of the percept-genetic theory, since it concerns not only perceptual processing in isolation, but also the wider context of personality.

There is another advantage in using a single core instrument in our studies. The instrument can be applied at all age levels from 4 years upwards. It thus makes possible a consistent view of creativity development. Since the creative functioning test is akin to a group of methods previously applied to children and adolescents, it has also been possible to interpret our findings broadly in terms of personality development.

RELATION TO OTHER FORMULATIONS ON CREATIVITY

As the present project has proceeded it has become increasingly difficult to relate our findings to the mainstream of creativity research as represented by such people as Guilford, Barron, Perkins, De Bono, and others. The obvious reason is that the psychometric tradition has focused on problem solving and other cognitive activities, viewed in the light of trait psychology, while our studies have emphasized relations between the experienced self and the experienced outside reality in a process perspective. Obviously, however, we have derived advantages from their pioneering studies of originality and cognitive flexibility, one example being our evaluation of the works of the professional artists, another being some of the interview dimensions used in the studies of children. On the other hand, many psychometric studies incur the risk of confounding with true creativity a certain "pseudo-creative" attitude, often combined with verbal fluency. Still, it appears more fruitful to relate our thinking to the writings of such key researchers in the field as Kris and Rothenberg in order to mark more decisively where we stand and also, very briefly, to actualize the classic psychoanalytic concept of sublimation.

CREATIVITY, ANXIETY, AND MENTAL ILLNESS

Ernst Kris was for decades the undisputed authority for most dynamically oriented researchers in the field of creativity. Even more cognitively oriented students have reason to feel indebted to him. His distinction between an inspirational and an elaborational phase in creation, for instance, still remains useful. Among his many astute observations, this one deserves to be quoted: ". . . the shift from consciousness to preconsciousness may account for the experience of clarification that occurs when after intense concentration the solution to an insoluble problem suddenly presents itself following a period of rest" (Kris, 1952, p. 312). His hypothesis about regression in the service of the ego can be summarized thus, in his own words: ". . . the integrative functions of the ego include self-regulated regression and permit a combination of the most daring intellectual activity with the experience of passive receptiveness" (p. 318).

On closer examination, however, a critique of his ideas appears justified. As mentioned already in Chapter 1, Kris did not really conceive creativity to be a process in the meaning of the term presented in Chapter 2. This is probably one reason why the place of intentionality in creative work remained unclear in his writings. Another criticism concerns his use of the term "ego regression," which really implied "primitivization of ego functions." In spite of his work as an art historian, his dominant interests were clinical. In the insane artists he described, regression was a central pathological characteristic, a sign of permanent withdrawal from reality-oriented activity.

Typically, regression seems to precede conscious elaboration, even as far as nonschizophrenic artists are concerned.

In contrast, Rothenberg (1979) believed that intentional, conscious activities open the sluices to unconscious (preconscious) material and are themselves partly motivated by an attempt to gain better control over this material (or its reflections in the external world). This seems to be an attractive synthesis of psychoanalytic theorizing and modern cognitive psychology. Many years earlier, Maslow (1962) wanted to free the theorizing about creative (self-actualizing) individuals from all psychopathological connotations inherent in psychoanalytic thinking. Still, the present authors cannot fully free themselves from thinking that regressive strategies in the meaning of Kris may be the only possible way for some rare type of artist or poet, etc., to function creatively. If regression involves too large a risk of being overwhelmed by internal conflicts, then partial regression might be a strategic alternative.

Adaptive regression is subsumed in our model under the conception of reconstruction, which always operates from the present level of reality adaptation (the C-phase). Reconstruction has no immediate pathological connotations and may actualize material from any part of the PG process, regardless of whether it is very distant from the C-phase or relatively close to it. Reconstruction involves an intentional effort but may be facilitated by relaxation (removal of defensive barriers or lowering of the anxiety level). Most important of all, the term "reconstruction" is part and parcel of a process perspective on creative functioning. The reconstructed materials are nothing but ingredients of the constructive process that shapes and upholds the individual's view of reality, including his own self.

As Arieti (1976) points out, Kris remained to a large extent within the energetic-libidinal framework of Freudian theory, where the main adaptive function of anxiety is to serve as a warning signal. In artistic work, for example, if primary-process mechanisms such as displacement and condensation remain incongruous with ego functioning, it is assumed that anxiety may result. Rothenberg's material clearly illustrates that anxiety can also function to stimulate arousal. This finding agrees well with our own experimental work, in which anxiety appears to be a common companion of creativity.

Typically, for the creative individual, artistic production does not proceed harmoniously but entails great tolerance for discomfort and even agony. In this respect, the creative person is the opposite of the neurotic (Kubie, 1958). Anxiety should not, however, be viewed only as an epiphenomenon of creative work but also as an incitement to it. Our experiments have shown that an extra dose of anxiety—triggered by a threatening subliminal stimulus—significantly increases creative activity (as defined in the experiment), above all in people who have once functioned creatively but have become more and more blocked and indifferent over the years. Anxiety seems to raise the creative temperature (Chapter 5). It is instructive that this positive effect of anxiety fails to appear in psychiatric patients inclined toward strong anxiety reactions but with low anxiety tolerance. Even if these people have strong creative intentions, their work is blocked by dread of its accompanying discomforts (Chapter 6).

JANUSIAN THINKING AND HOMOSPATIAL IMAGERY

In his intensive studies of creative people from various fields, Rothenberg (1979) claimed to have found two characteristics distinguishing them from other people: Janusian thinking and homospatial imagery. As the term suggests, a Janusian thought carries its own antithesis. The thought of A+ is accompanied by the thought of A−. A model intended to explain certain scientific data gives birth to its own diametrical opposite. One of the best recent examples of this kind of creative thinking is the double helix structure proposed for the DNA molecule. The first hypothesis of a simple helix was inadequate. But the notion of one helical molecule invoked its mirror image. Watson and Crick solved the problem by combining both spirals. Similarly, the poet, the painter, and the composer are not content with the simple, harmonious front view of a theme; they have the backside, the complex variations, and the shadows in mind at the same time. They not only tolerate ambiguity, indispensable part of their creation.

The term "homospatial imagery" relates to the mo side of creative cognitive processing—i.e, to the in visualize simultaneously or conceive in some other more discrete entities occupying the space" (Roth Sobel, 1980, p. 371)—in other words, entities that do ... . together either logically or conventionally. To paraphrase Rothenberg, the elements of the inventor's new machine come together in his inner (preconscious) eye, although the combination may at first seem improbable, abstruse, or even silly. Homospatial imagery is apt to lead to the articulation of new and unusual visual combinations, bold poetic metaphors, or unexpected leaps from one scientific field to another.

PERCEPT-GENETIC REFORMULATIONS

In his attempt to distinguish between creative functioning and primary-process modes of functioning, and thus to demarcate the cleft between his own position and that of Kris and his followers, Rothenberg obviously wishes to avoid the concept of regression, even "adaptive" regression. Yet homospatial imagery and Janusian thinking could very easily be thought of as aspects of primary-process functioning. Rothenberg (1981) argues that "primary process is a literal and obfuscating cognitive mode whereas both homospatial and Janusian thinking are figurative, abstract, and revelatory." He prefers to regard the latter modes as mirror images of primary-process functioning, occurring on a more advanced level and not representing a primitivization of mental functioning even though they utilize certain primary-process characteristics.

Rothenberg's mirror-image analogy may at first seem to be a mere play with words. The analogy, however, is apparently meant to convince us that unconscious processes are not really constituents of the creative act—they are only mirrored in it. In effect, Rothenberg claims that the creative pause is beneficial, not because it gives unconscious processes time to continue their constructive activity, but simply because the organism needs rest to work efficiently. If some confusion still remains in the mind of the reader—partly because Janusian thinking and homospatial imagery do not generally appear in one's field of attention while one is working—and are therefore all the more likely to be referred to the primitive pole of cognitive functioning—it may be possible to illuminate this tangled issue by returning to the PG concept of reconstruction.

As we have seen, reconstruction implies that unconscious (preconscious) steps in the process of reality construction are made conscious and adapted to the subject's present frame of reference or, to give it a more psychoanalytic twist, are allowed to enter consciousness because they have become adapted. The reconstructions of early process stages can be reflections only of the originals; reconstructions and originals are related to each other in the same way as the manifest dream content is related to the inferred latent content. The fact that Janusian thinking and homospatial imagery can be made conscious and reconstructed does not mean that when operative in the creative process, these modes of functioning are close to the level of rational, reality-adapted cognitive operations. We would prefer to place them somewhere in that part of the PG process which at some distance augurs the final stage but still carries hallmarks of nonrealistic ways of functioning. Too great a distance, on the other hand, would mean inaccessibility to the feedback stimulation necessary for the dialectical progress of creative work.

By no means are all people willing to let such peculiarities as homospatial and Janusian conceptions enter their conscious, ordered, everyday cogitation. Our experiments have clearly demonstrated that many persons, once they have been confronted with the conventional solution of a perceptual problem, simply refuse to acknowledge, much less use, the dubious contents of early PG phases—phases often reflecting ambiguities and combinations of apparently unrelated structures, i.e, Janusian thinking and homospatial imagery in Rothenberg's sense. Creative individuals differ from noncreative ones, not because they are endowed with special talents, but because they are able and willing to make conscious and exploit cognitive structures which deviate from the formal logic (in the Piagetian sense) and to represent these deviations in pictures, symbols, and cognitive models. They do not hesitate to retreat from the dead-end streets of convention in order to be able to proceed.

In this connection it is necessary to get rid of the misconception, perhaps lying close at hand, that creative activity entails only some sort of recurrent regrouping of the creative person's private experience. Reconstructive and recreative activity are, among other things, necessary to make the present meaningful to the individual and to provide a personal sounding board for the task ahead. The perceptual process laid bare in PG experiments can be described in terms of *cumulation* (successive determination from phase to phase) and *emergence* (the sudden appearance of contents with only marginal ties to previous phases). The "revolutionary" principle of emergence is always combined with the conserving influence of cumulation. This is not to say that these two principles of PG transformation inhibit each other. Rather, a broad contact with early P-phases seems to facilitate the emergence of new content in percept-genesis. Thus, although the creative work is produced in the here-and-now—in an intimate dialogue with contemporary knowledge and conceptions of reality—it is simultaneously rooted in the individual's history.

THE CONCEPT OF SUBLIMATION

In spite of the central role played by the concept of sublimation, particularly in Sigmund Freud's own writings on creativity, we have only incidentally mentioned it in Chapter 14. It seems to have become more and more entangled in contradictory usages and definitions and has eventually lost much of its attraction even to psychoanalytic students of creative functioning. However, by clearly distinguishing between sublimatory activity and neurotic symptom formation, Elliott (1985) seems again to have made sublimation a useful alternative to other formulations about creativity. We are not going to try to include it in our model but would just like to show, by quoting Elliott at some length, that a cleansed concept of sublimation is not incompatible with the substance of our own model:

The distinction between sublimatory activity and neurotic symptoms as entities is logically determined when the processes of neurotic symptom-formation and the formation of sublimatory activity are delineated. It is suggested that sublimatory activity results from the regulation of unconscious feeling states involving the symbolic representation of pleasurable infantile self and object relationships, the feelings and wishes involved having only become conflictual with further development but not having been conflictual at the appropriate developmental stage. Because of the gratification inherent in the unconscious symbolic expression of these relationships with the attendant gratification derived from the object's approval of the activity, the individual's capacity for further development is enhanced. Conflict in this sense is managed without the impairment of the individual's ability to perceive, judge, and adapt to the demands of reality. Neurotic symptoms, on the other hand, although they also have the character of unconscious symbolic representation of internal object relationships, differ in at least two respects: Firstly, they derive from a developmental phase (the Oedipal phase) in which the object relationships are intrinsically conflictual, independent of the external object's attitude. Thus, developmental considerations are of crucial importance. Secondly, the unconscious symbolic representation of infantile object ties in a symptom involves regression and is not an adaptive solution to conflict. The compromise involved impairs the individual's ability to perceive, judge, and adequately adapt to the demands of reality [p. 244].

Accordingly, what seems most compatible with sublimatory activity in this sense is the "successful repression" or metaphoric transformation discussed in Chapter 14.

Problems That Remain

Our model is meant to encompass various fields of creativity, scientific and artistic, amateurish and professional, immature and mature, at one and the same time. Many students of creativity are probably inclined to criticize such inclusiveness as contrary to well-known biographical facts. One way to counter this criticism would be to refer to differences in talent between, for instance, artists and mathematicians, as an explanation why people choose different fields of work even if their ways of functioning creatively are formally quite similar. Such an answer would be unsatisfactory, however. There are obviously other differences between artists and mathematicians than those accounted for by differences in intelligence profiles.

Some of these differences can be taken care of by our model. The reader may remember that none of our creative researchers received XX scores in the inverted part of the CFT while many amateur artists did, and professional artists placed themselves somewhere in between. These differences obviously reflected how close these people are to an established reality context in their creative endeavors. For scientists, the matching of fantasy and fact is a *sine qua non* to succeed in their constructive work; for amateur artists and writers the conventional view of the world may be worth little more than a shrug of the shoulders. The fact that professional artists place themselves in between probably mirrors the great differentiation of their creative specter, from a subject-centered to an object-centered pole of processing.

But these differences do not exhaust the possibilities of our model to accommodate creative diversities. In their reconstructive attempts, some persons actualize process content very far from the C-phase, i.e., nonadapted, subjective meanings, while others take care of what we have previously (Chapter 14) called contents at a middle distance. These latter contents may very well have their original roots farther down in the individual's experimental hierarchy (his personal history) but have remained dormant until reactualized many years later (Kragh and Smith, 1974; Smith and Kragh, 1975). Another difference concerns the kind of nonadapted P-phase content reclaimed in creative work. In our artists we found many who returned to concrete meanings in their inverted PGs, but a few who preferred abstract forms to concrete interpretations. The latter way of functioning is, we believe, more typical of some scientists.

The interplay between more primary and more secondary types of functioning is one of those problems that remains to be thoroughly highlighted. We believe that intensive studies of creative individuals is a necessary part of such an attempt. An enormous amount of valuable material has been collected by biographers of prominent people. However, it should be supplemented with the kind of material that our methods can supply. The PG model is constructed to illustrate how early, stimulus-distant process phases are transformed into more stimulus-proximal ones, and how, in building up his creative product, the individual utilizes the emotional energy of the highly charged, early roots of his PGs.

As an illustration we would like to use the protocol from an experiment where a professional artist, unknowingly, was presented with one of his own pictures. The stimulus in this percept-genetic presentation was a black-and-white photo of a relief in cement with painted contours. A beaklike form can also be distinguished and there are some other lines and small circles with no distinct meaning. The protocol is reproduced with the artist's permission.

At first it seems very difficult for the artist to find anything meaningful in the brief flashes on the screen. A few exposures later a landscape is reported. When asked after the experiment to associate to this landscape he says that there was something negative in it: "There are so many bad paintings of alps." Apropos such paintings he remembered that his mother lay ill and had a painting of a peak on the wall of her sickroom. Eventually the peak attained monstrous dimensions to her; it had to be removed in order for her to recover.

A few stimulus presentations later he sees a drawing by the Swedish artist C. F. Hill, from the period of his life when he had become irrevocably mentally ill. Some of the drawings are sad, our artists says, others are melancholy. Afterwards he adds that there is nothing negative in this because he loves Hill's drawings.

We continue to quote from the protocol:

> A hand. . . .
> A fragment of something . . . a bird's plumage.
> If I combine the alpine landscape with the plumage . . . I cannot get a unitary conception.
> The hand is there all the time.
> [Afterwards, associating to this report:] It was not a recognizable face, but like being very close to a woman: skin, embroidery.
> Something happened: the black edges glided to the side and I saw something in the middle . . . perhaps half a face with a hand over it. . . . It's not two fingers. . . . The plumage is a gray-

white darker section . . . now there is an organic interplay of
forms.

Something abstract.

Perhaps some kind of embroidery, different dark
forms . . . perhaps a piece of a skirt and skin.

[Comments afterward:] Much of my work is rooted in my
childhood. My childhood was happy. But there are also many
frightening things in the child's world. I am not afraid of returning to it.

We cannot decipher everything in this protocol. We know
that the artist had very early memories of separation from his
mother. Once he thought she was going to leave him for good.
Nightmares and anxiety are part of his adult existence. The
beginnings of his PG are charged with emotions, even personal
recollections of the mother's illness. A little later these emotions
are transformed to an artistic level, but the associations to illness
remain (Hill). New fragments enter the protocol. The first attempts to reconcile these fragments are unsuccessful. The final
reconciliation is achieved at a formal level, with the help of a
hand which may be the artist's own. Everything is still very close
to sensual impressions. The final product is a synthesis of contradictions in the artist's own life.

As we have shown, creative periods at the age of 5–6 and
10–11 years are followed by relatively uncreative, consolidating
periods in what seems to be a natural rhythm. We know less
about what happens later in life. Obviously, all creative individuals are not creative all the time without interruptions. But
why are the ups and downs so marked in some people where
creative oases stand out in deserts of sterility? And why do
others lose their creativity forever after a fertile period early
in life? The study described in Chapter 5 demonstrated that it
was possible to revive a latent creative set by using threatening
subliminal stimulation, i.e., by raising the anxiety level. Increasing dread of the discomforts of creative work may be one possible explanation for a dwindling urge to create or, to express
it the other way around, a more and more importunate yearning
for a life in quiet comfort. Pauses in creation needed for rest
and for the collection of new material and fresh experiences
imply no great problem. It is the shift between two entirely

different life styles, the creative and uncreative ones, that is puzzling. Careful investigations of life stories are apparently needed, investigations especially designed to highlight this problem.

Among important problems that remain to be better illuminated, we particularly want to mention the ego identity (in Erikson's meaning of the term) of creative people. The problem was touched on previously especially in Chapters 10 and 11. How does the creative individual look upon himself and his work? How narcissistic is his involvement, how inflationary his ego, etc.? Since this is one of the main themes of our present and future work on creative functioning, we need not further specify the other research problems in this area. We would rather emphasize their central and exciting nature, ego identity being one of the main organizing principles of mental life.

However, one result of our continuing work should be mentioned because it directly supports one of the main assumptions of the present monograph: that creative functioning involves reconstruction of early experiential material. The technique used is reminiscent of the one described in Chapters 10, 11, and 14, where a brief verbal message was presented on a screen in front of the subject immediately before a presentation of a picture, the picture being supraliminal while the sentence remained subliminal. In our new project we used a rather vague photograph of a human face and messages such as "I GOOD" or "I BAD" or similar opposites. The subject was simply asked to describe the picture.

The most interesting difference between subjects differing in creativity was that, intermittently, the more creative ones saw a young or even a childish face instead of the adult face usually reported. We interpreted this as suggesting that the self-image of creative people not only represents the mature adult "end product" but also represents a more primitive identity or open contact with its developmental roots. Thus, in creative adults the child or youngster is still very much alive. Our results also indicate that the reconstruction of a childish self-image is more pronounced when the "I BAD" combination introduces an identity conflict.

REFERENCES

ALMGREN, P.-E. (1971). Relations between perceptual defenses, defined by the Meta-Contrast Technique, and adaptive patterns in two serial tests. *Psychol. Res. Bull., Lund Univ.*, 11(3).

ANDERSSON, A. L. (1983). Cognitive growth, psychoanalytic conceptions of the mind, aftereffect experience and disavowal as a defense against percept-genetic threat. *Arch. Psychol.*, 135:103–114.

—— (1984). Toward a dialectical conception of the percept-genetic approach to perception-personality. In *Psychological Processes in Cognition and Personality*, ed. W. D. Frölich, G. J. W. Smith, J. G. Draguns & U. Hentschel. Washington, D.C.: Hemisphere, pp. 125–133.

—— FRIES, I. & SMITH, G. J. W. (1970). Change in afterimage and spiral aftereffect serials due to anxiety caused by subliminal threat. *Scand. J. Psychol.*, 11:7–16.

—— NILSSON, A., RUUTH, E. & SMITH, G. J. W., Eds. (1972). *Visual Aftereffects and the Individual as an Adaptive System*. Lund, Sweden: Gleerup.

—— RUUTH, E. & AGEBERG, G. (1977). Patterns of perceptual change in the ages 7–15 years: a cross-sectional study of the Rod-and-Frame Test and the Spiral Aftereffect Technique. *Scand. J. Psychol.*, 18:257–265.

ANTELL, J. A. & GOLDBERGER, L. (1986). The effects of subliminally presented sexual and aggressive stimulation on literary creativity. In *The Roots of Perception: Individual Differences in Information Processing within and beyond Awareness*, ed. U. Hentschel, G. J. W. Smith & J. G. Draguns. Amsterdam: North-Holland, pp. 75–92.

ARIETI, S. (1976). *Creativity: The Magic Synthesis*. New York: Basic Books.

BARRON, F. (1963a). The disposition toward originality. In *Scientific Creativity, Its Recognition and Development*, ed. C. W. Taylor & F. Barron. New York: Wiley, pp. 139–152.

—— (1963b). The needs for order and for disorder as motives in creative activity. In *Scientific Creativity. Its Recognition and Development*, ed. C. W. Taylor & F. Barron. New York: Wiley, pp. 153–160.

—— (1968). *Creativity and Personal Freedom*. Princeton, N.J.: Van Nostrand.

BELLAK, L. (1958). Creativity: some random notes to a systematic consideraton. *J. Project. Tech.*, 22:363–380.

—— (1967). Toward systematic consideration of the nature of the genesis of the creative process. In *The Broad Scope of Psychoanalysis*, ed. D. P. Spence. New York: Grune & Stratton.

BRIM, O. G. & KAGAN, J., Eds. (1980). *Constancy and Change in Human Development*. Cambridge, Mass.: Harvard Univ. Press.

228

BUSH, M. (1969). Psychoanalysis and scientific creativity. *J. Amer. Psychoanal. Assn.*, 17:136–191.

CARLSSON, I. (1986). A visual half-field study of anxiety and defense. *Psychol. Res. Bull., Lund Univ.*, 26(9).

—— & SMITH, G. J. W. (1985). Construction of a parallel version of the PG test. *Psychol. Res. Bull., Lund Univ.*, 25(3).

—— —— (1986). Identification with an aggressor or a victim and its relation to creativity. *Scand. J. Psychol.*, 27:252–257.

—— —— (1987). Gender differences in defense mechanisms compared with creativity in a group of youngsters. *Psychol. Res. Bull., Lund Univ.*, 27(1).

CHASSEGUET-SMIRGEL, J. (1984). Thoughts on the concept of reparation and the hierarchy of creative acts. *Int. Rev. Psychoanal.*, 11:399–406.

CORNSWEET, T. (1970). *Visual Perception.* New York: Academic Press.

CRAMER, P. (1979). Defense mechanisms in adolescence. *Devel. Psychol.*, 15:476–477.

DERI, S. K. (1984). *Symbolization and Creativity.* Madison, Conn.: Int. Univ. Press.

DIXON, N. F. (1971). *Subliminal Perception: The Nature of a Controversy.* New York: McGraw-Hill.

—— (1981). *Preconscious Processing.* New York: Wiley.

DOMINO, G. (1976). Primary process thinking—dream reports as related to creative achievement. *J. Consult. Clin. Psychol.*, 44:929–932.

DRAGUNS, J. G. (1961). Investment of meaning in schizophrenics and children: studies of one aspect of microgenesis. *Psychol. Res. Bull., Lund Univ.*, 1(5).

—— (1963). Responses to cognitive and perceptual ambiguity in chronic and acute schizophrenia. *J. Abnorm. Soc. Psychol.*, 66:24–30.

—— (1984). Microgenesis by any other name. . . . In *Psychological Processes in Cognition and Personality*, ed. W. D. Frölich, G. J. W. Smith, J. G. Draguns & U. Hentschel. Washington, D.C.: Hemisphere, pp. 3–17.

DRÖSLER, J. & KUHN, W. F. (1960). Ein experimenteller Vergleich der visuellen Wahrnehmung von Kindern, Schizophrenen und Alkoholikern mit der tachistoskopischen Wahrnehmung normaler Erwachsener. *16th Internat. Congress Psychol. Individual Papers.* Göttingen: German Psychological Society. *Congress Report*, 1:1–2.

DUDLEY, G. E. (1978). Effects of sex, social desirability, and birth order on the defense mechanisms inventory. *J. Consult. Clin. Psychol.*, 46:1419–1422.

EIDUSON, B. T. (1962). *Scientists: Their Psychological World.* New York: Basic Books.

EKVALL, G. (1971). *Creativity at the Place of Work.* Stockholm: Swedish Council for Personnel Administration. Report 62.

ELLIOTT, C. J. (1985). *Application of the Repertory Grid Model to the Study of the Psychoanalytic Concept of Sublimation.* Lund, Sweden: Gleerup.

ERIKSON, E. H. (1963). *Childhood and Society.* New York: Norton.

—— (1968). *Identity: Youth and Crisis.* New York: Norton.

—— (1977). *Toys and Reasons.* New York: Norton.

FENICHEL, O. (1945). *The Psychoanalytic Theory of Neurosis.* New York: Norton.

FITZGERALD, E. T. (1966). Measurement of openness to experience: a study of regression in the service of the ego. *J. Personal. Soc. Psychol.*, 4:655–663.

FLAVELL, J. H. & DRAGUNS, J. G. (1957). A microgenetic approach to perception and thought. *Psychol. Bull.*, 54:197–217.

FREUD, S. (1905). Jokes and their relation to the unconscious. *S. E.*, 7.

FRÖHLICH, W. D. (1964). *Umstimmigkeit, Erwartung und Kompromiss.* Habilitationsschrift, Univer. Bonn.

—— SMITH, G. J. W., DRAGUNS, J. G. & HENTSCHEL, U., Eds. (1984). *Psychological Processes in Cognition and Personality.* Washington, D.C.: Hemisphere.

GARDNER, H. (1973). *The Arts and Human Development.* New York: Wiley.

GARDNER, R.; HOLZMAN, P. S.; LINTON, H.; SPENCE, D. P. & KLEIN, G. S. (1959). *Explorations of Consistencies in Cognitive Behavior. Psychol. Issues,* Monogr. 4. New York: Int. Univ. Press.

GEDO, J. E. & GOLDBERG, A. (1973). *Models of Mind: A Psychoanalytic Theory.* Chicago: Univ. Chicago Press.

GEMELLI, A. (1928). Contributo allo studio della percezione, IV. *Contributi del Laboratorio di psicologia e biologia, università cattolica del Sacro Cuore, Milano,* 3:385–436.

GIOVACCHINI, P. I. (1960). On scientific creativity. *J. Amer. Psychoanal. Assn.,* 8:407–426.

GLESER, G. C. & IHILEVICH, D. (1969). An objective instrument for measuring defense mechanisms. *J. Consult. Clin. Psychol.,* 33:51–60.

GÖTZ, K. O., & GÖTZ, K. (1979a). Personality characteristics of professional artists. *Percept. Motor Skills,* 49:327–334.

—— —— (1979b). Personality characteristics of successful artists. *Percept. Motor Skills,* 49:919–924.

GRAUMANN, C. F. (1959). Aktualgenese. *Zschr. exper. angew. Psychol.,* 6:410–448.

GREENACRE, P. (1957). The childhood of the artist. *Psychoanal. Study Child,* 12:47–72.

—— (1971). *Emotional Growth,* Vol. 2. New York: Int. Univ. Press.

GRIPPEN, V. A. (1933). A study of creative artistic imagination in children by constant contact procedure. *Psychol. Monogr.,* 45:63–81.

GUILFORD, J. P. (1967). *The Nature of Human Intelligence.* New York: McGraw-Hill.

—— WILSON, R. C. & CHRISTENSEN, P. R. (1952). *A Factoranalytic Study of Creative Thinking. I. Administration of Tests and Analysis of Results.* Los Angeles: Univ. So. Calif. Press.

HAMMER, E. F. (1975). Artistic creativity: giftedness or sickness. *Art Psychother.,* 2:173–175.

HANSSON, S. B. & RYDÉN, O. (1987). Relationship between differentiation and integration of self and nonself: an investigation in terms of modes of perceptual adaptation. *Percept. Motor Skills,* 64:523–538.

HARRINGTON, D. M., BLOCK, J. & BLOCK, J. H. (1983). Predicting creativity in pre-adolescence from divergent thinking in early childhood. *J. Personal. Soc. Psychol.,* 45:609–623.

HARTMANN, H. (1939). *Ego Psychology and the Problem of Adaptation.* New York: Int. Univ. Press, 1958.

HENTSCHEL, U. (1980). Kognitive Kontrollprinzipien und Neuroseformen. In *Experimentelle Persönlichkeitspsychologie,* ed. U. Hentschel & G. J. W. Smith. Wiesbaden: Akademische Verlagsgesellschaft, pp. 227–321.

—— & SCHNEIDER, U. (1986). Psychodynamic personality correlates of creativity. In *The Roots of Perception: Individual Differences in Information Processing within and beyond Awareness*, ed. U. Hentschel, G. J. W. Smith & J. G. Draguns. Amsterdam: North-Holland, pp. 249–275.

—— & SMITH, G. J. W., Eds. (1980). *Experimentelle Persönlichkeitspychologie*. Wiesbaden: Akademische Verlagsgesellschaft.

—— —— & DRAGUNS, J. G., Eds. (1986). *The Roots of Perception: Individual Differences in Information Processing within and beyond Awareness*. Amsterdam: North-Holland.

HINDE, R. A. & BATESON, P. (1984). Discontinuities versus continuities in behavioral development and the neglect of process. *Int. J. Behav. Devel.*, 7:129–143.

HOLLEY, J. W. & GUILFORD, J. P. (1964). A note on the G index of agreement. *Educ. Psychol. Meas.*, 24:749–753.

—— & RISBERG, J. (1972). On the D estimate of discriminatory effectiveness. *Psychol. Res. Bull., Lund Univ.*, 12(12).

KOGAN, N. (1973). Creativity and sex differences. *J. Creat. Behav.*, 6:1–13.

KRAGH, U. (1955). *The Actual-Genetic Model of Perception-Personality*. Lund, Sweden: Gleerup.

—— (1960). Pathogenesis in dipsomania. *Acta Psychiat. Scand.*, 35:207–222, 261–288, 480–497.

—— (1962). A case of infantile animal phobia in adult precognitive organization. *Vita Humana*, 5:111–124.

—— (1969). *DMT-Defense Mechanism Test*. Stockholm: Skandinaviska Testförlaget.

—— (1980). Rekonstruktion verschiedener Aspekte einer Persönlichkeitsentwicklung mit dem Defense Mechanism Test. Eine Fallbeschreibung. In *Experimentelle Persönlichkeitspcyhologie*, ed. U. Hentschel & G. J. W. Smith. Wiesbaden: Akademische Verlagsgesellschaft, pp. 107–131.

—— (1986). Life panorama under the microscope: a paradigmatic case study. In *The Roots of Perception: Individual Differences in Information Processing within and beyond Awareness*, ed. U. Hentschel, G. J. W. Smith & J. G. Draguns. Amsterdam: North-Holland, pp. 145–159.

—— & SMITH, G. J. W., Eds. (1970). *Percept-Genetic Analysis*. Lund, Sweden: Gleerup.

—— —— (1974). Forming new patterns of experience: a classical problem viewed within a percept-genetic model. *Psychol. Res. Bull., Lund Univ.*, 14(6).

KRIS, E. (1952). *Psychoanalytic Explorations in Art*. New York: Int. Univ. Press.

KUBIE, L. S. (1958). *Neurotic Distortions of the Creative Process*. New York: Noonday Press.

KUHN, T. (1962). *The Structure of Scientific Revolutions*. Chicago: Univ. Chicago Press.

LANGER, J. (1969). *Theories of Development*. New York: Holt.

LINSCHOTEN, J. (1959). Actualgenese und heuristisches Prinzip. *Zschr. exper. angew. Psychol.*, 6:449–473.

MACKINNON, D. W. (1962). The personality correlates of creativity: a study of American architects. *Proc. Fourteenth Congr. Appl. Psychol.*, 2:11–39.

—— (1965). Personality and the realization of creative potentials. *Amer. Psychol.*, 20:273–281.

MAHLER, M. S. (1971). A study of the separation-individuation process, and its possible application to borderline phenomena in the psychoanalytic situation. *Psychoanal. Study Child*, 26:403–425.

MAINI, S. M. (1973). Personality and cognitive differences between an original and a non-original group. *Percept. Motor Skills*, 37:555–563.

MARR, D. (1982). *A Computational Investigation into the Human Representation and Processing of Visual Information*. San Francisco: W. H. Freeman.

MASLOW, A. (1962). *Toward a Psychology of Being*. Toronto: Van Nostrand.

MILGRAM, R. A., YITZHAK, V. & MILGRAM, N. (1977). Creative anxiety and sex-role identity in elementary school children. *Percept. Motor Skills*, 45:371–376.

NEUMAN, T. (1978). *Dimensionering och validering av perceptgenesens försvarsmekanismer: En hierarkisk analys mot pilotens stressbeteende*. Stockholm: Försvarets Forskningsanstalt.

NIEDERLAND, W. G. (1976). Psychoanalytic approaches to artistic creativity. *Psychoanal. Q.*, 45:185–212.

NILSSON, A. (1982). *The Mechanisms of Defence within a Developmental Frame of Reference*. Lund, Sweden: Gleerup.

NORDBECK, B. (1976). Critical factors in research work. *Committee on Research Economics*, Report 7. Stockholm.

NOVICK, J. & KELLY, K. (1970). Projection and externalization. *Psychoanal. Study Child*, 25:69–95.

NOY, P. (1969). A revision of the psychoanalytic theory of the primary process. *Int. J. Psychoanal.*, 50:155–178.

——— (1972). About art and artistic talent. *Int. J. Psychoanal.*, 53:243–249.

PERKINS, D. N. (1981). *The mind's best work*. Cambridge, Mass.: Harvard Univ. Press.

PHILLIPS, L. & FRAMO, J. (1954). Developmental theory applied to normal and psychopathologicaL perception. *J. Pers.*, 22:464–474.

PIAGET, J. & INHELDER, B. (1941). *Le développement des quantitées chez l'enfant*. Neuchâtel: Delachaux & Niestle.

——— ——— (1956). *The Child's Conception of Space*. London: Routledge & Kegan Paul.

PRITCHARD, R. M., HERON, W., & HEBB, D. O. (1960). Visual perception approached by the method of stabilized images. *Canad. J. Psychol.*, 14:67–77.

ROE, A. (1946a). The personality of artists. *Educ. Psychol. Meas.*, 6:401–408.

——— (1946b). Painting and personality. *Rorschach Res. Exchange*, 10:86–100.

——— (1951). A psychological study of eminent biologists. *Psychol. Monogr.*, 65(14).

——— (1953). A psychological study of eminent psychologists and anthropologists, and a comparison with biological and physical scientists. *Psychol. Monogr.*, 67(2).

ROGOLSKY, M. (1968). Artistic creativity and adaptive regression in third grade children. *J. Proj. Techn. Personal. Assmnt.*, 32:53–62.

ROSE, G. J. (1980). *The Power of Form: A Psychoanalytic Approach to Esthetic Form*. *Psychol. Issues*, Monogr. 49. New York: Int. Univ. Press.

ROSÉN, M. (1975). The effect of the psychotherapeutic process upon the creative process. *Art Psychother.*, 2:137–147.

ROTHENBERG, A. (1979). *The Emerging Goddess*. Chicago: Univ. Chicago Press.

——— (1981). A protest for creative theory. *Contemp. Psychol.*, 7:568.

———— & SOBEL, R. S. (1980). Adaptation and cognition: an experimental study of creative thinking. *J. Nerv. Ment. Dis.*, 168:370–374.

RUTSTEIN, E. H. & GOLDBERGER, L. (1973). The effects of aggressive stimulation on suicidal patients: an experimental study of the psychoanalytic theory of suicide. In *Psychoanal. Contemp. Sci.*, 2:157–174.

SACKEIM, H. A., PACKER, I. K. & GUR, R. C. (1977). Hemisphericity, cognitive set, and susceptibility to subliminal perception. *J. Abnorm. Psychol.*, 86:624–630.

SANDER, F. (1927). Experimentelle Ergebnisse der Gestaltpsychologie, *Berichte X Kongress für experimentelle Psychologie in Bonn*, pp. 23–28.

SCHILDER, P. (1928). Über Gedankenentwicklung. *Zschr. Neurol. Psychiat.*, 59:250–263.

SILVERMAN, L. H. (1976). Psychoanalytic theory: "The reports of my death are greatly exaggerated." *Amer. Psychol.*, 31:621–637.

———— & GEISLER, C. J. (1986). The subliminal psychodynamic activation method: comprehensive listing update, individual differences and other considerations. In *The Roots of Perception: Individual Differences in Information Processing within and beyond Awareness*, ed. U. Hentschel, G. J. W. Smith & J. G. Draguns. Amsterdam: North-Holland, pp. 49–74.

———— ROSS, D. L., ADLER, J. M. & LUSTIG, D. A. (1978). Simple research paradigm for demonstrating subliminal psychodynamic activation: effects of Oedipal stimuli on dart-throwing accuracy in college males. *J. Abnorm. Psychol.*, 87:341–357.

SINGER, J. L. (1973). *The Child's World of Make Believe: Experimental Studies of Imaginative Play*. New York: Academic Press.

SJÖBERG, M. P. (1984). På bräcklig is (On thin ice). In *Studia Psychologica et Paedagogica, Series altera*, 72. Lund, Sweden: Gleerup.

SMITH, G. J. W. (1949). *Psychological Studies in Twin Differences*. Lund, Sweden: Gleerup.

———— (1952a). *Interpretations of Behavior Sequences*. Lund, Sweden: Gleerup.

———— (1952b). Development as a psychological reference system. *Psychol. Rev.*, 59:363–369.

———— (1963). Process—a biological frame of reference for the study of behavior. *Scand. J. Psychol.*, 4:44–54.

———— (1981). Creation and reconstruction. *Psychoanal. Contemp. Thought*, 4:275–286.

———— (1983). Stabilization and automatization of perceptual activity over time. In *Psychological Processes in Cognition and Personality*, ed. W. D. Frölich, G. J. W. Smith, J. G. Draguns & U. Hentschel. Washington, D.C.: Hemisphere, pp. 135–142.

———— (1984). Plea for a process-oriented psychology. In *Psychology in the 1990's*, ed. K. Lagerspetz & P. Niemi. Amsterdam: North-Holland, pp. 367–381.

———— (1986). *Upplevande och verklighet* (Experience and reality). Lund, Sweden: Studentlitteratur.

———— ALMGREN, P.-E.; ANDERSSON, A. L.; ENGLESSON, I.; SMITH, M. & UDDENBERG, G. (1980). The mother-child picture test. *Int. J. Behav. Devel.*, 3:365–380.

———— & CARLSSON, I. (1983a). Creativity and anxiety: an experimental study. *Scand. J. Psychol.*, 24:107–115.

———— ———— (1983b). Can preschool children be creative? *Arch. Psychol.*, 135:37–53.

———— ———— (1983c). Creativity in early and middle school years. *Int. J. Behav. Devel.*, 6:167–195.

———— ———— (1985). Creativity in middle and late school years. *Int. J. Behav. Devel.*, 8:329–343.

———— ———— (1986). Creativity and aggression. *Psychoanal. Psychol.*, 3:159–172.

———— ———— & DANIELSSON, A. (1985). Identification with another person, manipulated by means of subliminal stimulation. *Scand. J. Psychol.*, 26:74–87.

———— ———— & SANDSTRÖM, S. (1985). Artists and artistic creativity. *Psychol. Res. Bull., Lund Univ.*, 25 (9–10).

———— & DANIELSSON, A. (1976). A new type of instrument constructed to explore the generative qualities of perception. *Psychol. Res. Bull., Lund Univ.*, 16(5).

———— ———— (1976–1977). From open flight to symbolic and perceptual tactics: a study of defense in preschool children. *The Royal Society of Letters at Lund, Scripta Minora*, No. 7.

———— ———— (1978). Richness in ideas, ego-involvement and efficiency in a group of scientists and humanists: a study of creativity using a process-oriented technique. *Psychol. Res. Bull., Lund Univ.*, 18(4–5).

———— ———— (1979). The influence of anxiety on the urge for aesthetic creation: an experimental study utilizing subliminal stimulation and a percept-genetic technique. *Psychol. Res. Bull., Lund Univ.*, 19(3–4).

———— ———— (1982). *Anxiety and Defensive Strategies in Childhood and Adolescence. Psychol. Issues*, Monogr. 52. New York: Int. Univ. Press.

———— & HENRIKSSON, M. (1955). The effect on an established percept of a perceptual process beyond awareness. *Acta Psychol.*, 11:170–179.

———— ———— (1956). Studies in the development of a percept within various contexts of perceived reality. *Acta Psychol.*, 12:263–281.

———— & JOHNSON, G. (1962). The influence of psychiatric treatment upon the process of reality construction. *J. Consult. Psychol.*, 26:520–526.

———— ———— & ALMGREN, P. E. (1982). *MCT-metakontrasttekniken* (MCT-the meta-contrast technique). Stockholm: Psykologiförlaget. (English edition, 1989).

———— & KRAGH, U. (1967). A serial afterimage experiment in clinical diagnostics. *Scand. J. Psychol.*, 8:52–64.

———— ———— (1975). Creativity in mature and old age. *Psychol. Res. Bull., Lund Univ.*, 15(7).

———— & MARKE, S. (1958). The internal consistency of the Humm-Wadsworth temperament scale. *J. Applied Psychol.*, 42:234–240.

———— & NYMAN, G. E. (1961). A serial tachistoscopic experiment and its clinical application. *Acta Psychol.*, 18:67–84.

———— & SJÖHOLM, L. (1974). Can our theory of reality influence our perception of it? *Psychol. Res. Bull., Lund Univ.*, 14(1).

———— SJÖHOLM, L. & NIELZÉN, S. (1974). Sensitive reactions and afterimage variegation. *J. Personal Assmnt.*, 38:41–47.

———— & WESTERLUNDH, B. (1980). Percept-genesis: a process perspective on perception-personality. In *Review of Personality and Social Psychology*, Vol. 1, ed. L. Wheeler. Beverly Hills, Calif.: Sage, pp. 94–124.

SPENCE, D. P. (1982). *Narrative Truth and Historical Truth: Meaning and Inter-pretation in Psychoanalysis.* New York: Norton.
STARKWEATHER, E. K. (1964). Problems in the measurement of creativity in preschool children. *J. Educ. Meas.*, 1:109–113.
—— & COWLING, F. G. (1964). The measurement of conforming and non-conforming behavior in preschool children. *Proc. Oklahoma Acad. Sci.*, 44:168–180.
STARVIG, G. R. (1981). Operational interpretations for the G and Gm indexes of agreement. *Scand. J. Psychol.*, 22:311–312.
STEIN, M. J. (1949). Personality factors involved in the temporal development of Rorschach responses. *J. Project. Techn.*, 13:355–414.
SULER, J. R. (1980). Primary process thinking and creativity. *Psychol. Bull.*, 88:144–165.
SZÉKELY, L. (1976). *Denkverlauf, Einsamkeit und Angst.* Bern: Huber.
TORRANCE, E. P. (1962). *Guiding Creative Talent.* Englewood Cliffs, N.J.: Pren-tice-Hall.
WEISBERG, P. S. & SPRINGER, K. J. (1961). Environmental factors in creative function: a study of gifted children. *Arch. Gen. Psychiat.*, 5:554–565.
WERNER, H. (1927). Über die Ausprägung von Tongestalten. *Zschr. Psychol.*, 101:181–195.
—— (1956). Microgenesis in aphasia. *J. Abnorm. Soc. Psychol.*, 52:347–353.
WESTERLUNDH, B. (1976). *Aggression, Anxiety and Defence.* Lund, Sweden: Gle-erup.
—— (1979). Conflict activation: Two experimental operations and their influence on percept-genesis. *Psychol. Res. Bull., Lund Univ.*, 19(8).
—— (1983). Personal organization in the visual field. *Arch. Psychol.*, 135:17–35.
—— (1984). Percept-genesis and the experimental study of conflict and defence. In *Psychological Processes in Cognition and Personality*, ed. W. D. Fröhlich, G. J. W. Smith, J. G. Draguns & U. Hentschel. Washington, D.C.: Hemisphere, pp. 145–164.
—— & SJÖBÄCK, H. (1986). Activation of intrapsychic conflict and defense. In *The Roots of Perception: Individual Differences in Information Processing within and beyond Awareness*, ed. U. Hentschel, G. J. W. Smith & J. G. Draguns. Amsterdam: North-Holland, pp. 161–215.
—— & SMITH, G. J. W. (1983). Percept-genesis and the psychodynamics of perception. *Psychoanal. Contemp. Thought*, 6:597–640.
WINNICOTT, D. W. (1971). *Playing and Reality.* London: Tavistock Publications.
YANDO, R., SEITZ, V. & ZIGLER, E. (1979). *Intellectual and Personality Charac-teristics of Children: Social Class and Ethnic Group Differences.* Hillsdale, N.J.: Erlbaum.

NAME INDEX

237

SUBJECT INDEX

PSYCHOLOGICAL ISSUES